MVFOL

SECOND EDITION

TOUCHSTONE

STUDENT'S BOOK 3

MICHAEL MCCARTHY

JEANNE MCCARTEN

HELEN SANDIFORD

CAMBRIDGE
UNIVERSITY PRESS

CAMBRIDGE
UNIVERSITY PRESS

32 Avenue of the Americas, New York, NY 10013-2473, USA

Cambridge University Press is part of the University of Cambridge.

It furthers the University's mission by disseminating knowledge in the pursuit of education, learning and research at the highest international levels of excellence.

www.cambridge.org
Information on this title: www.cambridge.org/9781107627949

First published 2005
Second Edition 2014
3rd printing 2015

Printed in Dubai by Oriental Press

A catalog record for this publication is available from the British Library.

ISBN 978-1-107-66583-5 Student's Book
ISBN 978-1-107-62875-5 Student's Book A
ISBN 978-1-107-69446-0 Student's Book B
ISBN 978-1-107-64271-3 Workbook
ISBN 978-1-107-62082-7 Workbook A
ISBN 978-1-107-65147-0 Workbook B
ISBN 978-1-107-62794-9 Full Contact
ISBN 978-1-107-63739-9 Full Contact A
ISBN 978-1-107-63903-4 Full Contact B
ISBN 978-1-107-68094-4 Teacher's Edition with Assessment Audio CD/CD-ROM
ISBN 978-1-107-63179-3 Class Audio CDs (4)

Additional resources for this publication at www.cambridge.org/touchstone2

Touchstone Second Edition has benefited from extensive development research. The authors and publishers would like to extend their thanks to the following reviewers and consultants for their valuable insights and suggestions:

Ana Lúcia da Costa Maia de Almeida and Mônica da Costa Monteiro de Souza from **IBEU**, Rio de Janeiro, Brazil; Andreza Cristiane Melo do Lago from **Magic English School**, Manaus, Brazil; Magaly Mendes Lemos from **ICBEU**, São José dos Campos, Brazil; Maria Lucia Zaorob, São Paulo, Brazil; Patricia McKay Aronis from **CEL LEP**, São Paulo, Brazil; Carlos Gontow, São Paulo, Brazil; Christiane Augusto Gomes da Silva from **Colégio Visconde de Porto Seguro**, São Paulo, Brazil; Silvana Fontana from **Lord's Idiomas**, São Paulo, Brazil; Alexander Fabiano Morishigue from **Speed Up Idiomas**, Jales, Brazil; Elisabeth Blom from **Casa Thomas Jefferson**, Brasília, Brazil; Michelle Dear from **International Academy of English**, Toronto, ON, Canada; Walter Duarte Marin, Laura Hurtado Portela, Jorge Quiroga, and Ricardo Suarez, from **Centro Colombo Americano**, Bogotá, Colombia; Jhon Jairo Castaneda Macias from **Praxis English Academy**, Bucaramanga, Colombia; Gloria Liliana Moreno Vizcaino from **Universidad Santo Tomas**, Bogotá, Colombia; Elizabeth Ortiz from **Copol English Institute (COPEI)**, Guayaquil, Ecuador; Henry Foster from **Kyoto Tachibana University**, Kyoto, Japan; Steven Kirk from **Tokyo University**, Tokyo, Japan; J. Lake from **Fukuoka Woman's University**, Fukuoka, Japan; Etsuko Yoshida from **Mie University**, Mie, Japan; B. Bricklin Zeff from **Hokkai Gakuen University**, Hokkaido, Japan; Ziad Abu-Hamatteh from **Al-Balqa' Applied University**, Al-Salt, Jordan; Roxana Pérez Flores from **Universidad Autonoma de Coahuila Language Center**, Saltillo, Mexico; Kim Alejandro Soriano Jimenez from **Universidad Politecnica de Altamira**, Altamira, Mexico; Tere Calderon Rosas from **Universidad Autonoma Metropolitana Campus Iztapalapa**, Mexico City, Mexico; Lilia Bondareva, Polina Ermakova, and Elena Frumina, from **National Research Technical University MISiS**, Moscow, Russia; Dianne C. Ellis from **Kyung Hee University**, Gyeonggi-do, South Korea; Jason M. Ham and Victoria Jo from **Institute of Foreign Language Education, Catholic University of Korea**, Gyeonggi-do, South Korea; Shaun Manning from **Hankuk University of Foreign Studies**, Seoul, South Korea; Natalie Renton from **Busan National University of Education**, Busan, South Korea; Chris Soutter from **Busan University of Foreign Studies**, Busan, South Korea; Andrew Cook from **Dong A University**, Busan, South Korea; Raymond Wowk from **Daejin University**, Gyeonggi-do, South Korea; Ming-Hui Hsieh and Jessie Huang from **National Central University**, Zhongli, Taiwan; Kim Phillips from **Chinese Culture University**, Taipei, Taiwan; Alex Shih from **China University of Technology**, Taipei Ta-Liao Township, Taiwan; Porntip Bodeepongse from **Thaksin University**, Songkhla, Thailand; Nattaya Puakpong and Pannathon Sangarun from **Suranaree University of Technology**, Nakhon Ratchasima, Thailand; Barbara Richards, Gloria Stewner-Manzanares, and Caroline Thompson, from **Montgomery College**, Rockville, MD, USA; Kerry Vrabel from **Gateway Community College**, Phoenix, AZ, USA.

Touchstone Second Edition authors and publishers would also like to thank the following individuals and institutions who have provided excellent feedback and support on *Touchstone Blended*:

Gordon Lewis, Vice President, Laureate Languages and Chris Johnson, Director, Laureate English Programs, Latin America from **Laureate International Universities**; **Universidad de las Americas**, Santiago, Chile; **University of Victoria**, Paris, France; **Universidad Technólogica Centroamericana**, Honduras; **Institut Universitaire de Casablanca**, Morocco; **Universidad Peruana de Ciencias Aplicadas**, Lima, Peru; **CIBERTEC**, Peru; **National Research Technical University (MiSIS)**, Moscow, Russia; **Institut Obert de Catalunya (IOC)**, Barcelona, Spain; Sedat Çilingir, Burcu Tezcan, and Didem Mutçalıoğlu from **İstanbul Bilgi Üniversitesi**, Istanbul, Turkey.

Touchstone Second Edition authors and publishers would also like to thank the following contributors to *Touchstone Second Edition*:

Sue Aldcorn, Frances Amrani, Deborah Gordon, Lisa Hutchins, Nancy Jordan, Steven Kirk, Genevieve Kocienda, Linda-Marie Koza, Geraldine Mark, Julianna Nielsen, Kathryn O'Dell, Nicola Prentis, Ellen Shaw, Kristin Sherman, Luis Silva Susa, Mary Vaughn, Kerry S. Vrabel, Shari Young, and Eric Zuarino.

Authors' Acknowledgments

The authors would like to thank all the Cambridge University Press staff and freelancers who were involved in the creation of *Touchstone Second Edition*. In addition, they would like to acknowledge a huge debt of gratitude that they owe to two people: Mary Vaughn, for her role in creating *Touchstone First Edition* and for being a constant source of wisdom ever since, and Bryan Fletcher, who also had the vision that has led to the success of *Touchstone Blended Learning*.

Helen Sandiford would like to thank her family for their love and support, especially her husband Bryan.

The author team would also like to thank each other, for the joy of working together, sharing the same professional dedication, and for the mutual support and friendship.

Finally, the authors would like to thank our dear friend Alejandro Martinez, Global Training Manager, who sadly passed away in 2012. He is greatly missed by all who had the pleasure to work with him. Alex was a huge supporter of *Touchstone* and everyone is deeply grateful to him for his contribution to its success.

Touchstone Level 3 Contents and learning outcomes

	Learning outcomes	Language		
		Grammar	Vocabulary	Pronunciation
Unit 1 **The way we are** pages 1–10	• Talk about people's behavior using adverbs • Describe people's personalities using adverbs before adjectives • Use *always* with a continuous verb to describe habits • Use *at least* to point out the positive side of a situation • Read online student profiles • Write a personal profile	• Adjectives vs. manner adverbs • Adverbs before adjectives and adverbs • Adjective prefixes ***Extra practice***	• Behavior and personality • Personal qualities	***Speaking naturally*** • Rising and falling intonation in questions giving alternatives ***Sounds right*** • Word stress
Unit 2 **Experiences** pages 11–20	• Talk about experiences and secret dreams using the present perfect • Ask about unusual experiences using present perfect questions • Keep a conversation going • Show interest with *Do you?*, *Have you?*, etc. • Read a travel blog • Write a post for a travel blog	• Present perfect statements • Present perfect and simple past questions and answers ***Extra practice***	• Past participles of irregular verbs	***Speaking naturally*** • Reduced and unreduced forms of *have* ***Sounds right*** • Different ways to pronounce the letter *o*
Unit 3 **Wonders of the world** pages 21–30	• Talk about the best, worst, and most beautiful things in your city and country • Describe natural features • Use short responses to be a supportive listener • Use superlatives for emphasis • Read an article about world records • Write a factual article about your country	• Superlatives • Questions with *How +* adjective . . . ? ***Extra practice***	• Buildings and structures • Natural features	***Speaking naturally*** • Linking and deletion with superlatives ***Sounds right*** • Which sound in each group is different?
Checkpoint Units 1–3 pages 31–32				
Unit 4 **Family life** pages 33–42	• Talk about family life using *let, make, help, have, get, want, ask,* and *tell* • Talk about your immediate and extended family • Describe memories using *used to* and *would* • Give opinions with expressions like *If you ask me* • Agree with opinions using expressions like *Absolutely* • Read a blog about family meals • Write a blog entry about a family memory	• Verbs *let, make, help, have, get, want, ask,* and *tell* • *Used to* and *would* ***Extra practice***	• Types of families • Relatives and extended family members	***Speaking naturally*** • Reduction of *used to* ***Sounds right*** • Matching vowel sounds
Unit 5 **Food choices** pages 43–52	• Talk about eating habits using containers and quantities • Talk about different ways to cook food • Talk about food using *too, too much, many,* and *enough* • Respond to suggestions by letting the other person decide • Use expressions like *I'm fine* to politely refuse offers • Read about snacks around the world • Write about a dish from your country	• Review of countable and uncountable nouns • Quantifiers *a little, a few, very little,* and *very few* • *Too, too much, too many,* and *enough* ***Extra practice***	• Containers and quantities • Different ways of cooking food	***Speaking naturally*** • Stressing new information ***Sounds right*** • Are the sounds the same or different?
Unit 6 **Managing life** pages 53–62	• Talk about future plans and schedules using *will, be going to,* present continuous, and simple present • Ask for and give advice about personal situations using modal verbs and expressions • Use expressions with *make* and *do* • End phone calls with expressions like *I'd better go* • Say good-bye in a friendly, informal way • Read a blog about multitasking • Write some advice about time management	• The future with *will, be going to,* the present continuous, and the simple present • Use *had better, ought to,* and *might want to* to say what's advisable • Use *have to* and *going to have to* to say what's necessary • Use *would rather* to say what's preferable ***Extra practice***	• Expressions with *make* and *do*	***Speaking naturally*** • Reduction of verbs *want to, you'd better, going to have to, ought to,* and *have got to* ***Sounds right*** • Matching vowel sounds
Checkpoint Units 4–6 pages 63–64				

Interaction	Skills				Self study
Conversation strategies	Listening	Reading	Writing	Free talk	Vocabulary notebook
• Use *always* and a continuous verb to talk about things people do more than is usual • Use *at least* to point out the positive side of a situation	***People I admire most*** • Listen to people talk about people they admire and fill in a chart ***Things you don't know about me*** • Predict what people will say next	***Student profiles*** • Online student profiles	***Your personal profile*** • Write a personal profile • Useful expressions for biographical writing	***What are we like?*** • Class activity: Ask questions to find out new things about your classmates	***Happy or sad?*** • When you learn a new word, find out if it has an opposite
• Keep the conversation going • Use response questions like *Do you?* and *Have you?* to show interest	***What have they done?*** • Listen to conversations about things people have done and choose the best responses ***A traveler's adventures*** • Listen to a conversation about travel and identify information; then answer questions about details	***Travel blogs*** • Read travel blogs	***Blog about it*** • Write a blog entry about an exciting experience • Use adverbs like *fortunately*, *unfortunately*, and *amazingly* to show your attitude or feeling	***I've never done that!*** • Group game: Play a game to find out things that your classmates have never done	***Have you ever . . . ?*** • When you learn a new verb, write the three main forms in a chart
• Use short responses with *really* and *sure* to agree and be a supportive listener • Use superlatives to emphasize your opinions and feelings	***What do you know?*** • Listen to a quiz and answer questions ***Travel talk*** • Listen to an interview about travel experiences and answer questions	***World records*** • Read an article about world records	***Interesting facts*** • Write a paragraph about an interesting place in your country • Adding information	***Where's the best place to . . . ?*** • Pair work: Think of advice to give to someone visiting your country for the first time	***From the mountains to the sea*** • Draw a map of your country and label it

Checkpoint Units 1–3   pages 31–32

• Give opinions with expressions like *It seems like . . .* and *If you ask me, . . .* • Use expressions like *exactly*, *definitely*, and *absolutely* to agree with people's opinions	***Reasonable demands?*** • Listen to people talk about demands their parents make on them ***Family memories*** • Listen to people talk about things they used to do	***Barbara's Blog*** • Read a blog about family meals	***Family memories*** • Write a blog about a family memory • Time markers to show the past and present	***Family histories*** • Group work: Prepare a short history of your family and share it with your group	***Remember that?*** • Use word webs to log new vocabulary about your family members
• Respond to suggestions by letting the other person decide • Refuse offers politely with expressions like *No, thanks. I'm fine.*	***That sounds good.*** • Listen to conversations and number pictures in order; then match each picture with the best response ***Snack habits*** • Listen to people talk about snacks and fill in a chart	***Snacks around the world*** • Read an article about popular snacks from around the world	***You should definitely try it!*** • Write an article about a popular snack from your country • Give examples with *like*, *for example*, and *such as*	***Whichever is easier*** • Group work: Plan a "pot luck" dinner with your group	***Fried bananas*** • Learn new words in combination with other words
• End phone conversations with expressions like *I'd better go*, *I've got to go*, and *I'll call you later* • Use informal expressions like *See you later* to end friendly phone conversations	***Fun invitations*** • Listen to three people respond to different invitations and fill in a chart ***When should I do that?*** • Listen to four people talk about their time management problems and identify how they solved them	***The art (and science) of doing less and achieving more*** • Read an article about multitasking	***When should I do that?*** • Write advice about time management • Link ideas using *as long as*, *provided that*, and *unless*	***Who's going to do what?*** • Group work: Plan a community event and tell the class about your event	***Do your best!*** • When you learn a new expression, use it in a sentence to help you remember it

Checkpoint Units 4–6   pages 63–64

	Learning outcomes	Language		
		Grammar	Vocabulary	Pronunciation
Unit 7 **Relationships** pages 65–74	• Talk about your circle of friends using relative clauses • Talk about dating using phrasal verbs • Soften comments with expressions like *sort of* • Use *though* to give a contrasting idea • Read an article about online dating • Write an article about your circle of friends	• Subject relative clauses • Object relative clauses • Phrasal verbs **Extra practice**	• Phrasal verbs, including expressions to talk about relationships	***Speaking naturally*** • Stress in phrasal verbs ***Sounds right*** • Which sound in each group is different?
Unit 8 **What if?** pages 75–84	• Talk about wishes and imaginary situations using *I wish* and *If* clauses • Discuss how to deal with everyday dilemmas • Give advice using expressions like *If I were you, . . .* • Use *That would be . . .* to comment on a suggestion or a possibility • Read a blog about regrets • Write an article about how you would change your life	• Use *wish* + past form of verb to talk about wishes for the present or future • Conditional sentences with *if* clauses about imaginary situations • Asking about imaginary situations or events **Extra practice**	• Expressions with verbs and prepositions	***Speaking naturally*** • Intonation in long questions ***Sounds right*** • Are these sounds the same or different?
Unit 9 **Tech savvy?** pages 85–94	• Talk about problems with technology using questions within sentences • Ask for help and describe how things work using *how to*, *where to*, *what to*, and separable phrasal verbs • Give different opinions with expressions like *On the other hand, . . .* • Ask someone to agree with you using expressions like *You know what I mean?* • Read an article about email scams • Write an article about protecting personal information	• Questions within sentences • Separable phrasal verbs with objects • *how to* + verb, *where to* + verb, and *what to* + verb **Extra practice**	• Phrasal verbs, including expressions to talk about operating electronic machines and gadgets	***Speaking naturally*** • Linking consonants and vowels ***Sounds right*** • Identifying unstressed syllables

Checkpoint Units 7–9   pages 95–96

	Learning outcomes	Grammar	Vocabulary	Pronunciation
Unit 10 **What's up?** pages 97–106	• Talk about news with the present perfect continuous, present perfect, *since*, *for*, and *in* • Use the present perfect with *already*, *still*, and *yet* • Describe different kinds of movies • Ask someone for a favor politely • Use *All right*, *OK*, and *Sure* to agree to requests • Use *All right*, *OK*, and *So* to change topic • Read a movie review • Write a review	• Present perfect continuous vs. present perfect • *Since*, *for*, and *in* for duration • *Already*, *still*, and *yet* with present perfect **Extra practice**	• Kinds of movies • Expressions to describe types of movies	***Speaking naturally*** • Reduction of *have* ***Sounds right*** • Matching vowel sounds
Unit 11 **Impressions** pages 107–116	• Speculate about people and things using *must*, *might*, *can't*, and *could* • Describe situations and people's feelings using adjectives that end in *-ed* and *-ing* • Show you understand situations or feelings • Use *you see* to explain a situation and *I see* to show you understand • Read an article about a music education program • Write an email to the founder of a charity	• Modal verbs *must*, *may*, *might*, *can't*, or *could* for speculating • Adjectives ending in *-ed* vs. adjectives ending in *-ing* **Extra practice**	• Feelings and reactions	***Speaking naturally*** • Linking and deletion with *must* ***Sounds right*** • *-ed* adjective endings
Unit 12 **In the news** pages 117–126	• Talk about news events using the simple past passive • Talk about natural disasters using the simple past passive + *by* • Use expressions like *Guess what?* to tell news • Introduce ideas with expressions like *The thing is . . .* • Read an interview with a foreign correspondent • Write a report using statistics	• The simple past passive • The simple past passive with *by* + agent • Adverbs with the passive **Extra practice**	• Extreme weather conditions • Natural disasters	***Speaking naturally*** • Breaking sentences into parts ***Sounds right*** • Matching words that have the same sounds

Checkpoint Units 10–12   pages 127–128

Interaction	Skills				Self study
Conversation strategies	Listening	Reading	Writing	Free talk	Vocabulary notebook
• Soften comments with expressions like *I think, probably, kind of*, and *in a way* • Use *though* to give a contrasting idea	**People I look forward to seeing** • Listen to someone describe three people; listen for the reasons he likes to see them **Getting back in touch** • Listen to a conversation about losing touch and fill in a chart	**Looking for love? Online is the way to go!** • Read an article about online dating	**Your circle of friends** • Write an article describing your circle of friends • Use *both* and *neither* to show what you have in common	**Your ideal partner** • Group work: Discuss your ideal partner and questions you should ask before you decide to get married	**Matching up** • When you learn a phrasal verb, it's a good idea to write down some other verbs you can use with the particle and some other particles you can use with the verb
• Give advice using expressions like *If I were you, . . .* and *You might want to . . .* • Use *That would be . . .* to comment on a suggestion or possibility	**Just one wish** • Identify four people's wishes; then write the reasons they can't have their wishes **Here's my advice** • Listen to a conversation about problems and advice	**If I could live my live over . . .** • Read a blog about regrets	**What would you change?** • Write an article about how you would change your life • Use adverbs like *probably* and *definitely* in affirmative and negative statements	**What would you do?** • Group work: Discuss what you would do in imaginary situations	**Imagine that!** • When you learn a new verb, find out what prepositions (if any) can come after it
• Give different opinions using expressions like *On the other hand . . .* and *I know what you mean, but . . .* • Use expressions like *You know what I mean?* when you want someone to agree with you	**What do you know about the Internet?** • Answer questions about the Internet; then listen to a conversation and check your answers **Technology matters** • Listen to a conversation about the pros and cons of technology; then agree or disagree with three opinions	**Savvy and safe** • Read an article about email scams	**Keeping it safe** • Write an article about protecting personal information • Planning your article	**Technology etiquette** • Pair work: Debate different opinions about technology etiquette	**On and off** • When you learn expressions with a new or complex structure, think of everyday situations where you might use them

Checkpoint Units 7–9   pages 95–96

• Ask for a favor politely using expressions like *I was wondering . . .* and *Would it be OK with you . . .* • Use *All right, OK*, and *Sure* to agree to requests and *All right, OK*, and *So* to move a conversation to a new topic	**Favors at work** • Match people with the favors they ask; then listen again for more information **I'd really recommend it** • Listen for details of a conversation about going to see a show	**Avatar is stunning, memorable, and mesmerizing!** • Read a movie review	**A Review** • Write a review of a concert, show, movie, or book • Contrast ideas with *although, even though*, and *even if*	**Who's been doing what?** • Class activity: Ask questions to find out interesting things your classmates have been doing lately	**Great movies** • When you learn a new word or expression, link it to something you have recently seen or done
• Show you understand another person's feelings or situation • Use *you see* to explain a situation • Use *I see* to show you understand	**People and situations** • Match four people and their situations; then write a response with *must* to each **People making a difference** • Listen for details of conversations about people and organizations; discuss which organization you would choose to get involved with	**El Sistema** • Read an article about a music education program	**My impression is . . .** • Write an email to the founder of a charity • Expressions to show impressions, reactions, and opinions	**That must be fun!** • Pair work: Make sentences to share with a partner. Then continue the conversation and speculate about what they say.	**How would you feel?** • When you learn new words for feelings, link them to different situations where you might experience each one
• Introduce news with expressions like *Did you hear (about) . . . ?* and *Guess what?* • Use *The thing is / was . . .* to introduce issues	**News update** • Listen to news stories and answer questions **What do they say next?** • Listen to people telling personal news and make predictions	**Life's work: Christiane Amanpour** • Read an interview with a foreign correspondent	**Are you up on the news?** • Write a report using statistics • Writing about statistics	**Here's the news!** • Pair work: Make up short TV news reports about pictures and take turns telling news stories to another pair.	**Forces of nature** • When you learn a new word, use a dictionary to find out what other words are typically used with it

Checkpoint Units 10–12   pages 127–128

Useful language for . . .

Working in groups

Does anyone else have anything to add?

What do you think, _____ ?

Let's take turns asking the questions. OK, who wants to go first?

Do you want me to make the list?

Should I write down the information this time?

Do you have any ideas?

Do you know what the answer is?

We're going to do a role play about . . .

In our survey, we found out that . . .

We agreed on these things. First, . . .

We're finished. What should we do next?

Checking your partner's work

Can you help me with this question? I'm stuck.

I can't figure out this answer. Can you help me?

Would you mind checking my work?

Let's compare answers.

Let's exchange papers.

I can't read your writing. What does this say?

I'm not sure what you mean. Do you mean _____ ?

I don't understand what this means. Are you trying to say _____ ?

Your blog was really interesting. I just wanted to ask you a question about _____ .

I was wondering about _____ .

The way we are

✓ Can Do! **In this unit, you learn how to . . .**

Lesson A
- Talk about people's behavior using manner adverbs and adjectives

Lesson B
- Describe people's personalities using adverbs like *extremely* before adjectives

Lesson C
- Use *always* with a continuous verb to describe habits
- Use *at least* to point out the positive side of a situation

Lesson D
- Read online student profiles
- Write a personal profile

1

2

3

4

Before you begin . . .

Who looks outgoing? shy? stylish? conservative?
Which people would you like to meet? Why?

Do you need to slow down?

Take this quiz to find out.

1

When I walk down the street, . . .

a I walk very fast and use the time to make phone calls.

b I enjoy the walk and look at the things and people around me.

2

When I go out to lunch with friends, . . .

a I eat quickly so that I can get back to my work.

b I eat slowly, and I enjoy the food and conversation.

3

When there's a family event, . . .

a I often have to miss it because I have too much to do.

b I try to plan my time well so that I can attend the event.

4

If traffic is heavy and some people are driving a bit recklessly, . . .

a I honk my horn a lot. I get mad easily in bad traffic.

b I automatically slow down and try to drive carefully.

5

If I'm waiting at the airport and find out that my flight is delayed, . . .

a I get impatient and complain to the people behind the counter.

b I wait patiently. I read something or make a few phone calls.

6

If I'm in a hurry and think people are talking too slowly, . . .

a I sometimes interrupt them to finish their sentences.

b I listen quietly and wait for them to finish before I talk.

7

If I play a game or sport with friends, . . .

a I take the game seriously, and I feel very bad if I lose.

b I think it's better to win than lose, but I don't feel strongly about it.

8

If I get an assignment with a very tight deadline, . . .

a I get very stressed – I hate it when I don't have time to do a job properly.

b I work hard to do the best I can in the time I have.

Mostly A answers?

It's time to slow down and enjoy life more. Try to plan your time differently. Make more time for family, friends, and fun.

Mostly B answers?

You're balancing work and play nicely. Just keep the balance right.

 Getting started

A Are you ever in a hurry? When? Tell the class.

"I'm usually in a hurry in the mornings when I have to get ready for class."

About you **B** ◀)) 1.02 Listen and take the quiz above. For each item, circle *a* or *b*.

C Pair work Compare your quiz responses with a partner. How are you alike? different?

Figure it out **D** Circle the correct words. Use the quiz to help you. Then tell a partner which sentences are true for you.

1. I have a lot of **tight** / **tightly** deadlines.
2. I plan my time **good** / **well**.
3. I often eat lunch **quick** / **quickly**.
4. I feel **strong** / **strongly** about my opinions.
5. I get **impatient** / **impatiently** in long lines.
6. I work **hard** / **hardly** to get good grades.

2 Grammar Adjectives vs. manner adverbs ◀ᴺ 1.03

Extra practice p. 140

Adjective + noun
I'm a **patient** person.
He's not a **good** singer.
He's a **fast** driver.
She's a **careful** driver.

Regular -ly adverbs
patient ▶ patient**ly**
careful ▶ careful**ly**
easy ▶ eas**ily**
automatic ▶ automatic**ally**

Verb + manner adverb
I wait **patiently** in lines.
He doesn't sing very **well**.
He drives very **fast**.
She drives **carefully**.

Irregular adverbs
good ▶ **well**
late ▶ **late**
fast ▶ **fast**
hard ▶ **hard**

be, feel, get, etc., + adjective
I'm **patient**.
His voice **sounds terrible**.
He **gets reckless** sometimes.
I **feel safe*** with her.
***But:** I **feel strongly** about it.

🗩 In conversation

The most common *-ly* manner adverbs are
*quickly, easily, differently, automatically,
slowly, properly, badly, strongly*, and *carefully*.

✖ Common errors

Don't use an adjective to describe
how someone does an action.

*Children learn languages **easily**.*
(NOT *Children learn languages ~~easy~~*.)

A Complete these opinions with the correct forms of the words given.

1. Young people talk really ___*fast*___ (fast) and don't speak _____
   (clear). And they use a lot of slang. It sounds _____ (terrible).
   They don't always communicate _____ (good).

2. People aren't very _____ (patient) when they have to wait in long lines.
   They don't speak to the clerks very _____ (polite), either.

3. Sometimes families argue because parents and children see
   things _____ (different).

4. A lot of people _____ (automatic) answer their cell phones when
   they ring, even at dinner. I think that's just _____ (rude).

5. People don't feel _____ (safe) on the roads because so many people
   are driving _____ (reckless). Driving can be _____ (dangerous).

6. A lot of people try _____ (hard) to do their job _____ (careful)
   and _____ (thorough) and they get stressed.

About you B Pair work Discuss the opinions. Are they true in your culture?

"People here talk very fast so you have to listen carefully."

3 Speaking naturally Questions giving alternatives

Are you usually on time for **class**? ↗ Or do you often arrive **late**? ↘

A ◀ᴺ 1.04 Listen and repeat the questions above. Notice how the intonation rises in
the first question and falls in the second question.

About you B ◀ᴺ 1.05 Now listen and repeat these questions. Then ask and answer the questions with a partner.

1. Do you do homework assignments carefully? Or do you just do them quickly?

2. Do you learn new English words easily? Or do you have to work hard at it?

3. Do you usually do well on tests? Or do you just get passing grades?

4. Do you practice English regularly outside of class? Or do you just use it in class?

5. Do you see things differently from your classmates? Or do you share their opinions?

6. Do you listen to class announcements carefully? Or do you ignore them?

1 Building vocabulary and grammar

A 🔊 1.06 **Listen and read. Who do these people admire? Why?**

Who is someone you really admire?

"My English teacher. She's incredibly **talented** and **creative**. And she **has a great sense of humor**. She's pretty **disorganized**, though. She forgets something almost every class, but her classes are absolutely wonderful!"
– Jessica Davis

"I really admire a guy in my karate class. He's extremely **competitive**, but when he wins, he's not **arrogant** like some of the other guys. He's not very **outgoing**, so some people think he's **unfriendly**, but I think he's basically just **shy**."
– Mike Kowalski

"I think my dad's a pretty cool guy. We get along really well. He's fairly **easygoing** and **laid-back**. And he's very **practical** and **down-to-earth**, so he always gives me good advice. Also, he's completely **honest** with me. I can trust what he says."
– Bryan Yuen

"My friend Luisa. She's so **helpful** and **generous**. I mean, she's always doing things for other people. She's not **selfish** at all. And she's totally **reliable**. If she says she'll help you with something, she does. You can always count on her."
– Emilia Perez

Word sort **B** **Which of the personality words or expressions above describe these qualities? Do you know any people with these qualities? Compare with a partner.**

Winning is very important to you.	*competitive*	You're relaxed about life.	
You handle small problems well.		You never cheat or steal.	
People can always count on you.		You're not well organized.	
You don't get along with people.		You can do lot of things well.	
You like to have fun with people.		You think you're the best.	
You're not relaxed around people.		You give a lot of time or money.	

Figure it out **C** **Find words in the article that make these adjectives stronger.** 📓 **Vocabulary notebook** p. 10

1. _incredibly_ talented
2. _____ practical
3. _____ disorganized
4. _____ honest
5. _____ competitive
6. _____ reliable

Figure it out **D** **Find words in the article that have the opposite meaning.**

1. friendly _____
2. organized _____
3. unreliable _____

2 Grammar Adverbs before adjectives and adverbs ◀)) 1.07

Extra practice p. 140

Use *incredibly*, *extremely*, *very*, *really*, and *so* to make some adjectives and adverbs stronger.	She's **incredibly** talented. She's **extremely** generous. He's a **really** cool guy. We get along **very** well.
Use *pretty* and *fairly* to mean "more than a little."	He's **pretty** easygoing. He's **fairly** laid-back.
Use *absolutely* or *really* (but not *very*) with adjectives that are already very strong.	She's **absolutely** wonderful. He's **really** fantastic.
The expression *at all* makes negatives stronger.	She's **not** selfish **at all**.
Completely and *totally* mean 100%.	He's **completely** honest. She's **totally** reliable.

Adjective prefixes
patient ► **im**patient
considerate ► **in**considerate
friendly ► **un**friendly
reliable ► **un**reliable
honest ► **dis**honest
organized ► **dis**organized

In conversation

People use *really* and *pretty* much more often in conversation than in writing.

really
pretty

conversation ■ : ■ writing

About you A Do you know people with these qualities? Write a sentence for each expression. Add an example.

1. totally laid-back
2. pretty generous
3. very honest
4. absolutely wonderful
5. not competitive at all
6. incredibly impatient
7. fairly disorganized
8. completely reliable
9. extremely talented
10. really inconsiderate

B Pair work Compare sentences with a partner.

A *My boyfriend is totally laid-back. He always goes along with my plans and everything.*
B *Really? He sounds incredibly easygoing.*

3 Listening and speaking People I admire most

A ◀)) 1.08 Listen. Who do these people admire? Write the people in the chart.

	John	Marina	Hiroyuki
1. Who do you admire?			
2. Why?			
3. What do you have in common?			
4. How are you different?			

B ◀)) 1.08 Listen again. What do they say about the people they admire?

About you C Pair work Ask and answer the questions. Then join another pair. Tell them about the person your partner admires.

A *Who do you admire?*
B *I admire my sister. She's extremely friendly and totally reliable. She ...*

Sounds right p. 137

1 Conversation strategy Describing individual habits

A Which two habits do you think are most annoying in a co-worker or classmate? Tell the class.

Someone who . . .

- ☐ smiles all the time
- ☐ disturbs people
- ☐ criticizes others
- ☐ wastes time
- ☐ stands around and talks
- ☐ talks about people behind their backs

B **1.09 Listen. What's Ellie's new co-worker like? How is he different from her last co-worker?**

Max Hey, how are you getting along with your new co-worker? He seems extremely friendly. He's always smiling.

Ellie You mean Jim? Well, yeah, he is, but he never does any work. He's always disturbing people. It drives me crazy. You know, he's always standing around and talking.

Max Well, at least he's pleasant.

Ellie Yeah. And he's not always criticizing people like that last guy.

Max Yeah. He was pretty bad. He was always talking about people behind their backs.

Ellie I mean, at least Jim's not like that. But like, he's always wasting time.

Max You mean like we're doing right now?

C **Notice** how Ellie and Max use *always* and a continuous verb to talk about things people do a lot or more than is usual. Find other examples in the conversation.

"He's always wasting time."

D Change the underlined parts of these sentences to describe habits. Use *always* and a continuous verb. Compare with a partner.

1. I'm pretty disorganized. I <u>lose</u> things. *I'm always losing things.*
2. Everyone in my family loves music. We <u>sing</u> together.
3. My brother is really generous with his time. He <u>fixes</u> my computer.
4. My father is a workaholic. He <u>comes</u> home late. And he <u>brings</u> work home with him, too.
5. My college roommate was really funny. She <u>made</u> us laugh. You know, she <u>told</u> jokes.
6. A friend of mine <u>complains</u> she's broke, but she <u>buys</u> herself expensive clothes.
7. One of my friends is totally unreliable. He <u>cancels</u> plans at the last minute.

About you **E** **Pair work** Do you know people like the ones above? Tell a partner.

"My sister is pretty disorganized. She's always losing her keys."

2 Strategy plus *At least*

You can use the expression *at least* to point out the positive side of a situation.

He's always standing around and talking.

Well, at least he's pleasant.

1.10 Add *at least* to each comment. Listen and check. Do you know anyone like these people? Tell a partner.

1. My girlfriend's always running <u>behind</u>, but she calls to say she'll be late. *(late / at least)*
2. My best friend is always borrowing my clothes. She returns them in good condition. *(At least)*
3. One of my classmates talks about himself a lot. His stories are always interesting. *(At least)*
4. My roommate sleeps all the time, but she doesn't snore. Thank goodness! *(at least)*
5. My parents and I see things differently. We don't have big fights or anything. *(At least)*

A *My dad's always running behind, but at least he says he's sorry when he's late.*

B *Well, my friend is always telling me I'm late, so . . .*

3 Strategies *Funny little habits*

A 1.11 Complete each conversation with *always* and a continuous verb. Add *at least* to each response. Then listen and check.

1. A My boyfriend <u>is always checking</u> (check) his messages, even at the movies!
   B Oh, that's annoying. But *(at least)* he doesn't answer his phone during a movie, right?

2. A My girlfriend <u>is always telling</u> (tell) jokes. She never takes anything seriously.
   B Well, *(At least)* she has a good sense of humor.

3. A Sometimes I'm so disorganized. I <u>am always losing</u> (lose) things, like pens and stuff.
   B Yeah, but *(at least)* you don't lose anything really valuable, right?

4. A My sister <u>is always asking</u> (ask) me for money. She asks nicely, so it's hard to say no.
   B Well, *(At least)* she asks politely.

B Pair work Practice the conversations above with a partner.

About you C Pair work Talk about people with habits like these. Think of something positive to say.

- texting
- chewing gum
- falling asleep in class
- singing or whistling
- forgetting things
- telling jokes
- losing things
- looking in mirrors
- daydreaming

"My friend is always texting, but at least she doesn't do it while she's crossing the street."

Lesson D / Is that a fact?

1 Reading

A Think of two questions you would ask a new classmate. Tell the class.

B Read the profiles. Who would you like to meet? Why?

Reading tip

As you read, think about your own answers to the questions. Can you find expressions you can use?

http://www.onlineenglishclass...

STUDENT PROFILES Meet your classmates in our online English class.

1. MARIANA BARELLI MATOS

What's your major? Fashion design. My dream is to create incredibly beautiful clothes for women all over the world.

Where are you based? In Milan. I was born and raised in São Paulo, Brazil, but my mother's Italian. She felt very strongly that I should experience her culture.

Why did you choose your major? I inherited my mother's love of fashion. She's very style-conscious and has impeccable taste in clothes.

What skills do you have? I speak Portuguese and Italian fluently and have some knowledge of Mandarin.

What do you do in your free time? I love the outdoors, and I'm fairly adventurous. During the summers I volunteer at a camp for disadvantaged children. It's extremely rewarding.

3. KATYA AKILOVA

Where are you based? In Moscow, Russia, though I'm from St. Petersburg, originally.

What do your friends say about you? That I'm very down-to-earth, hard-working, and incredibly organized, and that I'm always setting goals for myself.

What's your worst habit? I'm always doing something. I find it hard to relax.

What are your future plans? As a science major, I'm considering a career as an environmentalist because I feel strongly about protecting the environment.

What skills do you have? I'm an accomplished accordion player. I started playing at the age of eight. I'd love to play professionally with an orchestra.

2. MATEO REYES

Where are you from? I was born and raised in Veracruz, Mexico.

What do your friends say about you? They say that I'm extremely laid-back and even-tempered. And that I'm too humble about my talents.

What are your future plans? I have so many. Right now I'm working for a small production company called Film Fast. My major was film studies, and my goal is to tell real-life stories creatively through television and film.

What do you do in your free time? I like to cook, and I'm always trying out new recipes, especially for desserts.

What's something people don't know about you? When I was 12, I was on a reality TV show for young chefs. I didn't win, but at least I tried.

4. AHMED ABD EL-SALAM

What's your job? I'm an engineer. I work for a big company called Syntix.

Why did you choose to study online? You get to "meet" an incredibly diverse range of students, and the teachers are extremely supportive. I can be pretty shy and introverted and studying online feels safe somehow.

Do you have a secret talent? I play guitar in a band called All Kinds. We play all kinds of music. I feel like a totally different person in the band – outgoing and not shy at all.

What are your tips for new students? Take your studies seriously. Make the most of your opportunities to practice English with other students.

C Answer the questions about the students in the profiles. Which student (or students) . . .

- enjoys playing music? 43
- already has a job? 24
- is very serious? 3
- seems like fun? 1
- is very hard-working? 3
- is an outdoor type? 1
- wants a creative career? 12

8

D Find the adjectives on the left in the student profiles, and guess their meaning.
Then circle the best options to explain them.

1. experience   I should **have contact with** / **ignore** my mother's culture.
2. disadvantaged   The children are **poor** / **rich**.
3. humble   I **think** / **don't think** I am really good at things.
4. considering   This is something I **am** / **am not** thinking about.
5. diverse   The students are all **the same** / **different**.
6. introverted   I'm **very outgoing** / **not outgoing at all**.

About you **E** **Pair work** Ask and answer the questions in the profiles. Give your own answers.

2 Listening Things you don't know about me

A 🔊 1.12 Listen to five people talk about themselves. Match the people and the things they will
probably say next.

Name	Something you don't know about me
1. Ana	_____ I can play two instruments really well.
2. Kevin	_____ I'm a pretty good cook.
3. Jen	___Ana___ I'm a fairly good singer.
4. Patrick	_____ I'm extremely allergic to nuts.
5. Tom	_____ I speak two languages fluently.

B 🔊 1.12 Listen again. Write three pieces of information about each person above. Compare with a
partner. Did you write the same facts?

> 1. Ana started lessons in elementary school.

3 Writing and speaking Your personal profile

About you **A** Write a profile about yourself. Choose five questions from the student profiles, and include
information that other people don't know about you. Don't write your name.

Five things you don't know about me

1. **Where are you from?**

   I was born and raised in Istanbul, Turkey, but I
   moved here at the age of 14.

2. **Do you have a secret talent?**

Help note

Useful expressions

*I **was born and raised in** . . .*
***At the age of** 17, I . . .*
*I **can be** . . .*
*I work for a company **called** . . .*
*I'm an **accomplished** . . .*
*I **started playing** the flute . . .*

B **Class activity** Mix up all the profiles. Select one and guess who wrote it.
Tell the class. Were you right?

Free talk p. 129

Vocabulary notebook / Happy or sad?

Learning tip *Learning opposite meanings*

When you learn a new word, find out if it has an "opposite." Be careful –
sometimes a word has different meanings and different opposites.

This exercise is hard. ≠ *This exercise is easy.*
He's a hard worker. ≠ *He's lazy. He doesn't work hard.*
This chair feels hard. ≠ *This chair feels soft.*

In conversation

Adjectives without prefixes
are much more frequent in
conversation.

happy
unhappy
honest
dishonest

1 Rewrite the sentences so that they have an opposite meaning. Use the words in the box.

happy   polite   mean   well

1. My father drives really badly.
2. My best friend can be very kind.
3. My boss is an extremely rude person.
4. I was pretty unhappy in school.

2 For each of the underlined words, think of a word with an opposite meaning.

1. I have a pretty <u>loud</u> voice.
2. My classmate is extremely <u>outgoing</u>.
3. I'm usually <u>late</u> for appointments.
4. My brother eats very <u>slowly</u>.
5. I think English is <u>difficult</u>.
6. My sister and I have <u>different</u> tastes.

3 **Word builder** Use the prefixes *im-, in-, un-,* and *dis-* to create opposite meanings for these words.

1. He's **patient**. *impatient*
2. She's **honest**. _____
3. He's **friendly**. _____
4. He's **competent**. _____
5. They're **organized**. _____
6. He looks **healthy**. _____
7. She's **reliable**. _____
8. She's **considerate**. _____

 On your own

Make an online photo book. Write five things
about each person's personality and a sentence
about any funny little habits they have.

She's extremely funny.
She's always telling jokes and laughing.

 Can Do! Now I can . . .

✔ I can . . .   ? I need to review how to . . .

☐ talk about how people do things.
☐ describe people's personalities.
☐ make descriptions stronger.
☐ use *always* + continuous verb to say what people do a lot.
☐ use *at least* to point out positive things.
☐ understand people talking about people they admire.
☐ predict what people will say next.
☐ read online student profiles.
☐ write a personal profile.

Experiences

UNIT 2

☑ **Can Do!** In this unit, you learn how to . . .

Lesson A
- Talk about experiences and secret dreams using the present perfect

Lesson B
- Ask about unusual experiences using present perfect questions

Lesson C
- Keep a conversation going
- Use *Do you?*, *Have you?*, etc. to show interest

Lesson D
- Read a travel blog
- Write a post for a travel blog

Before you begin . . .

Think of some special experiences you hope to have in the future. Tell the class . . .

- a place you'd like to go someday.
- something you'd love to see.
- something you'd like to do.
- a person you'd really like to meet.

11

WE ASKED FIVE PEOPLE,

"What's your secret dream?"

"Actually, I've always wanted to be an actor. I haven't had any formal training, but I've been in a couple of college plays. So my dream is to study acting."

– Jill Richardson
Vancouver,
Canada

"Well, Carlos and I have gone sailing a few times with friends, and we've had a lot of fun. So our dream is to buy our own sailboat. But we haven't saved enough money!"

– Sonia and Carlos Silva
Brasília, Brazil

"My dream? To go surfing. I've never tried it before, but my brother goes surfing all the time! He's even surfed in Hawai'i."

– Raquel Garza
Monterrey,
Mexico

"Well, my parents have never traveled outside of Japan, so I want to take them to Europe. I've been there many times, so I know all the best places to go!"

– Hiro Tanaka
Osaka, Japan

1 Getting started

A What kinds of hopes and dreams do people have? Make a class list.

"Some people want to go traveling or meet their favorite pop star. . . ."

B 🔊 1.13 Listen. What is each person's secret dream? Do you have any secret dreams like these?

 C How do the people above express these ideas? Find what they say and underline the verbs.

1. **Jill** I always wanted to be an actor as a child. I want to be an actor now.

2. **Sonia** We didn't save enough money last year. We don't have enough money now.

3. **Raquel** My brother even surfed in Hawai'i — exactly when isn't important.

4. **Hiro** In the past, I went to Europe many times.

2 Grammar Present perfect statements 🔊 1.14

Extra practice p. 141

Use the present perfect for events at an indefinite time before now.

I **'ve been** to Europe.	I **haven't been** to Paris.
You **'ve done** a lot of things	You **haven't gone** sailing.
We **'ve had** a lot of fun.	We **haven't saved** enough money.
They **'ve traveled** in Asia.	They **haven't been** to Europe.
He **'s surfed** in Hawai'i.	She **hasn't tried** surfing before.

Regular past participles

travel	traveled	**traveled**
want	wanted	**wanted**
save,	saved	**saved**
try	tried	**tried**

The present perfect is often used with these frequency expressions.

I've **always** wanted to study acting.
We**'ve gone** sailing once / twice / many times.
She**'s never tried** it before.

Irregular past participles

be	was / were	**been**
do	did	**done**
go	went	**gone**
have	had	**had**
see	saw	**seen**

Notice how people use *been* and *gone* to talk about travel destinations.

I**'ve been** to Paris. (I went and came back.)
She**'s gone** to Paris. (She's still in Paris.)

❌ **Common errors**

Use the past participle, not the base form.

I've traveled a lot.
(NOT *I've travel* a lot.)

A Complete the conversations with the present perfect. Then practice with a partner.

1. A I _'ve always wanted_ (always / want) to try rock climbing.

   B Really? Not me. I _have never wanted_ (never / want) to do it. I _have always been_ (always / be) afraid of heights.

2. A I _haven't seen_ (not see) the Grand Canyon. I really want to go there someday.

   B Me too. My friend _has been_ (be) there. She had an amazing time.

3. A I _have gone_ (go) surfing three or four times. It's exciting.

   B Yeah? I _haven't tried_ (not try) it before. I _have never done_ (never do) any water sports.

4. A My dream is to be a tennis player. I _have had_ (have) a lot of training, and I _have played_ (play) with some professional tennis players.

   B No way! I love tennis. I _have always wanted_ (always / want) to meet Andy Murray.

5. A We _haven't traveled_ (not travel) much, but we want to go to Bogotá.

   B Me too. My cousin lives there. He _has invited_ (invite) me to visit several times, but I _haven't saved_ (not save) enough money to go.

About you **B** Pair work Start conversations like the ones above using your own ideas.

"I've always wanted to try hang gliding."   *"Really? My friend's been hang gliding."*

3 Talk about it What are your secret dreams?

Group work Talk about these things. Why haven't you done them? What has stopped you?

▶ something you've always wanted to buy
▶ a place that you've never been to but would like to visit
▶ something you've always wanted to learn how to do
▶ something else you've always wanted to do

1 Building language

A ◀)) **1.15** Listen. Which experience do you think was scarier?

HAVE YOU EVER DONE ANYTHING **SCARY**?

"Yes, I have. I went white-water rafting in Ecuador last year, and I fell off the raft. Luckily, my friends pulled me out of the river. But I've never been so scared in my life."

– Mei-ling Chen, Taipei, Taiwan

"No, I haven't. Well, maybe once. I entered a talent contest a couple of years ago and sang in front of a hundred people. That was scary. But I won third place!"

– Martín Suárez, Caracas, Venezuela

Figure it out **B** Unscramble the questions and complete the answers. Then practice with a partner.

1. A to Ecuador / you / been / Have / ever / ?
   B Yes, I _have_ . I _was/went_ there last year.

2. A entered / you / Have / a / talent contest / ever / ?
   B No, I _haven't_ . But I _sung_ in a concert in May.

2 Grammar Present perfect vs. simple past ◀)) 1.16

Extra practice p. 141

Use the **present perfect** for indefinite times before now.	**Have** you ever **gone** white-water rafting? No, I **haven't**. I've never **gone** rafting. Yes, I **have**. I **went** rafting **last May**.
Use the **simple past** for specific events or times in the past.	**Did** you **have** a good time? Yes, I **did**. But I **fell** off the raft.

In conversation

The most common questions with the present perfect are *Have you (ever) seen / been / heard / had . . . ?*

A Complete the conversations with the present perfect or simple past. Then practice.

1. A _Have_ you ever _heard_ (hear) of kitesurfing?
   B Yes, I _have_ . But I _have never done_ (never / do) anything like that.

2. A _Have_ you and your friends ever _gone_ (go) on a big roller coaster?
   B No, we _haven't_ . I _have_ always _hated_ (hate) roller coasters.

3. A _Have_ you ever _stayed_ (stay) up all night?
   B Yes, I _have_ . My family _went_ (go) camping two years ago, and none of us _slept_ (sleep) all night.

4. A _Did_ you _do_ (do) anything different last summer?
   B Yes, I _did_ . I _learned_ (learn) to play African drums. I _have_ always _wanted_ (want) to play them. I _'ve never gone_ (never / go) to Africa, though.

About you **B** Pair work Ask the questions above. Give your own answers.

3 Building vocabulary

About you **A** Ask your classmates about these good and bad experiences. For each question, find someone who answers yes. Write the student's name in the chart.

Good experiences		Bad experiences	
Have you ever . . .	Name	**Have you ever . . .**	Name
won a prize?	Bille	**broken** something valuable?	LuPida
gotten 100% on a test?		**lost** something important? Yes	LuPida
spoken to a famous person?		**had** the flu? Yes No	Kevin
taken an exciting trip? Yes	LuPida	**forgotten** someone's birthday? Yes	Kevin
found a wallet?	LuPida	**fallen** and **hurt** yourself? Yes	Jack

"Have you ever won a prize?" *"Yes, I have. I won a prize in a science fair in fifth grade."*

Word sort **B** Complete the verb chart. Make another chart with more verbs that you know.

Base form	win	get	speak		find				fall	
Simple past	*won*	got		took		lost		forgot		hurt
Past participle	*won*	got	spoken				had			

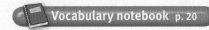 **Vocabulary notebook** p. 20

4 Speaking naturally Reduced and unreduced forms of *have*

> A ***Have*** you ever been to Mexico?
> B *No, I **haven't**. But my parents **have** been there several times. (parents'**ve**)*

A 🔊 **1.17** Listen and repeat the question and answer above. Notice how *have* is reduced in questions and full statements but not in short answers.

About you **B** 🔊 **1.18** Listen and complete the questions below. Then ask and answer the questions with a partner. If you answer yes, give a specific example.

1. Have you ever gone _bungee jumping_ ?
2. Have you ever been to a _rock festival_ ?
3. Have you ever seen a _famous person_ ?
4. Have you ever taken a _German_ class?
5. Have you ever had _North American_ food?
6. Have you ever won a _contest_ ?
7. Have you ever forgotten an _appointment_ ?
8. Have you ever broken _your arm_ ?

About you **C** **Pair work** Ask the questions above again, this time using your own ideas.

> A *Have you ever gone bungee jumping?*
> B *Actually, I have. I was terrified. I never did it again!*

🔊 **Sounds right** p. 137

I've heard good things . . .

1 Conversation strategy Keeping the conversation going

A What kinds of fun things do people do on the weekends? Make a list.

B 🔊 1.19 Listen. What fun things has Jason done lately?

Lea	Have you done anything fun lately?
Jason	Yeah, we went to a new club called Fizz last week. Have you been there?
Lea	No, but I've heard good things about it. How was it?
Jason	Yeah, it's neat. The DJ was really good. Do you like techno music?
Lea	Yeah, it's OK, um, not my favorite. I prefer hip-hop.
Jason	Do you? Have you seen that new movie about hip-hop artists?
Lea	No. Is it good?
Jason	Yeah. I've seen it a couple of times.
Lea	Have you? Well, I'm kind of in the mood for a movie. Do you want to see it again?
Jason	Well, I enjoyed it, but . . . I've never seen a movie *three* times!

C **Notice** how Lea and Jason keep the conversation going. They say things like *I've heard good things about it* to show interest and then ask a question. Find other examples in the conversation.

"Have you been there?"

"No, but I've heard good things about it. How was it?"

D Match each statement with a response. Then practice with a partner.

1. I just saw *Hereafter*. It was a good movie. Have you ever seen it? _____
2. Have you ever eaten a lychee? _____
3. I heard a really good band called Sunset recently. Do you know them? _____
4. One of my favorite restaurants is Spice House. Have you ever eaten there? _____

a. It's a fruit, right? I've never tried one. What do they taste like?
b. No, but I've walked by it. What kind of food do they serve?
c. No, but I've heard good things about them. What kind of music do they play?
d. No, but I've heard of it. What's it about?

About you **E** **Pair work** Practice the conversations above using your own ideas. Change the underlined words.

2 Strategy plus Response questions

You can show interest by responding with short questions like *Do you?* and *Have you?* Use the same tense as the other person.

I've seen it a couple of times.

Have you?

In conversation

To show surprise, you can respond with questions like *You do?* and *You have?* This is more informal.

Complete the conversations with response questions like *Do you? Are you? Did you?* or *Have you?* Then practice with a partner.

1. A I've never been up in a hot air balloon. I'm afraid of heights.

    B ___Are u___ ? Me too. I hate flying.

    A ___Do u___ ? I'm the same way. I get sick on airplanes, too.

2. A Have you ever performed in front of an audience?

    B Yes, I have. Actually, I do it all the time.

    A ___Do u___ ? Wow.

    B Yeah. I'm a drummer in a rock band.

    A ___Are u___ ? I'm impressed!

3. A Have you seen any good movies lately?

    B Actually, I went to see that new action movie that's out right now.

    A ___Did u___ ? The one with Liam Neeson? I've seen all his movies.

    B _____ ? So is he your favorite actor?

3 Listening and strategies What have they done?

A ◀⃞)) 1.20 **Listen to three people talk about things they have done. Match the people and the main topic they talk about. There are three extra.**

1. Albert ___D___
2. Reny ___A___
3. Melissa ___F___

a. a job
b. vacations
c. a sport
d. a hobby
e. a movie on TV
f. an accident

B ◀⃞)) 1.20 **Listen again. What did each person just do? Write a sentence.**

C ◀⃞)) 1.20 **Listen again. Respond to the last thing each person says. Check (✓) the correct response. Then write a question to keep each conversation going.**

1. Albert ☐ *You have?* ☒ *Did you?* ☐ *Were you?* _____
2. Reny ☐ *Did you?* ☐ *You were?* ☐ *You have?* _____
3. Melissa ☐ *You did?* ☐ *Are you?* ☐ *Do you?* _____

Free talk p. 129

17

1 Reading

Reading tip
After you read, think of a comment you could post to show you understood the blog.

A Look at the photographs. Which trip would you like to take? Tell the class. Then read the two blogs. Which blogger had the worst problems?

---

http://www.myblogguatemala...

JAKE'S JOURNEY   MARCH 2   GUATEMALA

When we arrived in Guatemala two weeks ago, we didn't know what to expect. But I have to say, we've had a great time. I've done a lot of traveling, and I think it's one of the most amazing places I've ever been to. We've done a lot in the last two weeks. We've gone hiking, explored some of the ancient Mayan ruins, and camped next to a volcano. We've also seen some beautiful birds. The quetzals are so colorful, and there are hummingbirds everywhere. There are lots of things we haven't had time to do. I've always wanted to go to the rain forest. I hope we get there.

 Camping was really fun. We drove up some rough dirt roads to Ipala Volcano and got a flat tire on the way. It was worth the trip, though. There's a really pretty lake up there that we hiked around. It rained really hard one night, and everything outside the tent got soaked, but at least the tent didn't leak. Fortunately, the weather's gotten better. Another place we found had these beautiful hot springs and a hot waterfall. Standing underneath it was just like taking a hot shower! I miss you all!

Comments

Linh: You do? That's hard to believe, Jake. It sounds like you're having a blast! I've never been to Central America, but I've always wanted to go there. Have you gone on one of the zip lines? I've heard you can do them there. Have fun!

---

http://www.myblogbrazil...

CHLOE'S TRAVELS   March 2   Brazil

After 36 hours of travel, we arrived in Brazil last Sunday. I can't believe it – we got stuck on our way here, and unfortunately, we missed Carnival in Rio! I've always wanted to see it – with all the costumes and dancing and music, but we just couldn't get here in time. And I lost my camera!

Fortunately, I've been good about uploading all my photos to the blog, so I haven't lost many. At least it wasn't an expensive camera. Anyway, we've been to the beach every day. We've gone surfing, and I went parasailing yesterday. The views were amazing!

We've done a lot of sightseeing – though we haven't taken the cable car up Sugar Loaf Mountain. We'll probably do that tomorrow. We've met some really nice people. They're so incredibly friendly and helpful. Amazingly, we managed to visit the family of one of our classmates from college. They were extremely generous. They made us some traditional *feijoada* – a bean and meat dish. It was delicious! I could happily spend another month here. We'll have to come back and visit again.

Comments

Steve: Hey Chloe. I miss you! It's cold and wet here, and I'm working, unfortunately. Have you been able to see any capoeira?

B **Pair work** Read the blogs again. Are the sentences true or false? Write *T* or *F*.

1. Guatemala is exactly what Jake expected. _____
2. The weather has been bad for his entire trip. _____
3. He had problems with his tent one night. _____
4. Chloe enjoyed Carnival. _____
5. She and her friends have finished sightseeing. _____
6. She would like to spend more time in Brazil. _____

2 Listening A traveler's adventures

A 🔊 **1.21** Listen to Suzanne's friends talk about her trip to New Zealand. Check (✓) the things Suzanne has done.

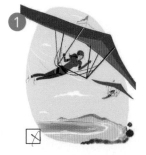

hiking

B 🔊 **1.21** Listen again. Answer the questions.

1. How does Suzanne's friend know about her trip?
2. Does Suzanne like to try new things?
3. What family does Suzanne have in New Zealand? Did she meet them on her trip?
4. What are Suzanne's photos like? Why are her friends surprised?
5. Have Suzanne's friends traveled a lot?

3 Writing and speaking Blog about it

A Read the excerpt from a blog below and the Help note. Underline the adverbs of attitude in the blog.

FLYING ABOVE THE RAIN FOREST

Last summer, I went on the Sky Trek in the rain forest in Monteverde, Costa Rica. I'm afraid of heights, so I almost didn't go. Fortunately, there were some great guides, and they really helped me. Amazingly, it wasn't really scary. It was the most exciting experience I've ever had! I didn't see a quetzal bird, unfortunately, so I'll just have to go back.

> ✏ **Help note**
>
> **Adverbs of attitude**
> Use adverbs like *fortunately*, *unfortunately*, *amazingly*, etc., to show your attitude or feeling about something.
>
> *Fortunately*, there were some great guides.
> I didn't see a quetzal bird, *unfortunately*.
> *Amazingly*, it wasn't really scary.

About you **B** Write a blog entry about an exciting experience you've had. Use *fortunately*, *unfortunately*, and *amazingly*. Do you have a photo to add to the blog?

C Class activity Take turns reading your classmates' blogs. Discuss who has . . .

- had the most exciting experience.
- done something you'd love to do.
- been somewhere you'd love to go.

Vocabulary notebook / Have you ever . . . ?

Learning tip *Verb charts*

When you learn a new verb, write the three main forms in a chart.

base form	simple past	past participle
go	went	gone

In conversation

The top 10 past participles after *I've never* . . . are:

1. been   6. done
2. heard   7. gone
3. had   8. read
4. seen   9. used
5. tried   10. watched

1 Word builder Complete the charts.

These verbs have three different forms.

be	was / were	been	drive	drove		break		broken
do	did		write		written	choose	chose	
go		gone	eat	ate		speak		spoken
see	saw		give		given	wake	woke	
drink		drunk	fall	fell		get		gotten
sing	sang		take		taken	forget	forgot	

2 Make a chart like the one above for the verbs below. Note the simple past form is the same as the past participle.

bring	catch	have	keep	make	read	sell	teach	think
buy	find	hear	leave	meet	say	sit	tell	win

3 Now complete these charts.

The base forms and past participles are the same.

become	became	become
come		
run		

All forms are the same.

cut	cut	cut
hurt		
put		

On your own

Make a "sentence string." Complete the sentence *I've never* . . . How many different ideas can you think of?

I've never flown a plane, danced in the rain,...

Can Do! Now I can . . .

✓ I can . . .   ? I need to review how to . . .

☐ talk about my dreams.

☐ describe experiences I've had or haven't had.

☐ keep a conversation going.

☐ show interest with *Have you?*, *Do you?*, etc.

☐ understand people talking about experiences.

☐ understand a conversation about travel.

☐ read a travel blog.

☐ write a blog about my travel experiences.

20

Wonders of the world

Can Do! In this unit, you learn how to . . .

Lesson A
- Talk about your country or city using superlative adjectives and superlatives with nouns

Lesson B
- Ask and answer questions about your country's natural features with *How* + adjective

Lesson C
- Use short responses with *really* and *sure* to be a supportive listener
- Use superlatives for emphasis

Lesson D
- Read an article about world records
- Write a factual article about your country

1

Arenal Volcano in Costa Rica has been continuously active since 1968.

2

The Great Pyramid of Giza in Egypt dates from around 2560 BCE.

4

This roller coaster at Six Flags Great Adventure in New Jersey, U.S.A., has a 139-meter (456-foot) drop and goes at 206 kilometers (128 miles) per hour.

3

The Great Canyon of Yarlung Tsangpo in Tibet is deeper than the Grand Canyon in the United States.

Before you begin . . .

Have you ever done any of these things? Which would you really like to do?

- See an active volcano.
- Go hiking in a beautiful canyon.
- Visit an ancient city or monument.
- Ride a scary roller coaster.

Test your knowledge. Can you guess the answers to these questions?

1. Which city has the tallest office building in the world?
   a. Kuala Lumpur   b. Taipei   c. Chicago

This building is 509 meters (1,670 feet) tall.

2. Where is the longest suspension bridge?
   a. Japan   b. Denmark   c. China

This is the longest suspension bridge in the world. It's 1,990 meters (6,529 feet) long.

3. Where is the largest shopping mall?
   a. Canada   b. China   c. The United States

This mall covers about 1.97 million square meters (6.46 million square feet).

4. Where is the busiest fast-food restaurant in the world?
   a. Seoul   b. Moscow   c. Hong Kong

This restaurant serves over 40,000 people each day.

5. Which city has the biggest soccer stadium in Europe?
   a. London   b. Dublin   c. Barcelona

This stadium has the most seats. It can hold nearly 100,000 people.

6. Which country has the most tourism?
   a. The United States   b. Spain   c. France

This is the most popular country with tourists. Eighty million people visit every year.

1 Getting started

A Look at the pictures. What is the quiz about? Are you good at these kinds of quizzes?

B ◀)) 1.22 Listen to the quiz. Can you guess the correct answers? Circle *a, b,* or *c.* Then compare with a partner. Check your answers on the last page of your book.

Figure it out **C** **Pair work** Complete the questions. Then ask and answer them with a partner. Can you guess the correct answers? Check your answers on the last page of your book.

1. What's the _____biggest_____ (big) train station in the world?
2. What's the _____busiest_____ (busy) airport in the world?
3. Where is the _____largest_____ (large) building in the world?
4. What's the _____most expensive_____ (expensive) city in the world?

2 **Grammar** Superlatives 1.23

Extra practice p. 142

For short adjectives *the* + adjective + *-est*	What's **the tallest** building in the world? What's **the busiest** restaurant?
For long adjectives *the* + *most / least* + adjective	What's **the most interesting** city in your country? What's **the least expensive** store?
Irregular superlatives *good* ▸ *the best*; *bad* ▸ *the worst*	What's **the best** country to visit? What's **the worst** problem in your country?
Superlatives with nouns *the most* + **noun**	Which country has **the most tourism**? Which stadium has **the most seats**?

A Complete these questions about your country. Use the superlative form of the adjectives or the superlative with nouns.

In conversation

The most + adjective is about 20 times more common than *the least* + adjective.

1. What's ___the largest___ (large) city?
2. Which airport has _the most_ (flights) every day?
3. What's _the fastest_ (fast) way to travel?
4. What's _the most beautiful_ (beautiful) region?
5. Which city has _the most_ (tourism)?
6. Where's _most_ (famous) monument?
7. What's _the best_ (good) university?
8. What's _the worst_ (bad) problem for people?
9. Which city has _the biggest_ (big) population?

X Common errors

Use *-est* with short adjectives.
*What's the **tallest** building in your city?*
(NOT *What's the most tall building in your city?*)

About you **B** **Pair work** Ask and answer the questions. Do you and your partner agree on the answers?

3 **Speaking naturally** Linking and deletion with superlatives

Link the final *st* to vowel sounds and the sounds / *h, l, r, w, y*/.	Delete the final *t* and link the *s* to most consonant sounds.
*What's the mo**st i**nteresting neighborhood?*	*What area has the mo**s(t) t**raffic?*
*What's the talle**st o**ffice building?*	*What's the busie**s(t) m**all or shopping area?*
*What's the bigge**st h**otel?*	*Where's the bigge**s(t) s**tadium?*
*What's the large**st l**ibrary?*	*What's the be**s(t) s**ports team?*
*What's the nice**st r**estaurant?*	*What neighborhood has the mo**s(t) c**lubs?*
*What's the faste**st w**ay to travel around?*	*What's the mo**s(t) p**opular dance club?*
*What's the olde**st u**niversity?*	*What's the be**s(t) m**ovie theater?*

A 1.24 Listen and repeat the questions above. Notice how the final *st* is linked to vowel sounds and the sounds /*h, l, r, w, y*/. However, the final *t* is deleted before – and the *s* is linked to – most consonant sounds.

About you **B** **Pair work** Ask and answer the questions above about your city. Agree on an answer for each question. Then compare with your classmates.

1 Building vocabulary and grammar

A Complete the facts below with seven of the natural features in the box. Which facts did you know?

archipelago	desert	island	mountain	rain forest	✓river
coast	glacier	lake	ocean	reef	volcano

http://www.didyouknow...

Did you know . . . ?

The Nile is the longest _river_ in Africa. It's 6,695 kilometers (4,160 miles) long.

The highest _Mountain_ in the world is Mount Everest in Asia. How high is it? It's 8,850 meters (29,035 feet) high.

The largest _Ocean_ is the Pacific. It covers one-third of the earth! The deepest part is about 11,000 meters (36,000 feet) deep.

How big is the largest _rain forest_? The Amazon in South America covers about 4 million square kilometers (1.5 million square miles).

The largest hot _desert_ is the Sahara in Africa. How large is it? It's about 9.1 million square kilometers (3.5 million square miles).

The most active _volcano_ is probably Kilauea on the _island_ of Hawai'i. It has been active since 1983, and it still erupts every day!

Word sort **B** What natural features are in your country? Complete the chart. Then compare with a partner.

Features we have		Features we don't have	
beaches		desert	

Vocabulary notebook p. 30

"We have a lot of great beaches. They're some of the best in the world."

Figure it out **C** Can you complete the questions and answers?

1. How _____ is the Nile River?
2. _____ high is Mount Everest?
3. It's 6,695 kilometers _long_ .
4. It's 8,850 meters _high_.

2 **Grammar** Questions with *How* + adjective . . . ? 🔊 **1.25**

Extra practice p. 142

How high is Mount Everest?	It's 8,850 meters (29,035 feet) **high**.
How long is the Nile River?	It's 6,695 kilometers (4,160 miles) **long**.
How wide is the Grand Canyon?	It's about 29 kilometers (18 miles) **wide**.
How deep is the Pacific Ocean?	It's about 11,000 meters (36,000 feet) **deep**.
How large is the Sahara Desert?	It's 9.1 million square kilometers (3.5 million square miles).
How hot does it get in Death Valley?	It can reach 48 degrees Celsius (120 degrees Fahrenheit).

Some measurements can be followed by an adjective: *high, tall, long, wide, deep*

A Write two questions about each of the natural features below.

Questions
1. the longest river in Canada
2. the highest mountain in South America
3. the smallest continent
4. the widest canyon in the world
5. the deepest lake in the world
6. the coldest place in the world

Answers
1. The Mackenzie River / 4,241 kilometers
2. Mount Aconcagua / 6,962 meters
3. Australia / almost 7.7 million square kilometers
4. The Grand Canyon / 29 kilometers
5. Lake Baikal / 1,741 meters
6. Antarctica / −89.6 degrees Celsius

What's the longest river in Canada? How long is it?

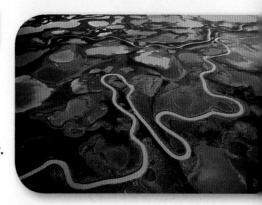

B **Pair work** Ask and answer your questions.
Use the information given above.

A *What's the longest river in Canada?*
B *The Mackenzie River.*

A *How long is it?*
B *It's 4,241 kilometers long.*

3 **Listening** What do you know?

A **Pair work** Take the quiz below. Circle *a*, *b*, or *c*, and guess the answers to the questions.

1. The world's tallest trees grow in _____ .
   a. Japan   ~~c.~~ the United States
   b. Brazil
   How tall are they? They're ___370 feet___

2. _____ is the highest lake in the world.
   a. Lake Victoria   c. Lake Superior
   b. Lake Titicaca *Peru*
   How high is it? It's ___3800___ .

3. The longest mountain range is _____ .
   a. the Andes   c. the Rocky Mountains
   b. the Himalayas
   How long is it? It's ___7600 km___

4. The world's largest archipelago is _____ .
   a. the Philippines   c. Indonesia
   b. Greece
   How many islands does it have? It has ___1300 island___

5. The world's deepest canyon is in _____ .
   a. the United States   c. Australia
   b. Tibet
   How deep is it? It's ___5000 meter deep___

6. The world's smallest volcano is in _____ .
   a. the Philippines   c. Mexico
   b. Italy
   How high is it? It's ___13 meter 43 feet high___

B 🔊 **1.26** **Pair work** Listen to the quiz show. Were your guesses correct?
Write the correct answers above.

Sounds right p. 137

1 Conversation strategy Being a supportive listener

A Are there any national parks in your country? Which one is the most beautiful? Which one is the largest?

B 🔊 1.27 Listen to Kim and Diego. What do they say about Sequoia National Park?

Kim   This is the most incredible place!

Diego Yeah, it really is. It feels good to be out of the city.

Kim   It sure does. You know, these trees are just awesome.

Diego They really are. Have you ever been to Sequoia National Park?

Kim   No. Have you?

Diego Yeah. I went last year. The trees there are the tallest in the world.

Kim   Really? I didn't know that.

Diego Yeah. I had the best time. I mean, it's just the greatest place to hike.

Kim   We should go hiking there sometime.

Diego You're right. We really should.

C **Notice** how Kim and Diego use short responses sometimes with *really* and *sure* to agree and to be supportive listeners. Find examples in the conversation.

"This is the most incredible place!"
"Yeah, it really is."

D Match the comments on the left with the responses on the right. Then practice with a partner.

1. The weather was great last Saturday. _____
2. This city doesn't have many parks. _____
3. We should go hiking sometime. _____
4. The lake here is a great place to go swimming. _____
5. I like being out of the city. You can hear the birds. _____

a. You're right. We really should.
b. Yeah, you sure can.
c. Yeah. It sure is.
d. It really was. I spent the whole day outdoors.
e. No, it really doesn't. That's too bad.

About you **E** **Pair work** Practice the comments and responses using your own ideas. Change the underlined words.

2 Strategy plus Using superlatives for emphasis

You can use superlatives
to emphasize your opinions
or feelings.

> This is the most incredible place!

> I had the best time.

About you | **Pair work** Complete the answers with the superlative form of the adjectives. Then practice with a partner. Practice again with your own information.

1. A Where's your favorite place to hang out?
    B Well, I really like going to cafés. You see _____ (interesting) people.
2. A Where's a good place to go to get out of the city?
    B I like going into the mountains. It's so quiet, and you can see _____ (amazing) wildlife.
3. A I heard that you can take a boat trip down the river.
    B You sure can. You can get _____ (good) views of the city. You really should do it.
4. A How was your vacation? Was it fun?
    B Yeah. We went sailing around some islands. I had _____ (good) time.

3 Listening and strategies Travel talk

A 🔊 1.28 Listen to a radio interview. Number the experiences 1 to 4 in the order you hear them.

☐ A Caribbean cruise   ☐ A visit to Petra, Jordan   ☐ A trip to Antarctica   ☐ A train ride through Copper Canyon in Mexico

B 🔊 1.28 Listen again. How does Jill answer these questions? Complete the sentences.

1. What's the most interesting place you've ever been to? Petra. It's _____.
2. What's the most beautiful place you've seen? Antarctica has _____.
3. What's the best trip you've taken? Copper Canyon. The colors _____.
4. What's the most exciting thing you've done on a trip? I rode _____.
5. What was your worst trip? A Caribbean cruise. The cruise was great, but I _____.

About you | **C** **Group work** Discuss the questions. What experiences have people in your group had?

> A *Well, I went to Rome one time. I had the best time. It's fun to explore new places.*
> B *Yeah, it sure is. I bet Rome was amazing.*

Free talk p. 130

Reading

Reading tip
Before you read, try and answer the questions. Then read to check your guesses.

A Read the questions in the article. Can you guess the correct answers? Then read the article. Were your guesses correct?

---

http://www.worldrecords...

World Records

What was more popular?

☐ A family video uploaded online showing a baby biting his older brother's finger

☐ A popular video war game

"Charlie bit my finger" made the record books as the most liked video in one year with 908,668 "likes." The video war game, however, sold 6.5 million copies in the first 24 hours of its launch in the United States and UK alone.

What's the longest?

☐ The longest snake in the world   ☐ The shortest street   ☑ The world record for the long jump

The world's longest snake, a python, is 7.67 meters (25 feet 2 inches) long. It's the scariest inhabitant at a haunted house attraction in Kansas City, Missouri.

Meanwhile, the shortest street in the world, in Caithness, Scotland, is only 2 meters (6 feet 9 inches) long. It consists of one house with the address 1, Ebenezer Place.

The world record for the long jump was set in 1991. Mike Powell from the United States jumped 8.95 meters (29 feet 4.36 inches) in Tokyo, Japan. More than two decades later, it was still the world record.

Which is more dangerous?

☐ The most dangerous road in world   ☐ The most dangerous animal

The most dangerous road in the world runs 69 kilometers (43 miles) from La Paz to Coroico in Bolivia. On average there are 300 deaths annually. The road is most dangerous in the rainy season when it is muddy and wet.

The deadliest animal is the mosquito. This tiny insect can carry a deadly disease, malaria. Malaria kills more than two million people a year.

Which is older?

☐ The oldest skyscraper city   ☐ The oldest living tree

The oldest skyscraper city in the world is in Yemen. Shibam, with approximately 7,000 citizens, has buildings up to 12 stories high. While they are not the tallest skyscrapers in the world (the tallest is currently in Dubai, UAE), they are the oldest. Most of the 500 skyscrapers were built in the sixteenth century. However, Hong Kong, the place with the *most* skyscrapers, has 2,354 towering buildings, which together would almost reach a space station orbiting Earth.

Some of the oldest forests in the world are in the Andes, a mountain range in southern Chile and Argentina. The average age of these forests is 2,500 years old. However, the oldest living tree, a pine tree in the White Mountains of California, is 4,800 years old.

B Read the article again. Circle the correct words to make the sentences true according to the article.

1. The most popular video war game sold 6.5 million copies in one **day** / **month**.
2. The longest snake is **shorter** / **longer** than the world's longest long jump.
3. The people at 1, Ebenezer Place have **no** / **a few** next-door neighbors.
4. The worst time for accidents on the road is during the **wet** / **cold** season.
5. **Shibam** / **Dubai** / **Hong Kong** has the most skyscrapers.
6. The oldest living tree **is** / **is not** in one of the oldest forests.

C Find the bold words in the article. Then choose *a* or *b* to complete the sentences.

1. After a **launch**, a company starts to _____ a product. a. sell b. design
2. An **inhabitant** is a thing or person that _____ a place. a. visits b. lives in
3. If a street **consists of** one house, it means it _____ one house. a. has b. is famous for
4. When something happens **annually**, it happens every _____ . a. month b. year
5. A city that has 7,000 **citizens** has 7,000 _____ . a. people b. buildings
6. A **towering** building is very _____ . a. short b. tall

2 **Speaking and writing** Interesting facts

A Group work Discuss these questions about your country. Find out as many facts as you can about each thing. Take notes.

What is . . .

- the highest mountain? the longest river?
- the longest bridge? the tallest building?
- the best-known natural feature?
- the best time of year to visit?
- the city with the most historic sites?

B Read the article and the Help note. Then write an article about an interesting place in your country. Add information as shown in the Help note. Include a photo if you can.

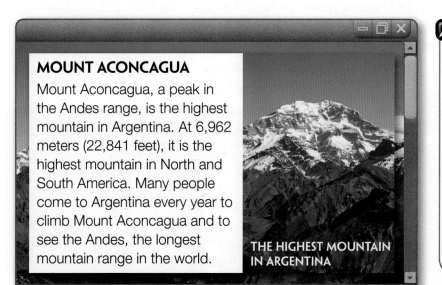

MOUNT ACONCAGUA

Mount Aconcagua, a peak in the Andes range, is the highest mountain in Argentina. At 6,962 meters (22,841 feet), it is the highest mountain in North and South America. Many people come to Argentina every year to climb Mount Aconcagua and to see the Andes, the longest mountain range in the world.

THE HIGHEST MOUNTAIN IN ARGENTINA

✎ Help note

Adding information

Mount Aconcagua is the highest mountain in Argentina. + It is a peak in the Andes range. =

*Mount Aconcagua, **a peak in the Andes range,** is the highest mountain in Argentina.*

Many people come to Argentina to see the Andes. + They are the longest mountain range in the world. =

*Many people come to Argentina to see the Andes, **the longest mountain range in the world.***

C Group work Take turns reading your articles aloud. What new information did you learn?

Learning tip *Drawing maps*

Draw a map of your country. Include natural features.
Label your map.

In conversation

The six natural features people talk
about most are:

1. lakes   3. mountains   5. oceans
2. beaches   4. rivers   6. valleys

1 **Fill in the missing labels
on this map of Australia.**

archipelago	mountains
bridge	ocean
coast	rain forest
desert	reef
island	river
lake	volcano

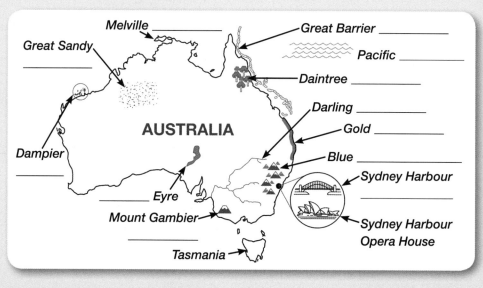

Melville _____
Great Sandy
Great Barrier _____
Pacific _____
Daintree _____
Dampier
Darling _____
Gold _____
Blue _____
AUSTRALIA
Sydney Harbour
_____
Eyre
Mount Gambier
Sydney Harbour
Opera House
_____
Tasmania

2 **Word builder** Sketch a map of your country. Draw and label
natural features. Are any of these features in your country?

bay	cliffs	geysers	hot springs	peninsula	sand dunes	waterfall

 On your own

Find out the highest, longest, biggest,
deepest, and largest natural features in your
country. Make a fact chart showing how
long, high, big, and deep the features are.

Can Do! Now I can . . .

☑ I can . . .   ? I need to review how to . . .

☐ talk about the best, worst, and most beautiful things in
my city and country.

☐ describe natural features.

☐ use short responses to be a supportive listener.

☐ emphasize my opinions and feelings using superlatives.

☐ understand a quiz about natural features.

☐ understand an interview about someone's
travel experiences.

☐ read an article about world records.

☐ write a factual article about my country.

How much do you know about your partner?

A Complete the sentences with an adverb or adjective. Then make guesses about your partner by circling the affirmative or negative form of the verb.

Your guesses My partner . . .	Are your guesses . . .	
	right?	**wrong?**
1. (eats)/ **doesn't eat** _slowly_ (slow).	☐	☐
2. **listens / doesn't listen** _____ (careful) to the weather forecast.	☐	☐
3. **can draw / can't draw** really _____ (good).	☐	☐
4. **gets / doesn't get** upset _____ (easy).	☐	☐
5. **feels / doesn't feel** _____ (bad) if he / she can't do a job _____ (proper).	☐	☐
6. **tries / doesn't try** _____ (hard) to be on time for appointments.	☐	☐

B Pair work Ask and answer questions to check your guesses. Show interest in what your partner says.

A *I guessed that you eat slowly. Do you?*

B *Actually, I do. I'm always the last person to finish a meal.*

A *You are? Well, it's probably a good idea to eat slowly.*

2 Have you ever?

Pair work Find out if your partner has ever done any of these things. Ask and answer questions. Give more information in your "yes" answers.

see someone famous	eat something unusual	win a prize or a competition	be late for an important event	break a bone
get sick and miss a class	have an argument	lose something important	buy yourself something special	throw a party

A *Have you ever seen someone famous?*

B *Yes, I have. I saw Taylor Swift in concert last July.*

3 What natural and human wonders would you like to see?

Complete the chart with four natural and four human wonders. Then discuss with a partner.

Natural wonders	Human wonders	
volcano - Mt. Fuji		

"I'd really like to see Mt. Fuji. I've never seen it before. Have you seen it?"

4 Can you complete this conversation?

Complete the conversation with the words and expressions in the box. Use capital letters where necessary. Then practice with a partner.

I've ever seen	We really should	Have you	at least	incredibly
✓ I've heard	We sure did	I saw	always	the coolest

Milton Have you been to the new sports complex?

Peter No, but ___I've heard___ it's fabulous. How about you?

Milton Actually, I've been there every weekend this summer.

Peter _____? What's it like?

Milton Great. You see _____ people there. _____ Jillian and Maggie there Saturday. They're _____ hanging out at the skating rink.

Peter Maybe we should go skating there sometime.

Milton Yeah. _____ .

Peter So, what's the pool there like?

Milton Gigantic. I think it's the biggest pool _____ .

Peter Do you remember that little pool in Lincoln Park?

Milton Yeah. We always had a lot of fun there.

Peter _____ . But it was _____ small.

Milton Yeah, but _____ it was free. It costs $20 to swim in this new pool!

5 What do you think?

Complete the questions with superlatives. Then ask and answer the questions with a partner.

1. What's ___the tallest___ (tall) building in this city?
2. What's _____ (nice) park around here?
3. Where's _____ (good) place to sit and enjoy the view?
4. Where's _____ (expensive) restaurant in this city?
5. What's _____ (delicious) thing you've ever eaten?
6. What's _____ (bad) movie you've ever seen?
7. Who's _____ (busy) person you know?

6 What are they like?

A Add an appropriate adverb before each adjective below. Use a different adverb each time.

___extremely___ generous _____ impatient _____ reliable _____ inconsiderate

_____ disorganized _____ talented _____ arrogant _____ dishonest

B **Pair work** Think of a person for each quality above. Think of one thing this person is always doing. Tell a partner.

"My friend Cecilia is extremely generous. She's always helping people."

Family life

☑ **Can Do!** In this unit, you learn how to . . .

Lesson A
- Talk about family life using *let, make, help, have, get, want, ask,* and *tell*

Lesson B
- Talk about your immediate and extended family
- Describe memories of growing up with *used to* and *would*

Lesson C
- Give opinions with expressions like *If you ask me*
- Agree with opinions using expressions like *Absolutely* and *That's true*

Lesson D
- Read a blog about family meals
- Write a blog entry about a family memory

Before you begin . . .

What activities do you and your family do together?
Tell the class three things.

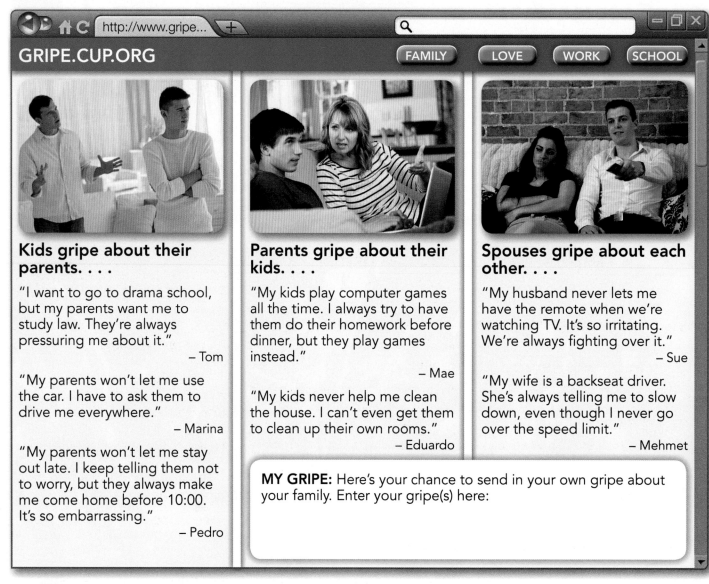

GRIPE.CUP.ORG   FAMILY   LOVE   WORK   SCHOOL

Kids gripe about their parents. . . .

"I want to go to drama school, but my parents want me to study law. They're always pressuring me about it."
– Tom

"My parents won't let me use the car. I have to ask them to drive me everywhere."
– Marina

"My parents won't let me stay out late. I keep telling them not to worry, but they always make me come home before 10:00. It's so embarrassing."
– Pedro

Parents gripe about their kids. . . .

"My kids play computer games all the time. I always try to have them do their homework before dinner, but they play games instead."
– Mae

"My kids never help me clean the house. I can't even get them to clean up their own rooms."
– Eduardo

Spouses gripe about each other. . . .

"My husband never lets me have the remote when we're watching TV. It's so irritating. We're always fighting over it."
– Sue

"My wife is a backseat driver. She's always telling me to slow down, even though I never go over the speed limit."
– Mehmet

MY GRIPE: Here's your chance to send in your own gripe about your family. Enter your gripe(s) here:

1 Getting started

A What are some things family members argue about? Add your own ideas. Tell the class.

chores   school   sharing things   staying out late

B 🔊 2.01 Listen and read the messages on the website above. What problems do the people have?

 C Complete sentences about the people above. Add verbs.

1. Marina's parents won't let her _____ the car.

2. Pedro's parents make him _____ home before 10:00.

3. Mae tries to have her kids _____ their homework before dinner.

4. Eduardo can't get his kids _____ their rooms.

5. Mehmet's wife always tells him _____ even when he's not driving fast.

About you D Pair work Do you have the same gripes as the ones on the website? Tell a partner.

2 Grammar *let, make, help, have, get, want, ask, tell* 🔊 2.02

Extra practice p. 143

let / *make* / *help* / *have* + object + verb	*get* / *want* / *ask* / *tell* + object + *to* + verb
My parents won't **let me stay out** late.	I can't **get them to clean up** their rooms.
They **make me come** home before 10:00.	My parents **want me to study** law.
My kids never **help me clean** the house.	I have to **ask them to drive** me everywhere.
I **have them do** their homework before dinner.	My wife is always **telling me to slow down**.

A Choose the correct verbs to complete the sentences.

1. When I was a kid, my parents never ___*let*___ me walk to school by myself. (got / let)

2. My parents made me _____ to bed at 8:00. (go / to go)

3. My mother couldn't _____ me to eat fish. I was a picky eater! (make / get)

4. My brother never lets me _____ his computer. (use / to use)

5. My parents _____ me to spend more time with them. I should, but I'm too busy. (want / have)

6. My dad's always telling me _____ more exercise. (get / to get)

7. I always _____ my husband make breakfast on weekends so I can sleep late. (have / get)

8. I think kids should _____ their parents clean the house. (get / help)

9. My parents always say they want me _____ happy, not rich. (to be / be)

10. I usually _____ my parents know when I'm going to be home late. (let / have)

In conversation

You can also say *help me to do something*, but this is much less common.

███████████████	*help* + verb
██ *help* + *to* + verb	

✕ Common errors

Don't use *to* with *let, make,* or *have*.

*They make me **come** home before 10:00.*
(NOT *They make me ~~to~~ come home . . .*)

About you **B Pair work Make five of the sentences above true for you. Tell a partner.**

A *When I was a kid, my parents never let me eat junk food.*

B *Really? My parents let me have soda and stuff, but they made me eat vegetables, too.*

3 Listening and speaking Reasonable demands?

A Read the list of demands that parents make on their children. What other demands do parents make?

My parents want me to . . .

1. _____ get married and start a family.
2. _____ study a subject I'm not interested in.
3. _____ work in the family business.
4. _____ change my appearance.
5. _____ call them every week.
6. _____ move nearer to them.

B 🔊 2.03 Listen to five people talk about their parents' demands. Number the demands they talk about above 1 to 5. There is one extra.

About you **C Pair work What demands do your parents or your friends' parents make? Why? Which demands are reasonable? Which are not? Tell a partner.**

"My parents don't want me to get married too soon. They want me to finish college first."

OCD obsessive – compulsive – disorder

Lesson B / Family memories

1 Building vocabulary and grammar

A 🔊 2.04 Listen and read the article. What memories do these people have?

Happiest Memories

We asked people to send us a photo and write about their happiest childhood memory.

My happiest memory is of my **great-grandmother**. She always used to keep candy in her pockets, and she'd always give us some when we came to visit. My dad used to tease us and say, "Grandma, don't give them any candy!" But she did anyway.

– Rosa, Guadalajara, Mexico

All my **aunts** and **uncles** used to come over for Sunday dinner, and there were always about 12 of us around a gigantic table. My **cousins** and I would crawl under it during dinner and play. I'm **an only child**, so it was nice to be part of a big **extended family**.

– Vasily, Saint Petersburg, Russia

My sister and **brother-in-law** used to live next door. I'm only a little older than my sister's kids, so I kind of grew up with my **niece** and **nephew**. I used to go over there a lot, and we'd play together. I was their favorite **aunt**!

– Haruka, Sendai, Japan

I used to love playing basketball with my four brothers. I grew up in a **blended family**, with two **stepbrothers** and two **half brothers**. After my parents **got divorced**, my father **married** a woman with two sons, and they had two more kids together. Anyway, the five of us used to play on a team, and we would always win.

– Justin, Vancouver, Canada

Word sort **B** Complete the chart with male or female family members and with other expressions. Add more ideas. Then tell a partner about your family.

Immediate family		Blended family		Extended family	
father	*mother*	stepfather			great-grandmother
	sister		stepsister	grandfather	
husband		stepson			aunt
	daughter		half sister	(first / second) cousin	
Other expressions					niece
only child		*fiancé*		brother-in-law	

"I'm an only child, but I have six first cousins."

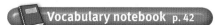 **Vocabulary notebook** p. 42

Figure it out **C** Underline all the examples of *used to* and *would / 'd* in the article. Are these activities and situations in the past or present? Are they finished, or do they still continue?

2 Grammar *used to* and *would* 🔊 2.05

Extra practice p. 143

Use *used to* for regular activities or situations in the past that don't happen now or are no longer true.	Use *would* or *'d* for regular activities in the past.
I **used to go** over to my sister's house a lot. My grandmother **used to keep** candy in her pockets. The five of us **used to play** on a team.	▶ I'**d play** with my niece and nephew. ▶ She'**d** always **give** us some. ▶ We **would** always **win**.
Negatives and questions with *use to* are less common.	Don't use *would* for situations in the past.
I **didn't use to like** jazz. What kind of music **did** you **use to like**?	My sister **used to live** next door. (NOT My sister ~~would live~~ next door.)

About you What family memories do you have? Complete each sentence and add a sentence with *would*. Then compare your memories with a partner.

> 📃 **In conversation**
> People often begin a story with *used to* and then continue with *would*.

1. My family used to go to *the beach* in the summer. *We'd go almost every weekend.*
2. My mother used to make _____ for us.
3. My brother / sister and I used to play _____ together.
4. My family used to watch _____ on TV.
5. I used to see my aunts, uncles, and cousins _____ .
6. My grandparents used to take me to _____ .
7. My family always used to _____ on Sundays.
8. My parents didn't use to _____ on weekends.

> ❌ **Common errors**
> Don't use *used to* to talk about your routines in the present.
> *I used to skip lunch, but now I usually have a sandwich.*
> (NOT . . . ~~now I used to~~ have a sandwich.)

    A *My family used to go to the beach in the summer. We'd go almost every weekend.*

    B *Really? I bet that was fun. My family used to visit my grandmother . . .*

3 Speaking naturally *used to*

> We **used to** visit my great-grandmother.　　I **used to** play with my cousins.

A 🔊 2.06 Listen and repeat the sentences above. Notice the reduction of *used to*.

B 🔊 2.07 Now listen and repeat these sentences.

1. I used to love jumping rope.
2. I used to hate spinach.
3. I used to be afraid of spiders.
4. We used to have a cat.
5. My sister used to tease me a lot.

About you **C Pair work** Use the ideas above to talk about your childhood.

    A *When I was a child, I used to love playing hopscotch.*

    B *Me too. And I also used to like . . .*

🔊 **Sounds right** p. 137

1 Conversation strategy Giving opinions

A Check the statements you agree with. Tell the class.

☐ People spend too much time at work.   ☐ Life is much simpler now than it used to be.

☐ Everybody's getting burned out.   ☐ People don't have enough time to relax.

B 🔊 2.08 Listen. Which of the statements above do Corey and Rob agree with?

Rob So, how are you and Charles doing? And the kids?

Corey Good, thanks. Just way too busy. I don't think we get enough time together. I guess it's the same for everybody.

Rob Oh, definitely. If you ask me, we all work too much these days.

Corey Absolutely. With all the long hours and running the kids around . . .

Rob Oh, I know. And my wife often brings work home on the weekends, too. Whatever happened to time off?

Corey Yeah. It seems like we don't get enough time to relax.

Rob Oh, that's for sure. And it seems to me that's why people often get burned out.

Corey Exactly.

C Notice how Rob and Corey use expressions like these to give opinions. Find examples in the conversation.

> I think . . .
> I don't think . . .
> It seems to me (that) . . .
> It seems like . . .
> If you ask me, . . .

About you | **D** Complete these sentences with expressions from above to give your opinions. Then compare with a partner.

1. _____ people work longer hours than they used to.

2. _____ people don't spend enough time with their families.

3. _____ it's not a good idea to take work home on the weekends.

4. _____ people should get more time off.

5. _____ there's a lot of pressure to work long hours.

6. _____ everyone is way too busy these days.

   A It seems to me that people don't spend enough time with their families.

   B Oh, I know. A lot of parents work long hours and have no time for their kids.

2 Strategy plus Agreeing

You can use these expressions to agree with people's opinions.

Absolutely.	*You're right.*	*I agree (with you).*
Definitely.	*That's true.*	*(Oh,) yeah.*
Exactly.	*That's for sure.*	*(Oh,) I know.*

If you ask me, we all work too much these days.

Absolutely.

In conversation

Exactly, definitely, and *absolutely* are in the top 600 words.

A 🔊 **2.09** Listen to the start of five conversations. Number the responses 1 to 5.

a. _____ Definitely. My kids love to spend time with my mother. They say she's more fun than me.

b. _____ Exactly. Some kids never want to sit down and eat with their families.

c. _____ Oh, I agree. I mean, a lot of kids stay up all night studying for exams.

d. _____ Oh, I know. But working a few hours a week can be a good experience for teenagers.

e. _____ That's true. But a lot of families need two incomes these days.

B 🔊 **2.10** Now listen and check. Do you agree with the opinions? Tell your partner.

3 Strategies In my opinion

A Choose the best responses to complete the conversations. Then practice.

a. I've heard that one in three marriages ends in divorce. I think it's terrible for the kids.
b. If you ask me, it's better to have lots of different friends at that age.
c. I mean, it takes a long time to plan a wedding.
d. It seems to me that it's better to wait until you're a little older.

1. A It seems like people are getting married much later these days.

    B Yeah, that's true. _____

    A Definitely. That way you have time to grow up and find a rewarding job.

2. A I don't think it's good for high school kids to have a serious boyfriend or girlfriend.

    B I agree. _____

    A Exactly. But it seems like teens want to grow up faster nowadays.

3. A It seems to me that long engagements are a good idea.

    B You're right. _____

    A Absolutely. And couples need time to decide where to live and everything.

4. A I think it's sad that so many people get divorced these days.

    B Oh, I know. _____

    A That's for sure. A lot of kids have a hard time when parents get divorced.

About you **B** **Group work** Give your opinions about the topics below. Which do you agree on?

- divorce and children
- spending time with family
- studying all night for tests
- taking work home
- teens having jobs
- the best age to get married

39

1 Reading

 A When you were a child, did you and your family use to eat together every day? What were family meals like? Tell the class.

B Read Barbara's blog. Why does Barbara think families should eat together more often?

 Reading tip

Sometimes writers state similar ideas in the first and last paragraph. This helps tie the reading together.

http://www.barbarasblog...

Barbara's Blog

It seems to me that families used to eat more meals together. And nowadays, there's often a TV nearby, or someone's talking on a cell phone or texting during dinner.

My family always used to eat dinner together, no matter what. We'd wait for everyone to get home, and then we'd all sit down together. My parents never let us take food into another room to watch TV, and if the phone rang, my mom would have us tell the caller to call back later. During dinnertime conversation, everyone had a chance to talk. Back then, I was a bit quieter than my siblings, so my dad would often ask me to talk about my day. That's how we learned to share and take turns, so everyone got to join in.

Speaking of taking turns, all of us kids used to take part in either preparing the meal or cleaning up. Sometimes my mom would let me help her in the kitchen – I'd wash and chop vegetables, or things like that. We'd always have fresh food, or at least leftovers from the night before . . . no fast food or take out.

Now, I won't pretend our mealtimes were absolutely perfect. There was plenty of sibling rivalry, especially between my little brother and me. We used to fight all the time and sometimes kick each other under the table. Then our parents would intervene, telling us to "get along or else!" Nobody knew exactly what "or else" meant, but we didn't want to risk finding out.

These days, it seems like families have little time together, especially at mealtimes. I was reading an article that said children who have regular meals with their families feel less stressed, have a healthier weight, get better grades, and are less likely to get into trouble than children from families that don't eat together. I wonder if those families know what they're missing.

C Find the expressions on the left in the blog. Match each one with a similar expression.

1. no matter what _f_
2. leftovers ____
3. pretend ____
4. sibling rivalry ____
5. intervene ____
6. or else ____

a. food remaining after a meal
b. competition between brothers or sisters
c. become involved in a difficult situation
d. act like something is true that is not
e. or something bad will happen (used as a threat)
f. in any situation

D Read the blog again. Are these sentences true or false? For each statement below, check (✓) *T* or *F*. Correct the false statements. Then compare with a partner.

		T	F
1.	Barbara's mother used to let her watch TV while she ate dinner.	☐	☐
2.	As a child, Barbara was less talkative than others in the family.	☐	☐
3.	The kids in Barbara's family helped make dinner and clean up.	☐	☐
4.	Barbara got along well with all her siblings at dinnertime.	☐	☐
5.	Barbara thinks kids are healthier when they eat with their families.	☐	☐

2 **Listening and writing** Family memories

A 🔊 **2.11** Listen to three people talk about their memories of family life. What did they use to do? Number the pictures.

_____   _____   _____

B 🔊 **2.11** Listen again. Why don't the people do these things now? Write a reason for each one on the line. Compare with a partner.

About you **C** **Pair work** Think of three things you used to do with your family. Tell a partner.

A *We used to go skiing every winter, but my dad hurt his knee, so we stopped.*

B *Really? My parents didn't let us go skiing because they thought it was too dangerous.*

D Read the blog below and the Help note. Underline the time markers. Then write a blog about a family memory from your childhood.

> ### Our roller-skating days
> When we were kids, my sister and I used to roller-skate a lot. We would skate on the sidewalk or on the school playground. In those days, we didn't have all the safety equipment kids use today. These days, kids wear helmets, knee pads, and wrist guards. Back then, we just had to skate carefully and try not to fall.

🖊 **Help note**

Using time markers
- Use these time markers to show the past:
  When we were kids, . . . / When I was . . . , In those days, . . . / Back then, . . .
- Use these time markers to show the present:
  today, now, nowadays, these days

E **Group work** Read your classmates' blogs. Then ask questions to find out more information.

"Did you use to skate to school?"   *"Did your parents let you play outside by yourself?"*

Free talk p. 131

Vocabulary notebook / Remember that?

Learning tip *Word webs*

Use word webs to log new vocabulary about your family members.
What memories do you associate with each person?

1 Look at the picture. Complete the word web with memories of the grandfather in the picture.

was interested in *old cars* .		used to drink _____ .

My grandfather

had _____ and a mustache.		used to wear _____ .

always listened to _____ .

2 Make word webs like the one above about two people in
your family. How many memories can you think of?

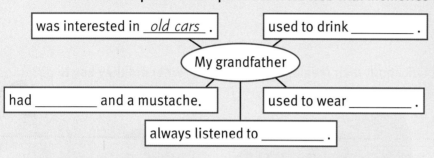

3 **Word builder** Do you know this vocabulary? Find out the meanings of any words you don't know.
Try to add some of the words to your word webs.

adopted   ex-husband   great-aunt   separated   single parent

On your own

Make a photo album of your family. Find
photos of each of your relatives. Write their
names and a short memory about each picture.

Aunt Emily used to bake me cookies.

✓ Can Do! Now I can . . .

| ✓ I can . . . | ? I need to review how to . . . |

- ☐ talk about my family life and habits.
- ☐ share my memories of growing up.
- ☐ describe things that happened in the past that don't happen now.
- ☐ give my opinions.
- ☐ use expressions like *Absolutely*, *Definitely*, etc.
- ☐ understand people talking about demands their parents make on them.
- ☐ understand people discussing things they used to do.
- ☐ read a blog about family meals.
- ☐ write a blog entry about a family memory.

42

Food choices

☑ Can Do! In this unit, you learn how to . . .

Lesson A
- Talk about eating habits using expressions like *a bottle of*, *a little*, *a few*, *very little*, and *very few*

Lesson B
- Talk about different ways to cook food
- Talk about food using *too*, *too much*, *too many*, and *enough*

Lesson C
- Respond to suggestions by letting the other person decide
- Refuse offers politely with expressions like *No, thanks. I'm fine.*

Lesson D
- Read about snacks around the world
- Write about a dish from your country

Before you begin . . .

Can you find these things in the picture? What other food items can you find? Have you bought any of these things recently?

- a bag of potato chips
- a bottle of ketchup
- a package of cookies

- some cartons of juice
- a box of cereal
- a loaf of bread

- a jar of mustard
- a can of soup
- a tub of margarine

What do you have in your refrigerator?

We visited three people to see what they keep in the fridge.

"Let's see, um, a carton of eggs, some milk, a pound of hamburger meat, a few slices of cheese, a jar of mustard, and a little butter. Um, there aren't many vegetables. There are just a few green peppers going bad in the vegetable drawer. I guess I should eat more vegetables."

– David Freeman

"Oh, there's lots of stuff. There's fruit – oranges, mangoes, a pineapple. And I always have plenty of fresh vegetables – broccoli, tomatoes, and carrots. And there's a carton of orange juice and a tub of margarine. I usually buy 1 percent milk because it has fewer calories. And then in the freezer there are one or two frozen dinners, but not many. We eat very few frozen meals."

– Marta Delgado

"Well, there's very little food in there because I eat out most nights. So there's just a loaf of bread, a bottle of soy sauce, a few cans of soda, and a jar of hot peppers. Yeah, there's not much food in the house."

– Chris Kim

1 Getting started

A How often does your family buy food? Do you buy groceries online? at a supermarket?

B 🔊 2.12 Listen to the people above. Who has the healthiest food in their refrigerator?

Figure it out **C** Each person above forgot to mention two things in their refrigerator. Circle the correct words in the sentences below.

1. Chris also has **a little** / **a few** butter and a **bottle** / **carton of** orange juice.
2. Marta also has **a few** / **not much** apples and a **loaf** / **jar** of bread.
3. David also has **a bottle of** / **bottle of** ketchup and some soda. He doesn't have **much** / **many** food.

Grammar Talking about quantities of food 🔊 2.13

Extra practice p. 144

Uncountable nouns	Countable nouns
We have **a little** butter in the fridge. = *some*	We have **a few** slices of cheese. = *some*
There's **very little** food. = *not a lot*	We eat **very few** frozen meals. = *not a lot*
I'm trying to eat **less** fat.	1 percent milk has **fewer** calories.
There's **not much** food in the house.	There aren**'t many** vegetables.

Food containers / items

a carton of juice ► two cartons of juice
a loaf of bread ► two loaves of bread

Weights and measures

a liter of / a quart of   *1 liter = 1.1 quarts*
a kilo of / a pound of   *1 kilo = 2.2 pounds*
kilo = kilogram

❌ **Common errors**

Don't use *a little, much* or *many* + *of* + noun.

There isn't **much cheese**.
(NOT There isn't ~~much of cheese~~.)

A Choose the correct words to complete the sentences.
Then compare with a partner.

1. In my refrigerator, there's always **a jar / a jar of** spaghetti sauce and **a quart of / a few** milk.

2. In my kitchen cabinet, there's **package of / a package of** rice and **a little / a bag of** chips.

3. I try to eat healthily, so I eat **a few / not much** vegetables and **a little / very little** fruit every day.

4. I've bought **very few / very little** meat and **very few / very little** cookies recently.

5. I should eat **less / fewer** junk food. I know it doesn't have **much / many** vitamins.

6. I eat **less / little** fast food than I used to, though I still enjoy **a little / a few** fries when I can!

7. Yesterday, I had **a little / a few** chocolate as a treat.

8. We always keep a few basics in the house: a couple of **loaves of / loaf of** bread, some **cartons of / carton of** milk, **a few slices of / a few** cheese, and **a few / a little** eggs.

About you **B** **Pair work** Make the sentences true for you. Compare ideas.

A *In my refrigerator, there's always a jar of mayonnaise, but there's not much else!*
B *Yeah? We don't eat much mayonnaise, but we have a few jars of salsa.*

Talk about it Is it good for you?

Group work Discuss these beliefs about food. Do you agree? What other beliefs are there?

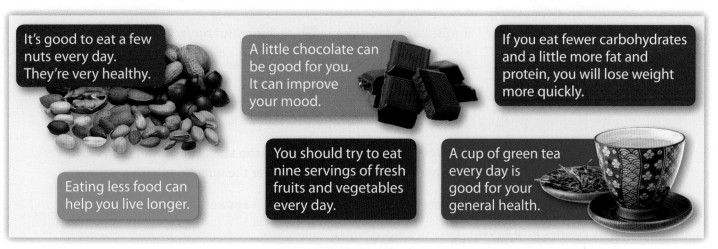

It's good to eat a few nuts every day. They're very healthy.

A little chocolate can be good for you. It can improve your mood.

If you eat fewer carbohydrates and a little more fat and protein, you will lose weight more quickly.

Eating less food can help you live longer.

You should try to eat nine servings of fresh fruits and vegetables every day.

A cup of green tea every day is good for your general health.

A *Do you believe it's good to eat a few nuts every day?*
B *Well, I don't eat many nuts, actually. They have a lot of fat in them.*

1 Building vocabulary

A Have you eaten any of these things recently? Which do you like best?

1. (stir-)fried noodles
2. grilled shrimp
3. steamed vegetables
4. boiled eggs
5. baked potatoes
6. pickled cabbage
7. roast lamb
8. barbecued beef
9. raw fish
10. smoked fish

Word sort **B** How do you like to eat different kinds of food? Make word webs like these using the words above. Then compare with a partner.

eggs
fried
potatoes

grilled

steamed

> **ℹ Note**
> Adjectives *fried, grilled, . . .*
> Verbs *fry, grill, . . .*

Vocabulary notebook p. 52

2 Speaking naturally Stressing new information

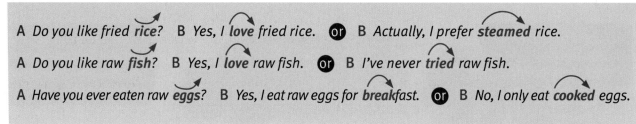

A *Do you like fried rice?*   B *Yes, I love fried rice.*   **or**   B *Actually, I prefer steamed rice.*

A *Do you like raw fish?*   B *Yes, I love raw fish.*   **or**   B *I've never tried raw fish.*

A *Have you ever eaten raw eggs?*   B *Yes, I eat raw eggs for breakfast.*   **or**   B *No, I only eat cooked eggs.*

A 🔊 **2.14** Listen and repeat the sentences above. Notice how the stress and intonation move to the new information in the answers. Then ask and answer the questions with a partner.

About you **B** **Pair work** Ask questions like the ones above. Give your own answers.

A *Do you like fried eggs?*
B *Actually, I prefer boiled eggs.*   OR   *No, I hate fried eggs.*

3 Building language

A 🔊 **2.15 Listen. What do Carla and Leo want to order? Practice the conversation.**

Carla Are you going to have dessert?

Leo No, I'm too full. I ate too many fries.

Carla Do you mind if I have something? My salad wasn't filling enough. I mean, is there enough time? I know I eat too slowly – probably because I talk too much!

Leo That's not true! Anyway, I want another iced tea. I'm really thirsty. I guess I put too much salt on my fries.

Carla OK. So I'm going to order some apple pie.

Leo Mmm. Sounds good. Maybe I'll have some, too.

Carla Well, as they say, there's always room for dessert!

Figure it out **B** **Can you complete these sentences with *enough*, *too*, *too much*, or *too many*?**

1. Leo ate _____ fries, and he put _____ salt on them.

2. Carla's still hungry because she didn't eat _____ food.

3. Leo is _____ full, but Carla isn't. Her salad wasn't filling _____ .

4. Carla eats _____ slowly. She doesn't eat fast _____ . She talks _____ .

4 Grammar *too, too much, too many, and enough* 🔊 2.16

Extra practice p. 144

	too / too much / too many	enough
With nouns	I ate **too much food** / **too many fries**.	I didn't eat **enough food** / **fries**.
As pronouns	I ate **too much** / **too many**.	I didn't eat **enough**.
With adjectives	He's **too full**.	Her salad wasn't **filling enough**.
With adverbs	She eats **too slowly**.	She doesn't eat **fast enough**.
With verbs	She **talks too much**.	Maybe she **doesn't listen enough**.

A **Complete these sentences with *too*, *too much*, *too many*, or *enough*. More than one answer may be possible.**

1. I eat _____ fast food and not _____ fruits and vegetables.

2. There's never _____ time to shop or cook during the week, so I eat out a lot.

3. During my exams, I study _____ and I don't sleep _____ .

4. I don't like fried foods – there's _____ fat in them. It's better to grill or steam food.

5. If I don't eat _____ for breakfast, or if breakfast isn't filling _____ , I'm usually _____ hungry to wait for lunch.

6. Sometimes, I eat _____ fast and I get a stomachache. Or I eat _____ .

7. I don't like ice cream. I find most desserts are _____ sweet for me.

8. I'm probably _____ careful about what I eat, but I get sick if I eat _____ fatty things.

About you **B** **Pair work** **Are the sentences above true for you? Discuss with a partner.**

A Actually, I don't eat too much fast food. I don't eat too many fries or anything.

B That's good. I eat too much fast food. I don't eat properly.

((• Sounds right p. 138

1 Conversation strategy Letting another person decide

A What drinks or snacks do you offer visitors to your home?

B 🔊 2.17 Listen. What snack does Laura offer Kayla? What drinks does she offer?

Laura	Can I get you something to eat?
Kayla	Oh, I'm OK for now. But thanks.
Laura	Are you sure? I have some cheese in the fridge and a box of crackers.
Kayla	No, thanks. I'm fine. Really. Maybe later.
Laura	Well, how about some tea or coffee?
Kayla	Um . . . are you having some?
Laura	Yeah. I need to wake up a bit. So tea or coffee?
Kayla	Either one is fine. Whatever you're having.
Laura	OK. I think I'll make some tea. Do you want it with milk or lemon?
Kayla	Oh. Either way. Whichever is easier. Are you sure it's not too much trouble?
Laura	No, no. It's no trouble at all.

C Notice how Kayla uses expressions like these because she wants Laura to decide. Find examples in the conversation.

> *Either one (is fine).* *Whatever you're having.*
> *Either way (is fine).* *Whichever is easier (for you).*
> *Whatever you prefer.*

D Pair work Write responses to these questions, letting the other person decide. Then start a conversation with a partner, and plan an evening out using the ideas below.

1. So what do you feel like doing this evening? Do you want to eat out or go to a movie?
2. OK. Let's go to a movie. What do you want to see? A thriller or a comedy or . . . ?
3. I guess we could eat out first. Do you want to eat Italian or Chinese or . . . ?
4. So, do you want to walk, or should we catch the bus? The buses run every 20 minutes.
5. Should we buy the tickets there, or should we get them online before we go?
6. Do you want a drink first? Would you like some lemonade or some iced tea?

> *A So what do you feel like doing this evening? Do you want to eat out or go to a movie?*
> *B Um, well, whatever you prefer.*

2 **Strategy plus** Polite refusals

**You can use expressions like these
to refuse offers of food and drink politely.**

No, thanks. Maybe later.
No, thanks. I'm fine. Really.
I'm OK for now. But thanks.

Can I get you something to eat?

I'm OK for now. But thanks.

**Imagine you are the guest at a party. How can you refuse your host's offers politely?
Complete the conversation. Then practice with a partner.**

Host   Would you like something to eat?

Guest _____

Host   Really? Are you sure? There are a few sandwiches or some vegetables and dip.

Guest _____

Host   Well, can I get you something to drink? I have juice, soda, . . . or would you prefer some water?

Guest _____

Host   Well, if you change your mind, just let me know.

3 **Listening and strategies** That sounds good.

A 🔊 **2.18 Listen to four conversations about food and drink. Number the pictures 1 to 4.**

☐   ☐   ☐   ☐

B 🔊 **2.18 Listen again. Choose an appropriate response to the last thing you hear. Write the number
of the conversation, 1 to 4.**

a. Actually, they all look really good. Whatever you prefer. _____

b. Either one is fine. Whatever you're having. _____

c. I could go either way. You choose. _____

d. Oh, no, thanks. I'm fine. Maybe later. _____

C Choose one of the pictures and role-play a conversation.

A *So would you like some dessert? How about chocolate cake or a little ice cream or . . . ?*

B *No, thanks. Maybe later. I'm too full.*

Free talk p. 131

1 Reading

A Brainstorm! How many different snacks can you think of? Which ones are popular in your country? Make a class list.

B Read the article. Which snacks have you heard of? Have you tried any of them?

> 📖 **Reading tip**
>
> Writers sometimes start a sentence with a short description of something before they name it. ***Originally from Spain***, *empanadas are baked or deep-fried pastries. . . .*

  http://www.snacksaroundtheworld...

SNACKS AROUND THE WORLD

BAOS

Baos are delicious steamed or baked buns with a variety of fillings such as spicy meat, sweet bean, pickles, or custard. A favorite in many Asian countries, they are delicious at any meal – even breakfast. Although they have been popular for over 2,000 years, people are still coming up with new ideas for fillings – like scrambled eggs or coconut!

MOCHI ICE CREAM

In the 1980s, a Japanese company showed the world a great new way to eat ice cream. They wrapped little ice cream balls in colorful sheets of sticky rice called *mochi*. You can hold these little treats in your hand as you eat them, and the ice cream won't melt on your fingers! Now popular in many countries, frozen mochi ice cream comes in flavors like green tea, chocolate, and mango.

DOLMA

Popular throughout Mediterranean countries, *dolma* are particularly popular as a snack food in Turkey. The best-known dolma are grape leaves stuffed with tasty ground-meat fillings or rice with herbs and spices and a few nuts. (In Turkish, *dolmak* means "stuffed.") Freshly steamed, dolma are delicious with yogurt.

FLAVORED POPCORN

People never get tired of popcorn. Native Americans first ate popcorn over 2,000 years ago, and people around the world still love it today! Buy it ready-made or cook it in a little oil until it "pops." Or make your own microwaved popcorn, and add your own flavors. How about a little cheese, chocolate, or caramel on yours? Some even more creative flavors are baked potato, curry, and taco. What new popcorn flavor can you think of?

EMPANADAS

If you're in Latin America, and you're looking for a quick snack, chances are you're not far from an *empanada* stand. Originally from Spain, empanadas are baked or deep-fried pastries that have a variety of different fillings depending on the region. Traditional fillings often have meat and potatoes or meat with spices, chopped onion, egg, olives, and raisins. In southern Europe, they often have a fish filling. They make a great snack at any time of the day.

C Read the article again. Complete the chart for each snack.

Name of snack	Popular where?	Cooked? How?	Ingredients / flavors
baos	Asia	steamed / baked	spicy meat, sweet bean, . . .

2 Listening and speaking Snack habits

A Have you tried any of the snacks below? Which countries do you think they come from originally?

 hummus  nachos  edamame  chocolate chip cookies

B 🔊 2.19 Listen. How would the three people answer the questions? Complete the chart.

	Zoe	Josh	Kate
1. What's your favorite snack?			
2. When do you eat it?			
3. Do you think it's healthy?			
4. Do you know how to make it?			

About you C Group work Discuss the questions above. Complete a chart like the one above with your classmates' information. Which snacks are healthy? Which do you like?

3 Writing You should definitely try it!

A Read the Help note and the article below. What do *like*, *for example*, and *such as* give examples of?

A THAI TREAT

If you visit Thailand, you should try some of the delicious desserts, like sweet sticky rice. People often eat it as an afternoon snack with tea or for dessert. You can order it in a restaurant or buy it on the street at a food stand.

There are many types of sweet sticky rice. For example, people make black sticky rice with a special type of wild rice, and they also make sticky rice with corn. You can put different toppings on sweet sticky rice, such as coconut custard, fresh coconut cream, and fresh mangoes.

Help note

Giving examples
You can introduce examples with:
like
for example
such as

B Choose a popular snack food or traditional dish in your country. Write an article about it for a food website. Include a photo if you can.

C Class activity Read your classmates' articles. Choose three to add to your website.

51

Learning tip *Collocations – words that go together*

Learn new words in combination with other words. For example, learn adjectives that often go before a noun.

boiled eggs, fried eggs, raw eggs

In conversation

The most common collocations in conversation with these six cooking words are:

1. *fried* chicken   4. *grilled* cheese
2. *boiled* eggs   5. *smoked* salmon
3. *baked* potatoes   6. *raw* fish

1 Cross out the adjective that doesn't go well with each noun.

a. fried
   pickled
   ~~smoked~~ ⎤ onions
   raw

b. barbecued
   steamed
   fried ⎤ rice
   boiled

c. stir-fried
   spicy
   boiled ⎤ noodles
   pickled

d. smoked
   fresh
   canned ⎤ fruit
   dried

2 How many cooking or taste words can you put before these foods? List them from your least favorite to your favorite ways of eating them in a chart like the one below.

carrots   chicken   eggs   fish   pineapple   red peppers

least favorite - - - - - - - - - - - - - → favorite				
boiled	*steamed*	*stir-fried*	*raw*	carrots

3 Word builder Which adjective goes best with each noun? Complete the expressions.

✓creamed   dark   grated   mashed   scrambled   sweet and sour   whole   whole wheat

| _____ eggs | _____ shrimp | _____ chocolate | _____ bread |
| _____ milk | *creamed* spinach | _____ potatoes | _____ cheese |

On your own

Find a restaurant menu online and translate five of the dishes into English.

Fried bananas

Now I can . . .

✓ I can . . .   ? I need to review how to . . .

☐ talk about quantities of food and eating habits.

☐ discuss different ways to cook food.

☐ respond to suggestions by letting the other person decide.

☐ use expressions like *I'm fine* to refuse offers.

☐ understand people offering and accepting or refusing food.

☐ understand conversations about snacks.

☐ read about snacks around the world.

☐ write about a dish from my country.

Managing life

 Can Do! In this unit, you learn how to . . .

Lesson A
- Talk about future plans and schedules using *will, be going to,* the present continuous, and the simple present

Lesson B
- Discuss problems and solutions using *ought to, have got to, would rather, had better,* etc.
- Use expressions with *make* and *do*

Lesson C
- Use expressions like *I'd better go* to end phone conversations
- Use expressions like *Catch you later* to say good-bye

Lesson D
- Read a blog about multitasking
- Write some advice about time management

Before you begin . . .

How good are you at managing your life? Are you good at . . .

- keeping your house neat and organized?
- organizing your social life?
- dealing with problems at work or school?

Hello?

● ● ● ● ● ● ● ● ●

Oh, hi, Brandon. How are you?

● ● ● ● ● ● ● ● ●

Good, really good. . . . No, it's OK. I'm on my way home.

● ● ● ● ● ● ● ● ●

What am I doing tomorrow night? Actually, I don't think I'm doing anything. . . .

● ● ● ● ● ● ● ● ●

Oh, wait. Tomorrow's Tuesday. I have my kickboxing class. That starts at 7:00, and then I'm meeting Anna afterwards. We're going to have dinner together. But, yeah, I'd love to catch up with you. How about Wednesday night?

● ● ● ● ● ● ● ● ●

Huh. So you're going to be out of town for a couple of days, . . . but you'll be back Friday, right? So what about Friday?

● ● ● ● ● ● ● ● ●

Uh-oh. I just remembered. My boss is going to have us all work late Friday. She mentioned it last week. We have this big deadline.

● ● ● ● ● ● ● ● ●

Yeah, yeah. We won't be finished on time. It's a long story. Uh, I'll tell you about it sometime.

● ● ● ● ● ● ● ● ●

Tonight? Actually, I'm not doing anything!

● ● ● ● ● ● ● ● ●

That's a fabulous idea. I'll just stop by my apartment to get changed, and then I'll come right over to meet you. I can get there by 7:30. And I'll call for a reservation.

● ● ● ● ● ● ● ● ●

Great. So, see you in about an hour. Bye.

1 Getting started

A What kinds of plans do you make in advance? at the last minute? Tell the class.

B 🔊 2.20 Listen. Stacy is talking on the phone to her friend Brandon. When do they decide to meet? Can you guess what they're going to do?

Figure it out **C** Complete the sentences. How does Stacy tell Brandon about these things?

1. Her plans with Anna tomorrow night: "We _____ together."

2. Not meeting the work deadline on Friday: "We _____ on time."

3. Not having plans tonight: "I _____ anything."

4. Why she can't meet tomorrow: "I _____ class."

54

2 **Grammar** Talking about the future 🔊 2.21

Extra practice p. 145

Use *will* when you decide to do something as you are speaking.	I**'ll** just stop by my apartment to get changed and then I**'ll** come right over to meet you. (NOT I ~~come~~ right over . . .)
Use *will* or *be going to* for factual information or predictions based on what you know.	You**'re going to** be out of town, but you'll be back Friday? My boss **is going to** make us work late Friday. Our project **won't** be finished on time.
Use the present continuous or *be going to* (not *will*) for decisions you've made and fixed plans.	I**'m meeting** Anna after my kickboxing class. We**'re going to** have dinner together. I**'m not doing** anything tonight.
Use the simple present for schedules.	I **have** my kickboxing class tomorrow. It **starts** at 7:00.

A Complete the conversations with appropriate ways to talk about the future, using the words given. There may be more than one possible answer. Then practice with a partner.

1. A So, what _____ you _____ (do) after class tomorrow?

   B Well, actually, I _____ (take) the afternoon off tomorrow. I _____ (have) lunch with my sister. So yeah, I _____ (not / work) in the afternoon.

   A That sounds nice. Where _____ you _____ (have) lunch?

   B I'm not sure. Do you want to meet us? I'm sure my sister _____ (not / mind).

   A OK. Sure. I _____ (text) you tomorrow when I get out of class.

2. A I _____ (have) a party at my place Friday night. Can you come?

   B Actually, I _____ (have) basketball practice at 7:00 on Friday. It _____ (not finish) until 9:00. Is that too late?

   A No, not at all. My guess is that most people _____ (not arrive) until after 9:00 anyway.

   B OK, great. So I _____ (come) over right after practice. It _____ (be) around 9:30.

3. A So _____ you _____ (go away) this weekend?

   B Actually, we _____ (go) on a boat trip on the lake on Saturday. The weather report says it _____ (not / be) too windy. So yeah, it _____ (be) fun, I think.

   A That sounds great. I've never done that.

   B You're kidding. Why don't you come with us? The boat _____ (leave) at 9:00. I _____ (call) my brother and ask him to get you a ticket.

About you **B** **Pair work** Ask and answer the questions above. Give your own answers.

3 **Listening and speaking** Fun invitations

A 🔊 2.22 **Listen. Complete the chart. Which invitation sounds the most interesting to you?**

	Anton	Clareta	Callie
What's the invitation for?	*a concert*		
What day? What time?			
What are his / her plans then?			
What does he / she decide to do?			

B **Pair work** Student A: Invite your partner to do something with you on a specific day.
Student B: Tell your partner your plans for that day, and make a decision about what to do.

Building vocabulary and grammar

A ◀)) **2.23** Read the posts and replies on the website. Complete the expressions with the correct form of *do* or *make*. Then listen and check.

Ask the LIFE COACH Do you have a personal problem that you'd rather not discuss with friends or family? Get some confidential advice from our online life coach.

Q1 Sometimes I think I ought to _____*do*_____ some **volunteer work** in a school or a hospital, but I'm too busy just trying to _____ **a living**. I have very little free time, so I think I'd better not add anything to my schedule right now. Am I right?

Coach Don't _____ **excuses**. You don't have to spend all your free time doing volunteer work – three hours a week is enough. _____ **some research**, and find an organization where you feel you can _____ **a difference** and _____ **some good** for other people.

Q2 My boss is a bully. He yells at me if I _____ **a mistake**, and he _____ **fun of** me in front of my co-workers. I've tried talking to him, but it doesn't _____ **any good**. He won't listen. I guess I'm going to have to _____ **something** about this problem, but what?

Coach It doesn't _____ **any sense** to ignore this problem, and you'd better do something quickly before it gets worse. _____ **an appointment** with your Human Resources representative. You might want to take a colleague with you, too.

Q3 I'm meeting my girlfriend's parents for the first time next weekend. They've invited me for dinner. I'm going to _____ **my best** to _____ **a good impression** on them, but I'm really nervous. Any advice?

Coach _____ **an effort** to dress nicely, and _____ **sure** you take them a small gift, such as flowers or chocolates. _____ **some nice comments** about their home, the food, etc., but don't overdo it. You ought to let them _____ **the talking** at first. The most important thing, however, is just to be yourself.

Q4 My boss recently offered me a promotion. I've _____ **a lot of thinking** about it, but I can't _____ **up my mind** if I should take it. Sometimes I think I'd rather stay in my current job. I've got to decide by next week. What should I do?

Coach _____ **a list** of the pros and cons of each job, and give each one a score from 1 to 5 (5 = the best). Then _____ **the math** – add up the points for each list, and subtract the con totals from the pro totals. Which job has the highest score? Does that help you_____ **a decision**?

Word sort **B** Make word webs like these for *do* and *make*. Add other expressions you know. Then discuss the life coach's advice with a partner. Do you agree? What advice can you add?

some volunteer work

 do

 make

 Vocabulary notebook p. 62

Figure it out **C** Find expressions on the website with the same meanings as the underlined words below.

1. I should do some volunteer work.
2. You really should do something quickly.

3. I have to make a decision soon.
4. I'd prefer to stay in the same job.

2 Grammar What's advisable, necessary, preferable 🔊 2.24

Extra practice p. 145

What's advisable	**You'd better** do something quickly. (*'d = had*) **I'd better not** add anything to my schedule. I **ought to** do some volunteer work. You **ought to** let them do the talking. You **might want to** take a colleague with you.
What's necessary	**I'm going to have to** do something about it. **I've got to** decide by next week. (*'ve = have*) You **don't have to** spend time on this.
What's preferable	**I'd rather (not)** stay in my current job. (*'d = would*)

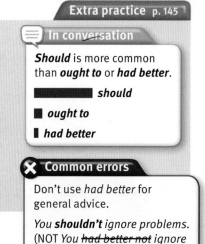

In conversation

Should is more common than ***ought to*** or ***had better***.

▮▮▮▮▮▮▮ should
▮ ought to
▮ had better

❌ Common errors

Don't use *had better* for general advice.

*You **shouldn't** ignore problems.* (NOT *You ~~had better not~~ ignore problems.*)

Pair work Complete the conversations with problems and solutions. Then compare with a partner. Did you have any of the same ideas?

1. A We have a test tomorrow, so I ought to _____ tonight, but I'd rather _____ .
   B You know, I think you'd better _____ because _____ .

2. A I don't know what to do. I received an offer for a job. It looks really interesting, but it doesn't pay very well. I'm going to have to make up my mind if I want to _____ .
   B That's a hard decision to make. You might want to _____ .

3. A I need more exercise. I ought to make an effort to _____ every day, but it takes so much time.
   B Well, you don't have to _____ , but you ought to _____ .

4. A I have a friend who makes fun of me all the time, but I'd rather not _____ .
   B That's not good. I think you're going to have to _____ .

5. A My sister hasn't applied to college. She's got to _____ if she wants to _____ .
   B She'd better decide soon because _____ she's got to _____ .

3 Speaking naturally Reduction of verbs

*You might **want to** try a new instructor. (**wanna**)*	*You **ought to** take more lessons. (**oughta**)*
*You'd **better** study the driver's manual. (**you better**)*	*You've **got to** pay attention! (**gotta**)*
*You're **going to have to** practice more. (**gonna hafta**)*	

A 🔊 2.25 Listen and repeat the sentences above. Notice the reduction of the verbs. In what situation might a person give this advice? Can you think of other advice?

About you **B** **Group work** Think of six pieces of advice for a student who's not doing well in class.

4 Talk about it What's your advice?

Group work Imagine a friend is in each situation. Give as much advice as you can.

1. You're tired and don't feel like going to a friend's party, but you know you ought to go.
2. You have time to do some regular volunteer work on the weekend or take a part-time job.
3. You had an interview for a job you really want, but it didn't go well.

"Well, you ought to just tell your friend, you know. And say you're not in the mood for a party."

(((· **Sounds right** p. 138

1 Conversation strategy Ending phone conversations

A When was the last time you were running late? Why? Tell the class.

B 🔊 2.26 Listen. Why can't Ling talk longer on the phone?

ASSERTIVENESS
SEMINAR
_____
4TH FLOOR

Ramon Hi, Ling. It's Ramon. Is this a good time to talk?

Ling Um, not really. I'm late for a seminar. I'm going to have to run.

Ramon Oh, OK. I just wanted to ask about this weekend.

Ling Well, can I call you back tonight? I've got to get going.

Ramon OK. I'll be home after 8:00. I'm going to the gym after work.

Ling Oh, good. I'll call you later. I'd better go now.

Ramon Yeah. So think about what you want to do on Saturday.

Ling Yeah, I will. Listen, Ramon, I've really got to go. I'm already late.

Ramon All right. I'll let you go. By the way, what's your seminar about?

Ling Being assertive. Bye now!

Ramon Oh, OK! Talk to you later.

C Notice how Ling tries to end the phone conversation with expressions like these. Find examples in the conversation.

I'd better go.	*Can I call you back?*
I've got to get going.	*I'll call you later.*
I'm going to have to run.	*I've really got to go.*

D Pair work Practice the phone conversation below six times. Think of a new excuse, and use a different expression to end the conversation each time.

> Hi, _____ (name). Is this a good time to talk?

> Not really. I'm just cooking dinner. (Give an excuse) Can I call you back? (Use an expression)

2 **Strategy plus** Friendly good-byes

In friendly or informal phone conversations, you can use short expressions like these to say *good-bye*. The words in parentheses are usually dropped.

(I'll) Talk to you later.
(I'll) Catch you later.
(I'll) See you later.
I('ve) got to go. / (I've) Got to go.
I('d) better go.
(It was) Nice talking to you.

In conversation

The shorter forms of these expressions are more common.

See you later.
I'll / We'll see you later.
Talk to you later.
I'll / We'll talk to you later.

Talk to you later.

Write the shorter forms of the underlined expressions to make these conversations more informal. Then practice the conversations with a partner.

1. A Hi, it's me. Are you on your way?
   B Yeah. I'll be there in about half an hour.
   A All right. <u>I'll see you soon.</u>

2. A Well, my appointment is at 2:00, so <u>I'd better go.</u>
   B OK. <u>I'll talk to you later.</u>
   A Yeah. <u>I've got to go.</u> <u>I'll see you later.</u>

3. A OK, well, <u>I'd better let you go.</u>
   B Yeah. <u>It was nice talking to you.</u>
   A Yeah. Take care. Bye.

4. A Listen, my train's coming. <u>I'll catch you later.</u>
   B Yeah. <u>I'll see you tomorrow.</u> Bye.

3 **Strategies** Role-play phone conversations

Pair work Student A: Choose a topic below. Call your partner. Try to keep the conversation going. Student B: Try to end the conversation. Then change roles.

- plans for the weekend
- how your week is going
- something you're looking forward to
- something you want to borrow
- some exciting news
- something you're busy with

A *Hey, Rick. How are things going?*
B *Not bad. Busy. Actually, I have an appointment at the dentist at 2:00. Can I call you back?*
A *Well, I was just calling about my band. We need someone to make a flyer for us.*

Free talk p. 132

1 Reading

A Do you ever multitask? What kinds of things do you do at the same time? Is multitasking a good thing to do?

B Read the blog. What does it say about multitasking?

📖 **Reading tip**
Writers often ask the reader questions to raise topics and organize their ideas.

http://www.theartandscienceof...

The Art (and Science) of Doing Less and Achieving More

"To do two things at once is to do neither." – Publilius Syrus, Roman philosopher, 100 BCE

Multitasking: An Effective Solution?

With the introduction of various technologies into our everyday lives, multitasking has become a normal feature of our busy days. Doing more tasks ought to mean that we get more done. But does it really? Take this example from a typical day at my job.

Last week, during a meeting, I decided to send a quick email to a client. A minute later, I had to send another email with the attachment I had forgotten. In my third email to him, I had to apologize for sending the *wrong* attachment. When I eventually focused on the meeting, I realized someone was asking me a question, but because I wasn't paying attention, I couldn't answer it and I had to ask him to repeat it. Embarrassing.

Sound familiar? Don't worry – you're not alone. Research shows that when we multitask, we are actually playing a trick on ourselves. We *think* we're doing more, but actually we're not. In fact, multitasking can lead to a 40 percent drop in productivity. Researchers say that we don't really multitask at all; we "switch-task," and when we switch from one thing to another, we're simply interrupting ourselves to do something else.

An Alternative Approach

I did some thinking about all of this and decided to do some research for myself. For one week, I would make an effort *not* to multitask. During that week, I discovered two surprising things.

First, I made great progress on challenging projects. I stayed with each project when it got hard, and it really made a difference. Now, I no longer avoid tough assignments, I don't get distracted by other things, and I finish one job before I go on to another – even if the job is driving me crazy!

Second, my stress levels dropped dramatically. Research shows that multitasking isn't just inefficient, it's stressful, and I found that was true. It was actually a relief to finish one thing before going on to the next. So how can we change our multi-tasking ways?

A Cure for Multitaskers

First, get rid of interruptions. I now know that when I'm working, I should resist the temptation to check email, and I make sure my phone is turned off.

Second, set yourself a tight deadline. If you think you have to give a presentation in 30 minutes, you might not want to answer that interrupting phone call! Single-tasking to meet a tight deadline will also reduce your stress levels – as long as you meet it, of course!

My experiment convinced me that I don't have to accept multitasking as a way of life. If you make up your mind to avoid distractions and concentrate on one job at a time, you really can achieve more.

About you **C** Replace the underlined words in each question with the correct form of an expression from the blog. Then ask and answer the questions with a partner.

1. Have you ever <u>done something to fool</u> someone? How did it turn out?
2. What do you do if you're not <u>moving forward on</u> an assignment?
3. Do you often <u>have your attention interrupted by</u> email or phone calls?
4. What kinds of personality traits <u>annoy you a lot</u>?
5. Do you ever <u>decide on a time to finish something that's hard to achieve</u>?
6. Do you find it easy to <u>make decisions</u> about things?

D Read the blog again. Answer the questions. Then compare your answers with a partner.

1. What happened when the writer tried to multitask?
2. What was the research the writer did?
3. What were the two things the writer learned?
4. What two things does the writer recommend we do to stop multitasking?
5. What is the writer's opinion of multitasking? Do you agree?

2 Listening and writing When should I do that?

About you **A** What do you do when you have a lot to do? How do you balance work, friends, and family time?

B 🔊 2.27 Listen to four people talk about their time management problems. Which problems did they have? Write the number of the speaker. There are two extra problems.

a. I left things until the last minute. ____
b. I couldn't set priorities. ____
c. I felt I had too much to do. ____
d. I couldn't meet deadlines. ____
e. I took on too many jobs. ____
f. I delayed difficult jobs. ____

C 🔊 2.27 Listen again and write the advice each speaker received.

D Read the Help note. Then read the question and answer and circle any sentences that link ideas with *as long as*, *provided that*, or *unless*.

I'm trying to be more organized, so I decided to record my lectures, but I never have time to watch them. Any ideas?

Unless you find time to watch the recordings, there is really no point in having them. So make time to review them - provided that they are worth watching again, of course!
Most people waste time when they are traveling to and from work or school, so use that time to watch your classes on your laptop - as long as you're not driving, of course!

 Help note

Linking ideas with *as long as*, *provided that*, and *unless*
- *As long as* and *provided that* mean "if" or "only if."
- *Unless* means "except if" or "if . . . not."

About you **E** **Pair work** Write a question about a time management problem. Then exchange papers and answer your classmate's question. Give advice.

Vocabulary notebook / Do your best!

In conversation

The most common collocations with the verb *make* are:

1. make **sure**   4. make **a decision**
2. make **sense**   5. make **a mistake**
3. make **a difference** 6. make **money**

1 Complete the sentences with these expressions.

do my best	make a difference	make a good impression	make up my mind

1. I'm going to try to _____ on my new boss. I want her to have a good opinion of me.
2. I'd like to do something useful in life. I want to _____ in people's lives.
3. I can't _____ if I want to buy a new cell phone. I can't decide if I need one.
4. I find exams very stressful, but I always _____. I try very hard to do well.

2 Write sentences to help you remember these expressions.

do some thinking	do volunteer work	make an effort
do something fun	make a decision	make fun of someone

3 **Word builder** Which expressions below can you complete with *make*? Find appropriate verbs to complete the other expressions. Write the words on the lines.

1. _____ changes
2. _____ a mess
3. _____ a dream
4. _____ progress
5. _____ a suggestion
6. _____ plans
7. _____ a walk
8. _____ a favor

On your own

Choose five expressions and make a "to do" list using them.

Now I can . . .

✔ I can . . .   ? I need to review how to . . .

- [ ] talk about the future.
- [ ] ask for and give advice about personal situations.
- [ ] end phone calls with expressions like *I'd better go.*
- [ ] say good-bye in a friendly, informal way.

- [ ] understand people discussing invitations.
- [ ] understand people discussing time management.
- [ ] read a blog about multitasking.
- [ ] write some advice about time management.

1 What do you think?

A Complete these opinions with a verb or *to* + verb. Compare with a partner.

1. Parents shouldn't let teenagers __*watch*__ violent shows on TV.
2. Parents ought to make their kids _____ books every night.
3. Teachers ask students _____ too much homework.
4. Parents shouldn't help their children _____ their homework.
5. Parents shouldn't let their children _____ too much junk food.
6. Parents should get their kids _____ more vegetables and fewer sweets.
7. We shouldn't let young people _____ cars until they're 21.
8. We ought to make all teenagers _____ some volunteer work.

B **Group work** Discuss three or four opinions above. Use the expressions in the boxes to give your opinions and to show when you agree.

   A *If you ask me, parents shouldn't let teenagers watch violent shows on TV.*
   B *Absolutely. It seems to me that teenagers are becoming more violent because of TV.*
   C *I don't know. I don't think people learn violent behavior from TV.*

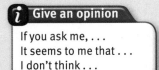

i Give an opinion
If you ask me, . . .
It seems to me that . . .
I don't think . . .

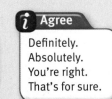

i Agree
Definitely.
Absolutely.
You're right.
That's for sure.

2 The way it used to be

Complete the story with the correct form of the verbs below.

| be | bring | buy | complain | get | hate | live | play | push | ✓ visit |

When I was a kid, we used to ____*visit*____ my grandparents every
month. They _____ two hours from our home, so we always
_____ some books to read in the car. I used to _____ the
drive, and I'd always _____ , so my dad would _____ us ice
cream. That _____ fun. When we _____ to my grandparents'
house, my grandma would always let us _____ in her yard. They
had a swing set, and my grandpa would _____ us on the swings.

3 How many words can you remember?

Write expressions with *do* or *make* about six family members or friends.
Then tell a partner about each person, using the expressions.

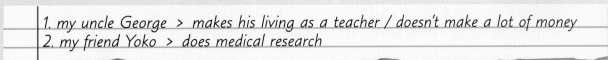

1. my uncle George > makes his living as a teacher / doesn't make a lot of money
2. my friend Yoko > does medical research

"My uncle George makes his living as a teacher. He doesn't make a lot of money, but he loves his work."

4 What's going to happen?

Complete the conversation with appropriate ways to talk about the future, using the verbs given. More than one correct answer is possible in some cases. Then practice with a partner.

Cindy What time does your train __leave__ (leave) today?

Dana I _____ (take) the 3:30 train. Oh, no, it's almost 3:00!

Cindy Don't worry. I _____ (drive) you to the station.

Dana Oh, you don't have to do that. I _____ (call) a taxi.

Cindy No way! I can take you. I _____ (go) to the mall this afternoon. It's not far from the train station.

Dana Are you sure it _____ (not be) a problem?

Cindy No problem at all. I _____ (meet) a friend there at 4:00.

Dana Well, OK. Thanks. I _____ (get) my suitcase.

Cindy Yeah. We _____ (have to) leave right away.

Dana OK. I _____ (be) ready in five minutes.

5 A healthy diet?

A Complete the sentences with different foods. Use your own ideas. Then discuss with a partner. Do you agree?

1. It's not healthy to eat too many __hamburgers__ .
2. If you want to lose weight, eat very few _____ .
3. If you eat too much _____ , you'll gain weight.
4. You should drink very little _____ .
5. A little _____ every day is good for you.
6. People should eat less _____ and more _____ .

B **Pair work** Replace the underlined words in these sentences. How many true sentences can you make? Compare with a partner.

1. I like <u>boiled eggs</u> better than <u>fried eggs</u>.
2. I drink about three cans of <u>soda a day</u>.
3. I'm trying to eat less <u>ice cream</u> and fewer <u>doughnuts</u>.
4. I always keep a <u>jar</u> of <u>mayonnaise</u> in my refrigerator.
5. I ate too much <u>candy</u> and not enough <u>fruit</u> yesterday.

> A *I like roast chicken better than fried chicken. How about you?*
> B *Actually, I prefer barbecued chicken.*

6 Get off the phone!

Role play Student A: You are planning a special dinner for an English-speaking visitor to your country. Call your partner to ask for advice about what kind of food to prepare.

Student B: Your partner calls to ask for advice just as you are leaving to meet a friend. Try to end the conversation politely.

Relationships

☑ Can Do! **In this unit, you learn how to . . .**

Lesson A
- Talk about your circle of friends using relative clauses

Lesson B
- Talk about dating using phrasal verbs like *get along* and *break up*

Lesson C
- Use expressions like *probably* and *sort of* to soften comments
- Use *though* to give a contrasting idea

Lesson D
- Read an article about online dating
- Write an article describing your circle of friends

Before you begin . . .

What relationships do you have with other people?
Are you a friend to someone? a family member? a co-worker?
Which relationships do you enjoy most?

CHRISTOPHER OWEN

talks about his circle of friends.

1 My running buddy . . .
"Well, Mike is the guy I run with in the morning. He's the one who got me started running when I was in college. It's convenient because he lives right down the street."

2 My most exciting friend . . .
"Jennifer is another friend from college. Jen plays in a rock band that's really hot right now, so her life is very different from mine. She still calls a lot to talk about all the things she's doing. That's kind of fun."

6 My oldest friend . . .
"Charlie is someone I grew up with. We've been through a lot together. I can tell him just about anything. He's just someone I can totally trust."

3 My roommate . . .
"Yuya is a guy that Jen introduced me to. He was looking for an apartment to share. It's great because he's a 'clean freak.' I've never lived in a place that's so clean."

5 A new friend . . .
"Then there's Angela. She's a new friend I met through Mike. She's cool. She's the kind of person you can just call and say, 'You want to go see a movie tonight?' That kind of thing."

4 A friend from work . . .
"Nina is an interesting woman who sits across from me at work. She used to have a company that planned weddings for people. She has some funny stories to tell."

1 Getting started

A Where do people make friends? How many places can you think of? Make a list.

B 3.01 Listen and read the article above. How did Christopher meet his friends?

Figure it out **C** How does Christopher express these ideas? Underline the sentences in the article.

1. Nina is an interesting woman. She sits across from me at work.

2. Jen plays in a rock band. It's really hot right now.

3. Angela is a new friend. I met her through Mike.

4. Jen calls me a lot to talk about things. She's doing a lot of things.

2 Grammar Relative clauses 🔊 3.02

Extra practice p. 146

Relative clauses begin with *who*, *that*, and *which*. They give information about people or things. Use *who* and *that* to refer to people and *that* and *which* to refer to things.

Subject relative clauses

Who, *that*, *which* are the subject of the verb.
Nina is an interesting woman **who** / **that** **sits across from me**.
Nina used to have a company **that** / **which** **planned weddings**.

Object relative clauses

Who, *that*, *which* are the object of the verb.
Charlie is someone (**who** / **that**) **I can trust**.   (**I can trust Charlie.**)
Jen talks about the things (**that**) **she's doing**.   (**Jen's doing things.**)

> **In conversation**
>
> In subject relative clauses:
> - *Who* is more common than *that* for people.
> - *That* is more common than *which* for things.
>
> In object relative clauses:
> - People often leave out *who* and *that*, especially before pronouns.
> - *Which* is not frequent.

A Combine each pair of sentences using relative clauses. More than one answer may be possible.

1. I have a really good friend. She works at a local radio station.
   _____

2. There was a really funny guy in my high school. He was always telling jokes.
   _____

3. One of my friends from class has a football. His favorite team signed it.
   _____

4. My best friend has a really pretty gold ring. Her grandfather gave it to her.
   _____

5. I have a new friend. I met him in my kickboxing class.
   _____

6. My friend and I saw a movie last night. It made us both cry.
   _____

> ✖ **Common errors**
>
> Don't use pronouns that repeat ideas in relative clauses.
>
> *Janet has a company **that** **makes** toys.* (NOT . . . *company that it̶ makes toys.*)
>
> *She's a friend **that I met** through Mike.* (NOT . . . *friend that I met h̶e̶r̶ through Mike.*)

About you **B** **Pair work** Make five true sentences about people you know. Take turns telling a partner. Ask questions to find out more information.

A I have a really good friend who works for an airline.
B Really? Which airline?

3 Talk about it Who's in your circle of friends?

Group work Discuss the questions. Give as much information as you can.

- ▶ Who's your closest friend? How did you meet?
- ▶ How many friends do you have on your social networking site?
- ▶ Do you have any friends that you only contact occasionally?
- ▶ Who were your friends when you were growing up?
- ▶ Are you still in touch with the friends that you grew up with?
- ▶ Do you have any friends that have exciting lives? Explain why.
- ▶ Do you have any friends who are very different from you? How are they different?

1 Building vocabulary and grammar

A ◀» 3.03 Put the story in the correct order. Number the parts from 1 to 6. Then listen and check your answers.

HIGH SCHOOL SWEETHEARTS ♥♥♥♥♥♥♥♥♥♥♥♥♥

☐ He discovered that Anna was a member. He wrote her an email, and she **wrote back** right away. It **turned out** that Anna was still single and was looking for him, too! They made plans to meet at a restaurant in her city.

☐ Steve and Anna **grew up** in a small town called Greenville. In high school, they **hung out** with the same crowd. They **got along** very well, and they started **going out** together. Anna was Steve's first love, and he was her first love, too.

☐ When Steve was 35, he was ready to **settle down** with someone, but no one seemed right. He still thought about Anna. Then he heard about a website that helps find old classmates. He signed up immediately.

☐ But the long-distance relationship didn't **work out**, and they decided to **break up**. A year later, Anna's family **moved away** from Greenville, and Steve lost touch with her.

Anna and Steve at their high school prom

A recent photo of the happy couple

☐ When they saw each other, all the old memories **came back**, and they started **going out** again. Within a few months they were married, and they are now living "happily ever after." Sometimes your first love **turns out** to be the best.

☐ After they graduated, Anna **went away** to college, while Steve attended a college nearby. They would get together about once a month, when Anna **flew back** home to visit her parents.

Figure it out **B** Which verbs in the story mean the same as the underlined expressions below?

1. Steve and Anna spent their childhood in the same town.
2. Steve and Anna started dating.
3. Anna went somewhere else to college.
4. Steve and Anna decided to stop dating.

Word sort **C** Complete the chart with phrasal verbs from the story. Then take turns retelling the story with a partner. How many verbs can you use?

along	away	back	down	up	out
		write back			

Vocabulary notebook p. 74

2 Grammar Phrasal verbs ◀)) 3.04

Extra practice p. 146

A phrasal verb is a verb plus a particle like *along*, *away*, *back*, *out*, *up*, etc.

Steve and Anna **grew up** in the same town.
They **got along** well and started **going out** together.
Anna **went away** to college.
She **flew back** home once a month.
Things didn't **work out**, so they decided to **break up**.

Notice

Steve and Anna **got along** well.
Steve **got along with** Anna.
Anna **got along with** Steve.
Steve and Anna **went out** together.
Steve **went out with** Anna.
Anna **went out with** Steve.

A Complete the opinions with the phrasal verbs in the box.

break up	go back	move away	sign up	work out
get along	✓go out	settle down	turn out	write back

1. It's more fun to _____*go out*_____ with someone you know than to go on a "blind date."
2. If you don't _____ well with your boyfriend's or girlfriend's family, your relationship won't _____ .
3. It's good to date a lot of different people before you _____ with one person.
4. After you _____ with someone, you should try and stay friends.
5. You should never _____ to someone you've broken up with.
6. If you want to meet someone, it's a good idea to _____ for a class.
7. First dates usually _____ to be a disaster!
8. Relationships never work out when one person has to _____ .
9. When a close friend sends you an email, you should _____ immediately.

About you **B** Pair work Discuss the opinions above. Do you agree?

3 Speaking naturally Stress in phrasal verbs

*Are you going **out** with anyone?*   *How are you getting **along**?*

A ◀)) 3.05 Listen and repeat the questions above. Notice that in phrasal verbs the particle is stressed more than the verb.

B ◀)) 3.06 Listen and repeat the questions below. Underline the stressed particles.

1. Do you think it's OK to go out with more than one person at the same time?
2. What should you do if you're not getting along with your boyfriend or girlfriend?
3. Do you think relationships can work out if you work in the same place?
4. Is it OK to go out with someone who is a lot older or younger than you?
5. What's a good age to settle down?
6. What's the best way to break up with someone?

About you **C** Group work Ask and answer the questions. How many different opinions do you have?

1 Conversation strategy Softening comments

A What are your neighbors like? Do you get along with them? Tell the class.

B 🔊 3.07 Listen. What does Olivia think about her new neighbor?
What are Adam's neighbors like?

Olivia	That woman by the mailboxes – she just moved in next door.
Adam	Yeah? She seems pretty friendly.
Olivia	She's OK. She's a little bit strange, though.
Adam	Yeah? How do you mean?
Olivia	Well, it's kind of weird. She's always coming over and borrowing things from me.
Adam	She's probably just a little lonely or something.
Olivia	Yeah. Maybe she is. But then other times she sort of ignores me. She's just a bit odd, I guess.
Adam	Yeah, in my building nobody ever speaks. I mean, we all smile but we don't really know each other.
Olivia	I guess that's OK in a way, though. I don't like to get too friendly with the neighbors.
Adam	Me either.

C **Notice** how Olivia and Adam use these expressions to "soften" their comments. Find examples in the conversation.

I guess / I think	*a little / a (little) bit*
probably / maybe	*just*
kind of / sort of	*in a way*

D Make the comments below softer. Add the expressions given.

1. The people in my neighborhood are unfriendly. (a little)
   They're just busy with their own lives. (maybe)

2. The people next door keep to themselves. (kind of)
   They don't like to go out. (I guess)

3. The people across the street are always looking out of their window. They seem nosy. (a little)
   They don't have anything better to do. (I guess)

4. The guy above me plays his music too loud. (a bit) It gets noisy. (kind of)
   It can be difficult to sleep. (a little bit)

5. One of my neighbors is always coming over. It's irritating. (in a way)
   She's lonely. (I think / probably / just)

About you **E** **Pair work** Do you know anyone like the people above? Take turns telling a partner. Can you "soften" your comments?

"Actually, the woman in our local store is a little unfriendly. She's not very helpful."

2 Strategy plus *though*

You can use *though* to give a contrasting idea.

> ▤ **In conversation**
>
> *Though* is one of the top 200 words.

She seems pretty friendly.

She's OK. She's a little bit strange, though.

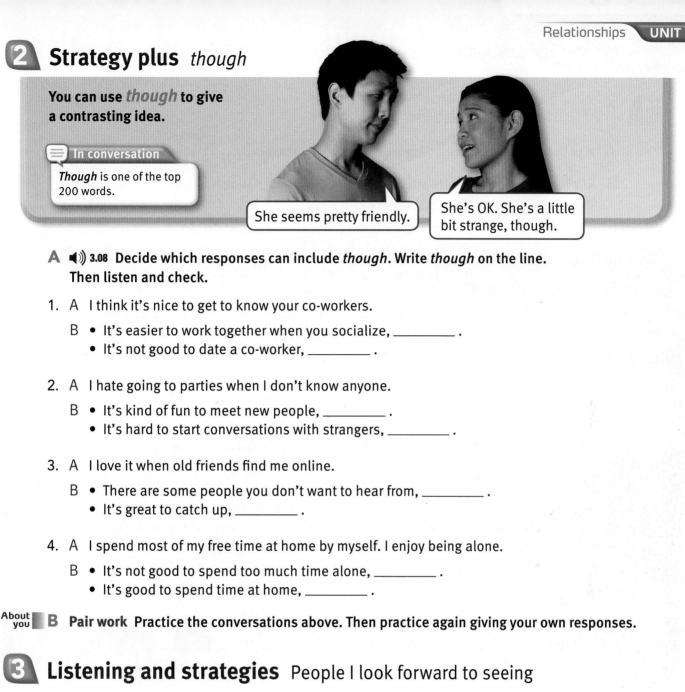

A ◀⫘ **3.08 Decide which responses can include *though*. Write *though* on the line. Then listen and check.**

1. A I think it's nice to get to know your co-workers.

   B • It's easier to work together when you socialize, _____ .
      • It's not good to date a co-worker, _____ .

2. A I hate going to parties when I don't know anyone.

   B • It's kind of fun to meet new people, _____ .
      • It's hard to start conversations with strangers, _____ .

3. A I love it when old friends find me online.

   B • There are some people you don't want to hear from, _____ .
      • It's great to catch up, _____ .

4. A I spend most of my free time at home by myself. I enjoy being alone.

   B • It's not good to spend too much time alone, _____ .
      • It's good to spend time at home, _____ .

About you | B Pair work Practice the conversations above. Then practice again giving your own responses.

3 Listening and strategies People I look forward to seeing

A ◀⫘ **3.09 Listen to Matthew talk about three people he looks forward to seeing. Complete the sentences.**

1. The woman in the coffee shop gets a little _____ .
   She's really _____ and positive, though.

2. My yoga teacher is really good. He's kind of _____ , though.
   The other students are nice. One guy is always _____ , though.
   It gets sort of _____ .

3. One of the guys that I go biking with is the worst biker.
   He's incredibly _____ , though. I guess the other guys are kind
   of _____ about biking.

B ◀⫘ **3.09 Listen again. Why does Matthew look forward to seeing each person?**

About you | C Pair work Who do you look forward to seeing? Tell a partner about three people. Ask and answer questions to find out more information.

⫘⫘⫘ **Sounds right** p. 138

1 Reading

A What are some good ways to make new friends? Make a list.

B Read the article. What have studies found about online dating? What are the reasons for its popularity?

 Reading tip

Writers often use different ways to present statistics, like *20 percent, one in five,* or *one out of (every) five.*

http://www.looking...

LOOKING FOR LOVE? Online is the way to go!

According to new research, people looking for romance need look no further than their laptops. Recent studies reveal that 17 percent of marriages are the result of an initial online encounter – making this the second most common way of meeting a potential partner, after meeting through friends.

Surveys show that more than one-third of singles looking for a partner have used an online dating site. Furthermore, one out of every five new relationships starts online. Although the results of online dating surveys may vary, the evidence points to the increasingly important role the Internet is playing in helping single people find romance.

The social stigma[1] that was attached to online dating in the past is fast disappearing as dating goes increasingly digital. These days, most people know someone who has tried online dating, so people are less afraid to talk about it or to try it. Online dating, it appears, has entered the mainstream.

But why is this? Experts say there are several factors that contribute to the popularity of online dating. Changes in lifestyle, geographic mobility, and the rise in social networking are largely responsible for changing how people meet potential partners. These days, people typically delay marriage as they concentrate on their careers, work longer and longer hours, and live farther away from family and childhood friends who might otherwise provide contacts with eligible[2] partners. Instead they turn to their tablets.

So has the Internet fundamentally changed *how* people date? According to Greg Blatt, former CEO of a popular dating website, the answer is no. "This is just meeting," Blatt says. "It's no different meeting on a dating website than it is meeting at a party, or at a restaurant, or on a subway. . . . Once you've met, it's real life; you either fall for each other, or you don't. You either have a great romance, or you don't."

"Computers are not taking the place of romance," he says. "They're just another way to put yourself in a position to meet somebody with a chance for romance."

1. *(a) stigma:* a bad opinion of someone or something
2. *eligible:* ideal as a marriage partner

C Read the article again. Circle the correct words to make the sentences true according to the article.

1. Seventeen percent of people who get married now meet **on the Internet / through friends.**
2. Meeting people through friends is **more / less** common than meeting online.
3. A third of people looking for romance **don't use / use** dating websites.
4. Online dating is now considered more **acceptable / dangerous.**
5. One reason why people try online dating is because they live farther away from their **place of work / original community.**
6. Blatt says that meeting online is **like / not like** meeting at an actual place, such as a party.

About you **D** **Pair work** Discuss the opinions expressed in the article. Which do you agree with? Why?

2 Speaking and listening Getting back in touch

About you **A Pair work** How do friends lose touch with each other? Add ideas to the list. Have you ever lost touch with a friend? Tell your partner how it happened.

Friends lose touch when one of them . . .

- moves away.
- gets married.
- gets interested in different things.
- gets too busy with school or work.
- _____ .
- _____ .

B 🔊 **3.10** Listen to Javier talk about his old friends. Does he want to get back in touch with them? Check (✓) the correct boxes in the chart below.

	Yes	No	Don't know	Why did he lose touch?
1. His college friends	☐	☐	☑	Got bored - recording songs
2. His running buddy	☑	☐	☐	got married - had baby
3. His old girlfriend	☐	☑	☐	They were different

C 🔊 **3.10** Listen again. Why did Javier lose touch with his friends? Complete the rest of the chart.

3 Writing Your circle of friends

About you **A Pair work** Think about three of your friends. Tell a partner about them. Discuss the questions below.

- What is your friend like?
- How did you meet?
- Why did you become friends?
- What do you have in common?
- What do you do together?

About you **B** Read the article below and the Help note. Then write an article like the one on page 66 about your circle of friends. Use *both* and *neither* to show what you have in common. Include photos if you can.

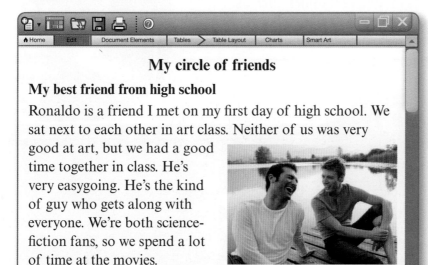

My circle of friends

My best friend from high school

Ronaldo is a friend I met on my first day of high school. We sat next to each other in art class. Neither of us was very good at art, but we had a good time together in class. He's very easygoing. He's the kind of guy who gets along with everyone. We're both science-fiction fans, so we spend a lot of time at the movies.

> **Help note**
>
> **Both** and **neither**
>
> *We're **both** science-fiction fans. **Both of us** are science-fiction fans.*
>
> *We **both** like going to the movies. **Both of us** like going to the movies.*
>
> ***Neither of us** was very good at art.*

C Pair work Read your partner's article. Ask questions about your partner's friends.

Free talk p. 132

Vocabulary notebook / Matching up

Learning tip *Phrasal verbs*

When you learn a phrasal verb, it's a good idea to write down

- some other verbs you can use with the particle.

  back: get back / call back / fly back

- some other particles you can use with the verb.

  go: go back / go out / go away

1 Circle the two verbs in each list that go with the particle on the right.

1. (go) /(move)/ hang **away**
2. wake /(eat)/(work) **out**
3. (come)/ break /(get) **back**
4. wake /(go)/(come) **over**
5. (sign)/(grow)/ sleep **up**
6. (fall)/ eat /(settle) **down**

2 Complete each expression with a different verb.

wake		in the morning
sign		for a class
get/wake	**up**	without an alarm clock
grow		in a small town
break		with your boyfriend / girlfriend

hang		with your friends
go		late
hang	**out**	to a club
eat		at a nice restaurant
work		at the gym

3 Word builder How many new phrasal verbs can you make from these particles?

away   back   down   out   up

 On your own

Make lists with headings for different topics such as "Relationships" or "Going out." Write phrasal verbs for each topic, and learn the words whenever you have a minute.

Relationships:
- work out
- get along
- break up

 Can Do! Now I can . . .

✔ I can . . .   ? I need to review how to . . .

- [ ] describe people and things using relative clauses.
- [ ] talk about friends and romantic relationships.
- [ ] soften comments with expressions like *sort of.*
- [ ] use *though* to give contrasting ideas.
- [ ] understand descriptions of people.

- [ ] understand a conversation about old friends.
- [ ] understand someone talking about losing touch with people.
- [ ] read an article about online dating.
- [ ] write about my circle of friends.

What if?

☑ Can Do! In this unit, you learn how to . . .

Lesson A
- Talk about wishes using *I wish* + past form
- Talk about imaginary situations or events in the present and the future with *If*-clauses

Lesson B
- Discuss how to deal with everyday dilemmas
- Ask about imaginary situations or events

Lesson C
- Give advice using expressions like *If I were you, . . .* or *I'd . . .*
- Use *That would be . . .* to comment on a suggestion or a possibility

Lesson D
- Read a blog about regrets
- Write an article about how you would change your life

Before you begin . . .

What are your priorities in life? Rank these things in order from 1 (most important) to 6 (least important).

- ☐ your health
- ☐ your career
- ☐ wealth
- ☐ your family
- ☐ relationships
- ☐ looking good

What other things matter to you?

How do you wish your life were different?

"I just wish I weren't so busy with my work. I have to work most weekends, so I never have enough time to do anything fun. If I had more free time, I'd go kayaking every weekend."

– Berta Palmas, Monterrey

"We just got married, and we're renting a tiny little apartment. It would be great if we could afford a bigger place to live. We don't have enough room for all our stuff."

– Min Sup and Jin Eun Cho, Seoul

"Well, I never get to go away on holiday. I just don't have enough money. So I wish I had enough money to go somewhere exciting. Yeah, if I could choose anywhere, I'd probably go to Egypt to see the pyramids. That would be great!"

– Bryan Gibson, Melbourne

"I wish I didn't live so far away from my family. My sister just had a baby – a little boy – and I never get to see him. I really miss everyone. If I lived closer, I'd be able to help out."

– Irene Chang, Taipei

1 Getting started

A What would you like more of in your life? Tell the class.

> fun   money   time   vacations   work

B 🔊 3.11 Listen to the people above talk about their wishes. What do they want?

Figure it out **C** Circle the correct verbs in the sentences below. Use the article above to help you. Then answer the questions. What do you notice about the verbs you circled?

1. Bryan wishes he **has** / **had** enough money to go away. Does he have enough money?

2. Berta says, "I just wish I**'m not** / **weren't** so busy." Is she busy now?

3. Irene says if she **lives** / **lived** closer, she would help her sister. Does she live close?

4. Min Sup and Jin Eun say it **would** / **will** be great if they could rent a big apartment. What's their place like?

2 Grammar Wishes and imaginary situations or events 🔊 3.12

Extra practice p. 147

Wishes for the present or future	Imaginary situations or events in the present or future
wish + past form of verb	*If* + past form of verb . . . *would* (*could*) + verb
I wish I **had** more free time. (*I **don't have** enough free time,* ▸	If I **had** more free time, I'**d** / I **would go** kayaking. *so I **don't go** kayaking.*)
She wishes she **didn't live** so far away. (*She **lives** very far away* ▸	If she **lived** closer, she'**d** / she **would be able to** help out. *so she **isn't able to** help out.*)
I wish I **weren't** so busy with my work. (*I'**m** very busy with my work,* ▸	If I **were** less busy, I **could go away** on the weekends. *so I **can't go away** on the weekends.*)
We wish we **could afford** to move. (*We **can't afford** to move,* ▸	If we **could afford** to move, we **wouldn't live** in this tiny place. *so we **live** in this tiny place.*)

In conversation

People say *I wish I was* . . . and *If I was* . . . more frequently than *I wish I were* . . . and *If I were* . . . , but this is not considered correct in written English.

▬▬▬▬ *I wish I was* . . .
▬▬ *I wish I were* . . .

A Complete the sentences with the appropriate form of the verbs given.

1. I wish I ___could do___ (can do) something more exciting with my life. If I ___had___ (have) the chance, I ___would travel___ (travel) around South America.

2. I wish I _____ (not be) so shy. If I _____ (have) more confidence, I _____ probably _____ (enjoy) going out more.

3. I wish I _____ (not have to) study so hard. If I _____ (not get) so much homework, I _____ (be able to) play on the soccer team.

4. I wish _____ (can finish) my degree this year. If I _____ (graduate) this year, I _____ (can get) a job, and I _____ (can start) to pay off my student loans.

5. I wish I _____ (can find) a job nearer to home. If I _____ (get) a new job, maybe I _____ (not have to) commute two hours a day.

6. I wish I _____ (be) famous. If I _____ (be) famous, I _____ (be able to) go to shows and get the best seats! And I _____ (not eat) in the cheapest restaurants anymore.

Common errors

Use the simple past form after *if*.

*If we **had** more money, we could go on vacation more often.*
(NOT ~~If we would have~~ more . . .)

About you **B** Pair work Discuss the sentences above. Do you have any wishes like these?

"I wish I could do something more exciting. If I had the chance, I would live in another country."

3 Listening and speaking Just one wish

A 🔊 3.13 Listen to four people talk about their wishes. Complete the sentences.

What do they wish for?

1. Daniel wishes _____ .
2. Martine wishes _____ .
3. Miguel wishes _____ .
4. Mi Yun wishes _____ .

Why can't they have their wish?

_____
_____
_____
_____

B 🔊 3.13 Listen again. Why can't they have their wishes? Write the reason(s) above.

About you **C** Class activity Ask your classmates about their wishes. What are the most popular wishes?

1 Building vocabulary and grammar

About you **A** ◀))) **3.14** Listen and take the quiz. Circle your answers. Then compare with a partner.

WHAT WOULD YOU DO?

1. What would you do if a friend accidentally spilled coffee all over your phone, and it stopped working? Would you . . .

   a. let your friend buy a new one?

   b. tell your friend not to **worry about** it and **buy** a new phone **for** yourself?

2. What would you do if you **borrowed** a camera **from** a friend and broke it? Would you . . .

   a. simply **apologize for** breaking it?

   b. take it to a store and **pay for** the repairs?

3. How would you react if a friend started dating someone you used to go out with? Would you . . .

   a. **talk to** your friend **about** your feelings?

   b. feel hurt but **say** nothing **to** either of them?

4. What would you do if a friend came for dinner and brought an expensive box of chocolates? Would you . . .

   a. **thank** your friend **for** the gift and not open it?

   b. **share** the chocolates **with** your friend after dinner?

5. What would you say if a friend **asked** you **for** a loan to buy a new laptop? Would you say . . . ?

   a. "Sorry, I never **lend** money **to** anyone."

   b. "I'll **think about** it and let you know."

6. What would you do if a friend borrowed $10 and forgot to pay you back? Would you . . .

   a. **remind** your friend **about** it several times?

   b. **forget about** it?

Word sort **B** **Pair work** Write the prepositions that are used in the quiz in the expressions below. Then ask and answer the questions with a partner.

1. What do you worry _about_ ?
2. Who do you talk to _____ problems?
3. Do you ever think _____ your diet?
4. How do you remind yourself _____ things?
5. Can you forget _____ your problems?
6. Do you buy gifts _____ your friends?
7. Do you use cash to pay _____ things?
8. Do you apologize _____ being late?
9. How do you thank people _____ gifts?
10. Did you ask a friend _____ a favor today?
11. Do you borrow clothes _____ friends?
12. Do you lend books _____ friends?
13. What can't you say no _____ ?
14. Do you ever share secrets _____ friends?

Figure it out **C** Complete these questions about imaginary situations. Use the quiz to help you. Then ask and answer the questions in pairs.

 **Vocabulary notebook** p. 84

1. What _____ you _____ (do) if your friend _____ (forget) your birthday?
2. How _____ you _____ (react) if a friend _____ (tell) everyone a secret about you?

2 Speaking naturally Intonation in long questions

How would you re**act** if a friend started **dat**ing someone you used to go **out** with?

What would you **do** if a friend came for **din**ner and brought an expensive box of **choc**olates?

A 🔊 **3.15** Listen and repeat the questions above. Notice how the intonation falls and then rises to show the question is not finished and then falls at the end.

About you **B** **Pair work** Find a partner. Take turns asking the questions in the quiz on page 78 and giving your own answers. Pay attention to the intonation of the long questions.

3 Grammar Asking about imaginary situations or events 🔊 3.16

Extra practice p. 147

What **would** you **do if** you **broke** a friend's camera?
  I**'d apologize** for breaking it.
  I**'d pay** for the repairs.
  I **wouldn't say** anything about it.

Would you **pay** for a new one?
  Yes, I **would**. / No, I **wouldn't**.

A Make questions with *would* using the ideas below. Compare with a partner.

1. a friend is 15 minutes late / call and remind him about it
   What would you do if a friend was 15 minutes late? Would you call and remind him about it?

2. you hear a strange noise in the middle of the night / go and see what it was
   _____

3. a salesperson charges you the wrong price for something / say something to her
   _____

4. you scratch a car with a shopping cart in a parking lot / leave a note with your name and number
   _____

5. you find a nice pair of gloves on the sidewalk / think about keeping them
   _____

6. you have an extra ticket for a show / offer it to a friend but ask him to pay for it
   _____

7. you get a gift that you hate from a friend / thank her for it and then get rid of it
   _____

8. your friend asks for help moving into an apartment / find an excuse to get out of helping him
   _____

9. your friend is in a bad mood / take him out for a fun night
   _____

About you **B** **Pair work** Take turns asking the questions above. Discuss your answers. Do you agree?

  A *What would you do if a friend was 15 minutes late for a date?*
  B *I'd probably just wait a little longer. Would you call and remind him about it?*

1 Conversation strategy Giving advice

A What tough decisions have you made? Did you ask for advice? Tell the class.

B 🔊 3.17 Listen. What advice does Nicole give Carlos about grad school?

Nicole	Hey, I hear you got accepted to grad school.
Carlos	Yeah. I got into MSU and Bracken Tech.
Nicole	Congratulations! So where are you going to go?
Carlos	I don't know. I got a full scholarship to Bracken Tech, but I think MSU has a better engineering department.
Nicole	Well, if I were you, I'd take the scholarship. Then you wouldn't have to borrow any money.
Carlos	Yeah, that would be great. But it's a tough decision.
Nicole	Well, Bracken Tech's a good school. I mean, you might want to go there and meet some of the professors.
Carlos	That'd be good. But then, everybody I know is going to MSU.
Nicole	Oh, I wouldn't worry about that. You can make new friends. And anyway, I might go to Bracken next year, you know, if I get accepted.
Carlos	Really? That would be awesome!

C Notice how Nicole gives advice to Carlos. She uses expressions like these. Find examples in the conversation.

If I were you, I'd . . .	You might want to . . .
I would / I'd . . .	You could . . .
I wouldn't . . .	

About you **D Pair work** Think of three pieces of advice for each problem below. Then take turns role-playing the problems and giving advice.

1. I wish I weren't majoring in economics. I just don't find it very interesting.
2. One of my co-workers just got a promotion, but I didn't get one.
3. I wish I knew what to do after college.
4. My boyfriend / girlfriend wants to get married, but I'm just not ready.
5. My parents want me to study law or accounting or something, but I don't want to.

"Well, if I were you, I'd try and switch to a different major. . . . "

2 Strategy plus That would be . . .

You can use
That would be . . .
to comment on a
suggestion or a
possibility.

You might want to go there and meet some of the professors.

That'd be good.

I might go to Bracken next year.

Really? That would be awesome!

Complete the responses. Practice with a partner. Then take turns asking and answering the questions.

1. A If you could do something really different, what would you do?

   B I'd really like to go skydiving.

   A Really? Wow! That would be _____ !

2. A If you could have any job, what would you do?

   B Something creative. I'd like to work in a design company or something.

   A Yeah. That'd be _____ .

3. A Would you ever like to get a Ph.D. in something?

   B Yeah, maybe one day. But it's impossible right now. I'm just too busy. I'd have to study at midnight!

   A Oh, yeah. That would be _____ .

3 Listening and strategies Here's my advice.

A 🔊 3.18 **Listen to Tom and Amy talk about their problems. What problems do they have? Complete the sentences on the left.**

What's the problem?

1. Tom wishes he _____ .
2. Tom wishes his boss _____ .
3. One of Tom's co-workers got _____ .
4. Amy can't decide which school to go to because _____ .

What's the advice?

"I wouldn't _____ . You could _____ ."

"I would _____ ."

"If I were you, I'd _____ ."

"I wouldn't _____ ."

B 🔊 3.18 **Listen again. What advice do Tom and Amy give each other? Complete the sentences above.**

C **Pair work Choose one of Tom or Amy's problems, or one of your own. Take turns describing the problem and offering advice.**

   A *I have a similar problem to Tom. I have a part-time job that I really like, but it doesn't pay very well.*

   B *Well, maybe you could ask for a raise.*

   A *Yeah, that would be good.*

 Sounds right p. 138

Reading

A What kinds of things do people regret in life? Make a class list.

B Read the blog. What impression do you have of the writer (age, gender, personality)? Compare ideas with a partner.

 Reading tip

As you read, try to imagine the situations, places, or people that the writer describes.

IF I COULD LIVE MY LIFE OVER . . .

If I could change the past and live my life over, I'd do a lot of things differently. I'd be more laid-back – I'd worry less about small or imaginary problems and maybe a little more about things that really matter. I'd complain less about unimportant things. I'd slow down and take each day as it comes. I'd be more patient with people.

I'd stop being afraid of making mistakes and make an effort to try new things. I'd learn to scuba dive and speak a new language. I'd do things I enjoyed, even if I wasn't good at them, like playing the piano. I'd continue with my lessons and wouldn't give up because I wasn't all that good. I would enjoy what I could do and not worry about what I couldn't do. Yes, I'd still be competitive – I wouldn't want to change that – but I wouldn't get upset if I didn't win.

I'd try to make a difference in people's lives. I'd be more generous – with my money and especially my time. Maybe do more volunteer work. I'd spend more time listening to the stories that older people have to tell without looking at my watch and thinking about the other things I could be doing. I'd get to know my neighbors and offer to help those I knew needed help or who had problems. I would ask people on the bus, "What's wrong?" if they seemed upset.

If I could change the last few years, I'd find more time to share long and laughter-filled meals with friends or family and spend less time shut away with my computer, working. I'd be more considerate. I'd send more handwritten thank-you notes and tell people what they mean to me. I would be completely reliable, someone that everyone can count on.

If I had another chance, I wouldn't read so much about celebrities' lives. I mean, who cares? I'd spend less time in malls and more time in parks, flying a kite, or watching the birds. I'd clean the house less and read more. I'd walk barefoot on beaches and feel the sand between my toes and the sun on my face. I'd spend a summer on a Greek island, see the Pyramids in Egypt, climb a mountain in Africa, watch more sunrises and sunsets.

Life is an incredibly enjoyable trip, but it's also incredibly short. Next time around, I'd focus more on the journey and less on the destination. You'll arrive sooner than you think.

C Find these words and expressions in the blog. Choose the best meaning and circle *a*, *b*, or *c*.

1. take each day as it comes
   - a. worry life is short
   - b. live for the present
   - c. do nothing

2. give up
   - a. start
   - b. stop
   - c. give something to a friend

3. upset
   - a. happy
   - b. disorganized
   - c. unhappy

4. considerate
   - a. intelligent
   - b. selfish
   - c. kind

5. barefoot
   - a. wearing leather shoes
   - b. wearing no shoes
   - c. quickly

D Group work Discuss these questions.

1. What have been the most important things in the writer's life?
2. What aspects of his or her life would he or she change?
3. Do you think the writer would be a better person "next time around"? How?
4. Does the writer remind you of anyone you know? Who?
5. Do you have anything in common with the writer? If so, what?

2 Speaking and writing What would you change?

A If you had last year to live over again, what would you change? Think of answers to the questions, and make notes below.

Is there . . .

*   a person you'd spend more time with? _____
*   something you'd spend more time doing? _____
*   something you'd spend less time doing? _____
*   a place you'd go more often? _____
*   something you'd take more seriously? _____
*   something you'd worry about less? _____
*   a sport or activity you'd try? _____
*   a subject you'd study? _____

B Pair work Take turns. Tell your partner about some things you'd change.

"I'd spend more time with my grandpa and less time on my social network."

C Read the Help note, and underline the examples of *definitely* and *probably* in the article below. Then write an article about changes you would make if you could live your year over again.

THINGS I'D CHANGE

If I had last year to live over again, I would definitely get more exercise. I definitely wouldn't watch so much TV, and I'd probably work out more at the gym. I'd try to stop eating so many snacks, but I probably would not give up ice cream because it's my favorite snack! If I got more exercise and ate less junk food, I'd lose some weight. I'd probably feel much healthier, too.

> **Help note**
>
> **Adverbs of certainty in affirmative and negative statements**
>
> Notice the position of the adverbs.
>
> *I would **definitely** get more exercise.*
> *I'd **probably** work out more at the gym.*
>
> But:
>
> *I **definitely** wouldn't watch so much TV.*
> *I **probably** would not give up ice cream.*

D Read your classmates' articles. Does anyone want to change the same things as you?

Free talk p. 133

Learning tip *Verbs + prepositions*

When you learn a new verb, find out what prepositions (if any) can come after it.
Remember that a verb coming after a verb + preposition has the form verb + *-ing*.

They apologized for making so much noise.

1 **Read the problem below. Complete the possible solutions with the prepositions *about*, *for*, and *to*.**

You forget you have a dinner date with a friend, and you don't show up.
Your friend calls you, and she is very upset. What would you do?

1. I wouldn't worry _____ it. People usually forget _____ things like that.
2. I'd apologize immediately _____ forgetting the date.
3. I'd offer to pay _____ dinner another time.
4. I'd tell her I was thinking _____ other things.
5. I wouldn't speak _____ her until she was less upset.
6. I'd blame my boss _____ keeping me in a meeting at work.
7. I'd wait _____ her to finish, and then I'd remind her _____ the time she didn't meet me.

2 **Word builder Find the prepositions that go with the verbs. Then complete the sentences.**

1. I agreed _____ my boss _____ the best solution.
2. He applied _____ a job with a software company.
3. I explained the problem _____ my boss.
4. I forgave my friend _____ losing my favorite sweater.
5. My neighbor invited me _____ a party last week.
6. We complained _____ the neighbors _____ the noise.
7. My parents blamed me _____ damaging their car.

On your own

Write six rules for living, using verbs that take prepositions.

My rules for living
1. Never blame other people for your problems.
2. Always forgive yourself.

✓ Can Do! Now I can . . .

✓ I can . . .   ❓ I need to review how to . . .

- ☐ talk about wishes and imaginary situations.
- ☐ say how I would deal with everyday dilemmas.
- ☐ give advice with expressions like *If I were you, . . .*
- ☐ use *That would be* to comment on a suggestion or possibility.

- ☐ understand people talking about their wishes.
- ☐ understand people giving advice.
- ☐ read a blog about regrets.
- ☐ write an article about how I would change my life.

Tech savvy?

✓ **Can Do!** In this unit, you learn how to . . .

Lesson A
- Talk about problems with technology using questions within sentences

Lesson B
- Describe how things work using separable phrasal verbs like *turn on* and *plug in*
- Ask for help with technology using *how to* + verb, *where to* + verb, etc.

Lesson C
- Give different opinions with expressions like *On the other hand*
- Use *You know what I mean?* to ask someone to agree with you

Lesson D
- Read an article about email scams
- Plan and write an article about protecting personal information

1

2

3

4

Before you begin . . .

How tech savvy are you? How do you use technology in your everyday life? Are you planning on buying any new electronic devices or gadgets soon?

85

Sean My computer won't turn on. Do you know what the problem is?

Mark I wonder if there's something wrong with your power cord.

Sue Mine did that, and I called tech support. But I can't remember what they said.

Pam There's something wrong with my tablet. It keeps freezing up. I have no idea why it's doing that.

Sally Do you know if the battery's charged?

Peter I wonder if you have a virus. Try running your antivirus software.

Olivia I don't know what the problem is, but I can't print anything.

Tom The last time that happened to me, I got the answer on a website. But I have no idea which site I used.

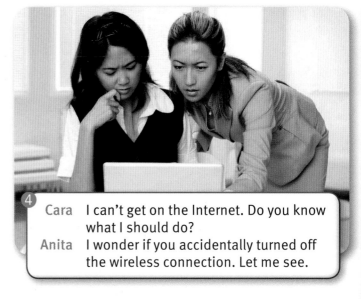

Cara I can't get on the Internet. Do you know what I should do?

Anita I wonder if you accidentally turned off the wireless connection. Let me see.

1 Getting started

A What kinds of problems do people have with their computers? Make a class list.

B 🔊 3.19 Listen. What problems are the people above having? What do their friends suggest?

Figure it out **C** How do the people say the things below in one sentence? Write what they actually say. Then compare with a partner.

1. **Sean** What's the problem? Do you know? _____

2. **Sally** Is the battery charged? Do you know? _____

3. **Tom** Which site did I use? I have no idea. _____

4. **Anita** Did you accidentally turn the wireless connection off? I wonder. _____

2 **Grammar** Questions within sentences 🔊 3.20

Extra practice p. 148

Direct questions	**Questions within questions**	**Questions within statements**
What's the problem?	Do you know **what the problem is**?	I don't know **what the problem is**.
Which site did you use?	Can you remember **which site you used**?	I have no idea **which site I used**.
What should we do?	Do you know **what we should do**?	I know **what we should do**.
Why is it doing that?	Do you have any idea **why it's doing that**?	I have no idea **why it's doing that**.
Is the battery charged?	Do you know **if* the battery is** charged?	I wonder **if* the battery is charged**.

*Use **if** for **yes-no** questions.*

Notice the word order: What **is** the problem?

Do you know what **the problem is**?

✗ Common errors

Don't use question word order for a question within a question or statement.

*I know what **you can do**.*
*Do you know what **you need to do**?*
(NOT *I know ~~what can you do.~~*
Do you know ~~what do you need to do?~~)

A Rewrite these sentences. Start with the expressions given.

1. Are there any useful new apps for students? *Do you know . . .*
   Do you know if there are any useful new apps for students?
2. What are the most popular sites for streaming movies? *I wonder . . .*
3. Which song did you last download? *Can you remember . . .*
4. Where can I get some cool accessories for a tablet? *Do you know . . .*
5. What's the most popular smartphone? *Do you know . . .*
6. How do you design your own website? *Do you have any idea . . .*
7. Will the price of tablets come down? *I wonder . . .*
8. What new technology is coming out? *Do you have any idea . . .*

About you **B** **Pair work** Start conversations using the sentences above. How tech savvy are you?

> *A **Do you know if there are any useful new apps for students?***
> *B **Well, I don't know if they're new, but you can get some good grammar apps.***

3 **Speaking and listening** What do you know about the Internet?

A 🔊 3.21 **Pair work** Discuss the questions. Can you guess the answers?
Then listen to a conversation about the Internet. Write the answers you hear.

1. Do you know when the public first used the World Wide Web? _____
2. Can you find out what the first webcam filmed? _____
3. Do you know what the most popular online activities are? _____
4. Can you guess how many new blogs people add to the Internet each day? _____
5. Do you know what the first email spam advertised? _____
6. Do you know what the three most common languages on the Internet are? _____

B 🔊 3.21 **Listen again.** Write one more piece of information about the answer to each question.
Then compare your answers with a partner.

C **Pair work** Student A: Read one of the answers to the questions above.
Student B: Can you remember what the question is without looking at your book? Take turns.

(((Sounds right p. 139

1 Building language

A 🔊 **3.22** Listen. What problem is Ken having? Practice the conversation.

Ken Pedro, do you know how to get this game controller to work?
I read the instructions, but I can't figure out how to do it.

Pedro Let's see. You have to turn it on first. Did you put the batteries in?

Ken Yeah. I turned the controller on — see? But the box won't work.

Pedro Oh, OK. Well, did you plug it in? Oh, yeah, you did. Oh wait, I think
you need to hook up another cable. Do you know where the blue cable is?

Ken Yeah, it's here. Do you know where to plug it in?

Pedro Yes. It goes here.

Ken Thanks. Now, can you show me how to set this game up?

Pedro OK, hand me the controller. Let me show you what to do.

Figure it out **B** Circle the two correct choices in each question. Then ask and answer the questions with a partner.

1. Can you **set up a game** / **set a game up** / **a game set up**?

2. If you have a game controller, can you **hook it up** / **hook up it** / **hook the box up**?

3. If there's a problem, do you know **what you do** / **what to do** / **to do**?

4. Can you show someone **how to use** / **how you use** / **to use** a game controller?

2 Grammar Separable phrasal verbs; *how to*, etc. 🔊 **3.23**

Extra practice p. 148

Separable phrasal verbs with objects	Question word + *to* + verb
How do you ⎰ **turn on** the game controller? **turn** the game controller **on**? **turn** it **on**? (NOT **turn on it**?)	Let me show you **what to do**. Can you show me **how to turn** it **on**? Do you know **where to plug** it **in**?

A Write A's sentences in two ways using the words given. Complete B's responses.

1. A Do you know how _to turn on the TV / to turn the TV on_ ? (the TV / turn on)

   B Yeah. You need to __turn it on__ with this remote – not that one.

2. A Do you know how _____ ? (this computer / turn off)

   B Oh, you can _____ here.

3. A I can't see where _____ . (these headphones / plug in)

   B Huh. I'm not sure where _____ , either. I think they go here.

4. A I don't know how _____ on my tablet. (the volume / turn down)

   B Here. I can show you how _____ . It's easy. Look.

5. A I can't figure out how _____ . (the air conditioning / turn up)

   B I have no idea how _____ either. Oh, you need to use the remote. Here – see?

B **Pair work** Practice the conversations above. Practice again using different gadgets.

"Do you know how to turn on the air conditioning?"

3 Speaking naturally Linking consonants and vowels

I'm not sure how to turn it on. I don't know where to plug it in.

A 🔊 **3.24** Listen and repeat the sentences above. Notice how the consonants are linked to the vowels. Then practice Exercise 2 on page 88 again with a new partner.

B 🔊 **3.25** Listen and complete the sentences you hear. Then imagine you have a new tablet. Take turns asking and answering the questions with a partner.

1. Can you show me how to _____ ?
2. Now tell me how to _____ .
3. Can you _____ to speakers?
4. Can you show me how to _____ ?

4 Building vocabulary

A Match the pictures with the sentences. Then compare with a partner. Say what's happening in each picture.

"He's hooking up his game system to the TV."

     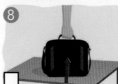  

a. Put them away.
✓ b. Hook it up.
c. Look it up.
d. Pick it up.
e. Put it down.
f. Print it out.
g. Put them on.
h. Take them off.
i. Take it apart.
j. Throw it away.
k. Turn it down.
l. Turn it up.

Word sort **B** What can you do with the things below? Write at least two expressions from above for each item. Add ideas. Then compare with a partner.

A computer	*hook it up*	A ringtone	
A photo		A phone number	
A cell phone		Batteries	
A pair of ear buds		A printer	

About you **C** Pair work Discuss the things below. Think of three . . .

 **Vocabulary notebook** p. 94

- different things you turn on every day.
- situations when you have to turn something off.
- different things you have to plug in before using.
- things you can turn up and down.
- useful pieces of information you can look up.
- things you have thrown away recently.

A Well, I turn my computer on every morning.
B Really? I leave it on all night.

1 Conversation strategy Giving different opinions

A What kinds of online games do people play? Do you or your friends play them?

B ◀)) 3.26 Listen. What does Hugo think about playing games online? What about Greg?

Hugo I'd get tired of playing that game by myself.

Greg Actually, I'm playing with two other guys. See? Starship and Bronco. We play together all the time. They're kind of like friends.

Hugo I don't know. You don't even know their real names. You know?

Greg That's true. It's still fun, though. We're like a team. You know what I mean?

Hugo Maybe. On the other hand, they're not *real* friends. I mean, you don't know anything about them. You know what I'm saying?

Greg Yeah. I know what you mean, but you don't have to *know* people to enjoy doing stuff with them.

Hugo Hmm. I'm not so sure. Don't you think it's good to spend time with real friends, face-to-face?

Greg Sure. So why don't you come and play?

C **Notice** how Hugo and Greg give different opinions. They use expressions like these. Find examples in the conversation.

> *I know what you mean, but . . .*
> *That's true. (You) . . . , though.*
> *Maybe. On the other hand, . . .*
> *I don't know. / I'm not (so) sure. Don't you think . . . ?*

D **Pair work** Respond to each comment by giving a different opinion. Then practice with a partner. Can you continue the conversations?

1. A Playing all those online games is a waste of time.

   B Maybe. On the other hand, _____ .

2. A I spend hours on my social networking site. It's a great way to keep in touch with people.

   B I don't know. Don't you think _____ ?

3. A I never call anyone anymore; I just text. Then you don't have to make all that small talk!

   B That's true. _____ , though.

4. A I hardly ever turn my cell phone off — even at night. I hate missing calls.

   B I know what you mean, but _____ .

2 Strategy plus *You know what I mean?*

When you want someone to agree with you, you can use expressions like these.

You know what I mean?
You know?
You know what I'm saying?

> It's still fun, though. We're like a team. You know what I mean?

In conversation

You know what I mean? is the most common five-word expression. It is five times more frequent than *You know what I'm saying?*

▬▬▬▬▬ *You know what I mean?*
■ *You know what I'm saying?*

Pair work Circle the best sentences to complete the comments. Then take turns saying each comment. Respond to your partner with a different opinion.

1. It seems to me that every student should have a laptop in school. **Kids need to know how to use them. / They can be distracting.** You know what I'm saying?

2. I don't think you can listen to music and study at the same time. **Music helps you concentrate. / You can't concentrate with music on.** You know?

3. They should ban cell phones from restaurants. People take business calls and everything. **It's important to be able to take business calls. / It's really annoying.** You know what I mean?

4. I guess we won't need books much in the future. Everything is online now. **We use the Internet for most things. / Books will always be more popular.** You know?

> A *It seems to me that every student should have a laptop in school. Kids need to know how to use them. You know what I'm saying?*
>
> B *But on the other hand, they can be distracting. You know what I mean?*

3 Listening and strategies *Technology matters*

A ◀)) 3.27 Listen to Karin and Sam. How would Karin answer these questions?

1. Do you know what to do when a computer freezes up?
2. What's one of the nice things about using technology?
3. How can technology help you be flexible?
4. Does it bother you if a friend you're with is always texting someone else?
5. What's one thing that annoys you about technology?

About you **B ◀)) 3.28 Listen again to three of Sam's opinions. Do you agree or disagree? Write responses.**

1. _____
2. _____
3. _____

About you **C Pair work** Discuss the questions in Exercise A above. Do you and your partner agree?

> A *Well, if my computer freezes up, I just turn it off and on again. It's easy, you know?*
>
> B *That's true. Most people don't know how to fix computer problems, though.*

1 Reading

A What is identity theft? What can happen when someone steals your identity?

B Read the magazine article. What scams does it describe? How do they work?

 Reading tip

If you don't understand words in the title of an article, read the first paragraph. It often explains the title.

SAVVY AND SAFE

Most people know how to stay safe in the city: Don't walk alone after dark, hold onto your bag on crowded subways, and only ride in registered cabs. However, many people are not so savvy when it comes to staying safe on the Internet and don't know what to look for. Identity theft – when thieves steal your personal information and use your identity to open bank or credit card accounts or take out home loans in your name – is on the rise. In some cases, thieves charge thousands of dollars to credit cards, empty bank accounts, and can ruin your credit. Criminals are getting better at cheating you out of your money. What's worse is that they sometimes do it with your help. To avoid becoming a victim of an Internet scam, know what to look for.

DON'T BE THE VICTIM OF A SCAM

The friend in need scam Have you ever received an email from a friend who is overseas and urgently needs you to send money? Emma Park did, and it cost her $2,000. Emma, 22, from Chicago, was the victim of a scam. Somebody hacked into her friend's email account and sent urgent messages to everyone in the contacts list. Emma didn't even think of calling her friend to check if the email really was from him. She sent the money, and by the time she realized it was a scam, it was too late. Emma never got her money back.

DON'T send money to anyone if you get an email like this.
DO contact your friend to ask if there is a problem.

Information-request scam Your bank sends an email saying it has lost customer data. It asks you to send your bank account details, including your full password and PIN[1]. At least the email *looks* as if it's from your bank. It has their logo and looks official.

DON'T reply! Banks and credit card companies *never* ask for your full password or PIN in this way.
DO check the spelling and grammar. If there are mistakes, the email is probably a scam.

The "make money fast" chain email scam Someone sends you an email with a list of names. It asks you to send a small amount of money to the person at the top of the list, delete that name, and add your name to the bottom. The email explains that when your name gets to the top of the list, you'll receive a lot of money. You might even become a millionaire! Usually, however, the scammer's name stays at the top of the list, so he or she gets all the money.

DON'T forward the email. Sending this type of chain email is not only expensive, but it's also illegal.
DO block the sender, and block any emails that come from names you don't recognize.

Being savvy about scams is the best way to stay safe. If something seems a little strange, it probably is. Don't fall for it.

1. *PIN*: Personal Identification Number

C Are these sentences true or false according to the article? Write *T* or *F*.

1. Most people know how to recognize scams on the Internet. _____
2. Identity theft is increasing. _____
3. Emma lost $2,000 of her own money. _____
4. Emma sent money to a friend who was traveling overseas. _____
5. Your bank may ask you for your password if they lose it. _____
6. Your name will never get to the top of the list in the chain email. _____

About you **D** **Pair work** Discuss the questions.

1. Have you or people you know received emails like the ones in the article?
2. How often do you get emails from people you don't know? What do you do with them?
3. How do you keep your personal information safe online?
4. What other scams have you heard about?

2 Speaking and writing Keeping it safe

About you **A** **Group work** Brainstorm ideas on how to keep your personal information safe. Discuss the questions and take notes.

1. Which documents should you shred? Do you shred them?
2. Do you memorize your PINs? Would you ever tell anyone your PIN?
3. Where do you keep important documents? Do you have copies of them?
4. What do you have passwords for? How can you choose a good password?
5. How can you shop safely online or on the phone?
6. What can you do to protect your credit or debit card information?
7. What precautions do you take when you use an ATM?
8. How else can people keep their personal information safe?

"Well, you should shred your bank statements. I don't usually do it, though. I forget. You know?"

B Read the Help note. Then write a short article like the one below.

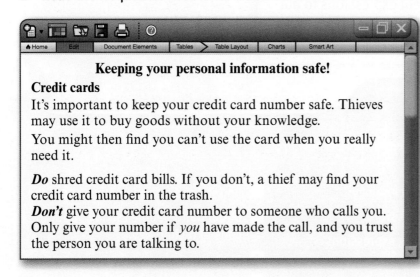

Keeping your personal information safe!

Credit cards

It's important to keep your credit card number safe. Thieves may use it to buy goods without your knowledge.

You might then find you can't use the card when you really need it.

Do shred credit card bills. If you don't, a thief may find your credit card number in the trash.

Don't give your credit card number to someone who calls you. Only give your number if *you* have made the call, and you trust the person you are talking to.

> **Help note**
>
> **Planning your article**
> - Write all your ideas down in any order. Don't worry about spelling and grammar.
> - Choose the best ideas you want to use.
> - Number your ideas to help you plan your article.
> - Write the article.
> - Check your spelling and grammar.

C Read your classmates' articles. What tips did you learn?

Free talk p. 134

Vocabulary notebook / On and off

Learning tip *Writing short conversations*

When you learn expressions with a new or complex structure, think of everyday situations where you might use them. Write short conversations using the expressions.

> **In conversation**
>
> The top six things people talk about *turning on* and *turning off* are their:
>
> 1. radio   4. phone
> 2. light(s)   5. computer
> 3. music   6. television

1 **Complete the conversations. Use the sentences in the box.**

I'll look it up.	✓ I'll turn it down.	Then I'd take them off.
I'll print it out.	I'll turn it up.	You can put them away in the closet.

1. A The music's too loud.   B   *I'll turn it down.*

2. A I don't know what to do with these boxes.   B _____

3. A What does this word mean?   B _____

4. A I need a copy of that document.   B _____

5. A I can't hear the radio.   B _____

6. A I think I'm allergic to these earrings.   B _____

2 **Word builder** Find the meaning of the phrasal verbs in the sentences below. Think of a situation for each one, and write conversations.

1. A _____
   B Sure. What time should I **pick** you **up**?

2. A _____
   B It's a nice color. Why don't you **try** it **on**?

3. A _____
   B **Take** it **back** to the store.

4. A _____
   B Can I **call** you **back** tonight? I'm late.

5. A _____
   B OK. I'd better **take** it **out** right now.

6. A _____
   B I'll show you how to **put** it **together**.

> **On your own**
>
> Make labels with different expressions to put around the house. When you have learned the expression, you can throw the label away.

✔ Can Do! Now I can . . .

✓ I can . . .   ❓ I need to review how to . . .

- ☐ talk about problems with technology.
- ☐ ask and describe how things work.
- ☐ give different opinions using expressions like *On the other hand* . . . .
- ☐ ask someone to agree with me using expressions like *You know what I mean?*

- ☐ understand a conversation about the Internet.
- ☐ understand people talking about the pros and cons of technology.
- ☐ read an article about email scams.
- ☐ plan and write an article about protecting my personal information.

1 How many words can you remember?

A How many different phrasal verbs can you use to complete the sentences below?

What can you say about relationships?		What can you do to a television?	
You can	*get along with someone.*	You can	*turn it on.*

B **Pair work** Compare with a partner. Score 1 point for each correct sentence. Score 2 points for a correct sentence your partner doesn't have.

2 Can you use these expressions?

Complete the conversation with the expressions in the box. Use capital letters where necessary. Then practice with a partner. There is one extra.

you might want to	✓ I know what you mean	don't you think	sort of
on the other hand	you know what I mean	I'm not so sure	though

Jan My boyfriend never picks up his phone. It drives me crazy.

Rob Oh, *I know what you mean* . My girlfriend never answers hers either.

Jan That's annoying. If you have a phone, you should answer it. It's rude to ignore it, _____ ? Well, I think so.

Rob _____ . Sometimes it *is* rude to answer it, like if you're having dinner or something. _____ ?

Jan Yeah, but you can always pick it up and say, "Can I call you back? I'm having dinner."

Rob Maybe. _____ , sometimes people start talking anyway, and you can't get them off the phone.

Jan Oh, no. I can't believe it. He's *still* not picking up.

Rob _____ leave him a message. Then you can eat.

Jan Yeah, I could I guess. He never checks his voice mail, _____ .

3 Here's my problem. Any thoughts?

Write a piece of advice for each person below. Then role-play conversations in groups.

1. My best friend doesn't study enough because he spends too much time on the Internet.

2. I wish I could email my parents, but they don't know how to use their computer!

3. My boyfriend / girlfriend wants to settle down and start a family, but I don't want children.

4. I wish I had more money for travel. If I did, I could go to some pretty exciting places.

    A My best friend doesn't study enough because he spends too much time on the Internet.

    B Well, you might want to talk to him about it.

    C I don't know. If I were you, I wouldn't say anything to him. But you could . . .

4 I wish, I wish . . .

A What do these people wish for and why? Complete the sentences. Compare with a partner.

1. I wish I __had__ (have) a car. If I __had__ (have) a car, I _could go_ (can go) places.

2. I wish I _____ (know) how to swim. If I _____ (can swim), I _____ (be able to) go snorkeling with my friends.

3. I wish I _____ (can speak) Portuguese fluently. If I _____ (be) fluent, it _____ (be) easier to travel around Brazil.

4. I wish I _____ (have) more money. If I _____ (find) a job, I _____ (earn) more money. On the other hand, I _____ (not have) enough time to study.

5. I wish I _____ (not have to) work tonight. If I _____ (be) free, I _____ (go out) with my friends.

6. I wish I _____ (know) how to use more software programs so I _____ (can get) a better job.

B **Pair work** Use the ideas above to tell a partner two things you wish. Explain why.

"I wish I had a motorcycle. If I had a motorcycle, I could ride it to work."

5 I wonder . . .

A Rewrite these questions about the picture. Compare with a partner.

1. What is it?   Do you know _____ _what it is_ _____ ?
2. How do you turn it on?   Can you tell me _____ ?
3. Does it still work?   I wonder _____ ?
4. How much did it cost?   Do you know _____ ?
5. How do you use it?   Can you tell me _____ ?

B **Pair work** Look at the picture and ask and answer your questions.

A *Do you know what it is?*
B *Yes, it's an old record player.*   **OR**   *I have no idea what it is.*

6 It's all relative.

A How many ways can you complete these questions? Use *who*, *that*, or *which*. Write them (in parentheses) if you can leave them out.

1. What do you do with electronic gadgets _____ don't work anymore?
2. What would you do if you got a gift _____ you didn't like?
3. What do you do when you see a word _____ you don't know?
4. What do you do with clothes _____ are out of style?
5. What would you do if you had neighbors _____ played their music too loud?

B **Pair work** Ask and answer the questions. Can you use phrasal verbs in your answers?

What's up?

Lesson A
- Talk about your news using the present perfect, present perfect continuous, *since*, *for*, and *in*

Lesson B
- Describe movies
- Talk about your social life using the present perfect with *already*, *still*, and *yet*

Lesson C
- Ask for a favor politely
- Use *All right*, *OK*, and *Sure* to agree to requests and *All right*, *OK*, and *So* to change topic

Lesson D
- Read a movie review
- Write a review

Before you begin . . .

Have you done these things lately? What else is happening in your life these days? Have you . . .

- been out with your friends?
- done anything special?
- had a party?
- gone dancing anywhere?

- eaten anywhere nice?
- joined any clubs?
- been to any concerts?
- seen any good movies?

1 Bob So, what have you been doing since I saw you last?

Lois Working. That's pretty much it. I haven't been out in months. What about you?

Bob Same here. I've been working late every night. Uh . . . do you have time to grab a bite to eat?

2 Maya I haven't seen you in ages! What have you been up to?

Gail Well, you won't believe it, but I've been seeing a guy from work. We've gone out three or four times now, so I guess it's getting serious.

3 Will What have you been up to recently? I haven't seen you at the gym.

Diane Well, I've been going to a pottery class since September.

Will Pottery . . . really! So, what kind of things do you make?

Diane So far I've made eight vases and two bowls. Here's something I just made.

4 Luis Hey, good to see you. I see you're still doing karate.

Ahmad Oh, yeah.

Luis How long have you been doing that? About three years?

Ahmad Actually, for nine years now.

Luis Wow! That's impressive.

1 Getting started

A What kinds of things do people talk about when they are catching up with friends? Make a list.

B 🔊 **4.01** Listen. What topics do the people above talk about? Were the topics on your list?

 C Circle the correct words to complete the sentences.

1. Bob has been **working** / **worked** late every night recently.

2. Ahmad has been doing karate **since** / **for** nine years.

3. Diane's been going to a pottery class **since** / **for** September.

4. Maya hasn't seen Gail **in** / **since** ages.

2 Grammar Present perfect continuous vs. present perfect 🔊 4.02

Extra practice p. 149

Use the present perfect continuous for an ongoing or repeated activity that started before now and continues into the present.	Use the present perfect to show the results of an activity or how many times it has happened.
What **have** you **been doing** lately? I**'ve been going** to a pottery class. Who **has** she **been seeing**? She's **been seeing** a guy from work.	What things **have** you **made** so far? I**'ve made** eight vases and two bowls. How many times **have** they **gone out** together? They**'ve been** out three or four times.

Since, *for*, and *in* for duration
Use *since* with points in time.

Use *for* and *in* with periods of time, but use *in* only in negative statements.

I've been going to a pottery class **since** September.
What have you been doing **since** I saw you last?

He's been doing karate **for** nine years. (NOT . . . ~~since nine years.~~)
I haven't been out to eat **in** months.

In conversation

The present perfect is about 10 times more frequent than the present perfect continuous.

▬▬▬▬▬ present perfect
■ present perfect continuous

A Complete the conversations with the present perfect or the present perfect continuous of the verbs given. Sometimes both forms are correct. Add *for*, *since*, or *in*.

1. A ___Have___ you __been working__ (work) a lot recently? I haven't seen you _____in_____ ages.

   B Actually, yeah. I _____ (not take) one day off _____ weeks. So yeah, I _____ (not go) out _____ ages. How about you? What _____ you _____ ? (do)

   A Well, I _____ (take) a weight training class at the gym _____ May.

2. A _____ you _____ (do) anything interesting lately?

   B Not really. I _____ (fill) out college applications _____ the last month.

   A Yeah? How many colleges _____ you _____ to? (apply)

   B Well, I _____ (send) three applications, but I _____ (not hear) anything.

3. A _____ you and your friends _____ (go) out a lot recently?

   B Actually, yeah. We _____ (go) to a few clubs lately. We _____ (have) fun.

4. A How long _____ you _____ (learn) English?

   B _____ I was in elementary school. I guess _____ 12 years now.

   A Wow. That's a long time. So, how long _____ you _____ (come) to this class?

   B _____ April.

About you **B** Pair work Practice the conversations above. Practice again and give your own answers.

3 Speaking naturally Reduction of *have*

What **have** you been doing for fun lately?	(What**'ve**)
How many times **have** you gone out this month?	(times**'ve**)
Where **have** you been hanging out?	(Where**'ve**)

A 🔊 4.03 Listen and repeat the questions above. Practice the reduction of *have* to *'ve*. Then ask and answer the questions. Continue your conversations.

About you **B** 🔊 4.04 Listen. Write the four questions you hear. Then ask and answer with a partner.

1 Building vocabulary

A What kinds of movies are these? Label the pictures with the words in the box.
Add other kinds of movies to the list. Which ones do you like? Which do you never watch?

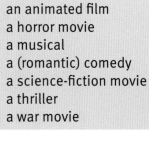

an action movie
an animated film
a horror movie
a musical
a (romantic) comedy
a science-fiction movie
a thriller
a war movie

B 🔊 **4.05** What kind of movie is each person talking about? Complete the descriptions with a type of movie. Then listen and check your answers.

1 It's a _____ . **It's about** these two people who **fall in love** over the Internet. It's a great **love story**, and it's **funny**, too.

2 It's a new _____ **set in** ancient China. Michelle Yeoh is in it. The **stunts** and the kung-fu **fight scenes** are amazing. It's kind of **violent**, though.

3 I just saw this _____ . A family moves into an old house, and they find a **monster** living in the attic. It was so **scary** that I couldn't watch most of it.

4 It's a _____ that **takes place** in Delhi. So, it's in Hindi, but it's **subtitled**. The **costumes**, the dancing, and the music are just wonderful.

5 It's a _____ . Matt Damon **plays** a spy who can't remember who he is. It was so exciting. I couldn't stand the **suspense**.

6 It's about **aliens** who come to take over the earth. It's a classic _____ . The **special effects** are incredible.

7 I saw this _____ about two soldiers who are brothers. It's a **true story** with a really **sad ending**. I cried a lot. It's a real **tearjerker**.

8 We saw this **hilarious** movie. It's one of those _____ for both kids and adults. Eddie Murphy is the voice of one of the **cartoon characters**.

Word sort **C** Make a word web about a movie. Use the words in bold. Then describe it to a partner.

It's a _____ .

It's about _____ .

_____ is in it .

It's set in _____ .

Movie: _____

He / She plays _____ .

It takes place in _____ .

It _____ .

I _____ .

📓 **Vocabulary notebook** p. 106

2 Building language

A 🔊 4.06 Listen. What do Carl and Jolene decide to do? Why? Practice the conversation.

Carl   Sorry I'm late. Have you been waiting long?

Jolene   No, just a few minutes.

Carl   So, which movie do you want to see? I've heard good things about *Starship*. Have you seen it yet?

Jolene   Yeah. I've already seen it. It was OK.

Carl   Oh. Well, there's *Funny Guy*. It's been playing for ages, and I still haven't seen it.

Jolene   Actually, I saw it when it first came out.

Carl   OK, well, how about *Joker*? I haven't seen that yet, either.

Jolene   I've seen it, but I'll go again. It was hilarious. At the end, the guy falls into a . . .

Carl   Hey, don't spoil it for me. Let's just go see it.

Figure it out **B** Write the name of a movie you've seen in A's question, and circle the correct word in each response. Then work with a partner. Take turns asking your questions and giving true answers.

A   I recently saw _____ . Have you seen it?

B   You know, I **already / still / yet** haven't seen that movie.

C   Actually, I haven't seen that movie **already / still / yet** either.

D   Yeah. I've **already / still / yet** seen it.

3 Grammar *already, still,* and *yet* with present perfect 🔊 4.07   **Extra practice** p. 149

Have you seen *Funny Guy* **yet**?	= *I imagine you're planning to see it.*
Yes, I've **already** seen it. / Yes, I've seen it **already**.	= *I saw it earlier.*
No, I haven't seen it **yet**. / No, not **yet**.	= *I haven't seen it, but I plan to.*
No, I **still** haven't seen it.	= *I've wanted to see it for weeks, but I haven't yet.*

💬 **In conversation**

With this meaning of *yet*, about 83 percent of its uses are in negative statements and about 17 percent are in questions.

A Complete the conversations. Add *already, still,* or *yet.* Then practice with a partner.

1. A   There's a new comedy out. Have you seen it _yet_ ?

    B   Oh, the Ben Stiller movie? Yeah, I've _already_ seen it. It was hilarious. Have *you* seen it _yet_ ?

    A   No, I haven't, not _yet_ . I'd like to, though.

2. A   Have you seen the latest James Bond movie _yet_ ?

    B   No. I haven't had a chance _yet_ . Actually, I _still_ haven't seen the last one.

3. A   So, do you want to go see a movie later?

    B   I don't know. I've _already_ seen most of the movies that are out now.

    A   Really? I _still_ haven't seen any of them.

About you **B** Pair work Take turns asking the questions above. Give your own answers.   🔊 **Sounds right** p. 139

Lesson C
Conversation strategies

I was wondering . . .

1 Conversation strategy Asking for a favor politely

A What kinds of favors might you ask a teacher for? Make a class list.

B 🔊 4.08 Listen. What favor does Jake ask his professor? Does his professor agree?

Jake	Excuse me, Professor Carlton. I was wondering if I could ask you something.
Professor	Sure. Let me just finish up here. All right. So, what can I do for you?
Jake	Well, I wanted to ask a favor, actually.
Professor	OK.
Jake	I was wondering if you could write a reference for me. I've been applying for jobs and . . .
Professor	Sure. Do you have the information I need?
Jake	Um, yes. But not with me. Um, would it be all right if I brought it tomorrow?
Professor	All right. As long as you come late afternoon. I have classes all morning. When do you need it by?
Jake	Well, I know it's short notice, but would it be OK if I picked it up next Monday?
Professor	OK. Sure. So, was that all? All right, well, see you tomorrow!

C **Notice** the expressions Jake uses to ask for a favor politely. These expressions are useful in formal situations or if you are asking someone for a big favor. Find examples in the conversation.

> *I was wondering . . .*
> *I was wondering if I / you could . . .*
> *I wanted to . . .*
> *Would it be all right / OK with you if I (picked it up / came back, etc.) . . . ?*

D Complete the favors below with expressions from the box above. Then match each favor with an explanation. Write the letters *a* to *f*.

1. *I was wondering if I could* miss the next class. __d__
2. _____ get help with my homework. ____
3. _____ write me a letter of recommendation. ____
4. _____ get an extension on my paper. ____
5. _____ took some more practice tests? ____
6. _____ stayed after class to talk about my college applications? ____

a. I'm applying for a job in a hospital.
b. I need some advice about the application essays.
c. I need a little more time to complete it.
d. I have to retake a math test that day.
e. I don't understand the calculus problems.
f. I want to improve my test-taking skills.

E **Pair work** Take turns playing the roles of a student and a professor. Ask and respond to the favors above.

2 Strategy plus *All right, OK, So, Sure*

You can use *All right*, *OK*, and *Sure* to agree to requests.

You can use *All right*, *OK*, and *So* to move a conversation to a new phase or topic.

I was wondering if I could ask you something?

Sure.

All right. So, what can I do for you?

🔊 **4.09** Listen. Write the missing words. Is the speaker agreeing to a request (*A*), showing understanding (*U*), or moving the conversation along (*M*)? Then practice.

> **In conversation**
>
> People also respond with just *Right* to show they understand or agree.

A I was wondering if you had a few minutes to talk.

B *Sure (A)* . Actually, I have time now before my next class. Do you want to grab a cup of coffee?

A _____ . Let's go to that place across the street.

B _____ . Let's walk over there. . . . _____ , what's up?

A Well, I wanted to ask you for a favor actually.

B Oh, _____ . _____ , what do you need?

A Well, you know I'm going away on an exchange program for two weeks.

B _____ . I heard you're going to Brazil.

A Yeah. _____ , I was wondering if you could feed my snake.

B Um, _____ . Sure.

A Thank you so much. That's great. _____ , well, can I get you a coffee?

3 Listening and strategies *Favors at work*

A 🔊 **4.10** Listen to four people ask their bosses for favors. Check (✓) the favors each person asks for. There is one extra favor.

	1. Peter	2. Sandra	3. Joel	4. Julia
1. a day off work	☐	☐	☐	☐
2. to leave work early on Friday	☐	☐	☐	☐
3. more time to write a report	☐	☐	☐	☐
4. a signature on an expense form	☐	☐	☐	☐
5. to do a presentation	☐	☐	☐	☐

B 🔊 **4.10** Listen again. Why do the people need to ask the favors? Write the reason. Do their bosses agree to the requests? Circle *Y* (Yes) or *N* (No).

1. _____ Y / N   3. _____ Y / N

2. _____ Y / N   4. _____ Y / N

About you **C** **Pair work** Take turns asking your partner for favors. Give reasons. Either agree to or decline the favor, and say why. How many favors can you think of?

"Arturo, I was wondering if you could give me a ride home after class tomorrow?"

1 Reading

A Do you ever read reviews before deciding to see a movie? Are the reviews usually accurate? Tell the class.

B Read the movie review and the comments. What kind of movie is it? Does the review encourage you to see the movie? Why or why not?

> **Reading tip**
> Scan reviews for adjectives. They will tell you if the review is positive or negative.

---

www.avatarmoviereview...

AVATAR is magnificent, mesmerizing, and memorable!

It's an action movie, science fiction, and fantasy all in one – with, of course, some romance. *Avatar*, directed by James Cameron, is 162 minutes of thrilling entertainment. Millions of people saw the movie worldwide on its opening weekend. It went on to win a string of awards and break box office records, including the record for the highest-grossing film of all time with more than $2 billion in sales, finally ending the 12-year reign of *Titanic*.

The story takes place in 2154 on the moon Pandora, where 10-foot tall, blue-skinned, human-like creatures – the Na'vi – live in complete harmony with their environment. Pandora is rich in minerals, and humans, who have an energy crisis on Earth, have traveled to Pandora to conquer it and to mine its minerals. Since humans cannot breathe in Pandora's atmosphere, they use Na'vi-like "avatars," which they control. Sam Worthington gives an excellent performance as Jake Sully, who becomes sympathetic to the Na'vi and their desire to protect their homeland. There is inevitably conflict that ends in a violent war.

The computer-generated special effects are stunning. The music is memorable, and the invented Na'vi language is mesmerizing. All in all, it's a movie that keeps you firmly glued to your seat.

I have already seen *Avatar* several times now – more recently in 3D. It's one of those movies that you could watch again and again. Sad, scary, exciting – I'm sure every viewer will find his or her own way to describe the movie. If you haven't seen it yet, I recommend it. At least then you'll be ready for the sequels. And I, for one, can't wait.

READERS' COMMENTS:

MIKI: I haven't seen this movie yet, and I can't comment on the acting or anything, but my friends say it's the best movie they've ever seen.

JON: Although it sounds good, I'm not going to see this movie. I heard it's violent in parts, and I don't like violent movies.

SUE-ANN: Even if you don't like sci-fi movies, you'll enjoy this one. I did!

MARIBETH: I loved this movie, even though I cried all the way through.

C Find the underlined expressions in the review or in the readers' comments. Match them with the definitions. Write *a* to *f*.

1. a string of awards _____
2. break box office records _____
3. highest-grossing film of all time _____
4. conflict that ends in violent war _____
5. keeps you firmly glued to your seat _____
6. you'll be ready for the sequels _____

a. you won't get up, so you don't miss anything
b. a fight
c. several, one after another
d. movies that continue a story begun in a previous movie
e. do better than ever before
f. earned more than any other has ever earned

D Read the review and comments again. Answer the questions below, and then compare your answers with a partner.

1. What movie was previously the highest-grossing film of all time?
2. Why do humans need Pandora's minerals?
3. How does Jake Sully feel about the Na'vi?
4. What are two things the reviewer really likes about the movie?
5. What is one thing that might keep some people from seeing *Avatar*?
6. Will someone who doesn't like science fiction or tearjerkers enjoy *Avatar*?

2 Listening and writing I'd really recommend it.

A ◀)) 4.11 Listen to Jim and Marissa talk about a Cirque du Soleil show. Does Marissa want to see the show? Would you like to see it? Tell a partner.

B ◀)) 4.11 Listen again. Are the sentences true or false? Check (✓) *T* or *F*. Correct the false sentences.

		T	F
1.	Cirque du Soleil performers are all Canadian.	☐	☐
2.	The group started in Quebec more than 20 years ago.	☐	☐
3.	They now perform all over the world.	☐	☐
4.	The acrobats perform with animals.	☐	☐
5.	Jim has already seen a Cirque du Soleil show.	☐	☐
6.	Jim is going to call to find out about tickets.	☐	☐

3 Writing A Review

A Read the review and the Help note. Circle the expressions in the review that show contrasting ideas.

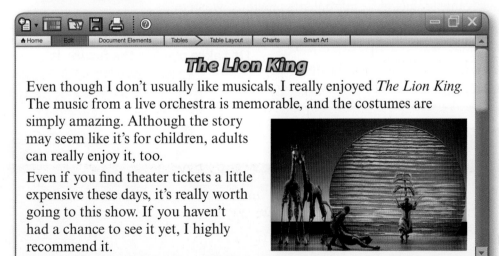

The Lion King

Even though I don't usually like musicals, I really enjoyed *The Lion King*. The music from a live orchestra is memorable, and the costumes are simply amazing. Although the story may seem like it's for children, adults can really enjoy it, too.

Even if you find theater tickets a little expensive these days, it's really worth going to this show. If you haven't had a chance to see it yet, I highly recommend it.

> **✏ Help note**
>
> **Contrasting ideas**
> ***Although*** the story may seem like it's for children, adults can really enjoy it, too.
>
> ***Even though*** I don't usually like musicals, I loved this one.
>
> ***Even if*** you don't like musicals, you might enjoy this one.

About you B Think of a concert, a show, a movie, or a book you have seen or read. Write a review about it. Then read your classmates' reviews. Can you find . . .

- a concert or show you'd like to go to?
- a play you've already seen?
- a book you've been wanting to read?
- a movie you haven't seen yet?

Free talk ᴄp. 135

Vocabulary notebook / Great movies

Learning tip *Linking new words to your experiences*

When you learn a new word or expression, link it to something you have recently seen or done.

In conversation

People say *movie* 15 times more frequently than *film*.

▬▬▬▬▬▬ *movie*
■ *film*

1 Think of a movie title for each of these kinds of movies.

1. an animated film _____
2. a thriller _____
3. a musical _____
4. a romantic comedy _____
5. a science-fiction movie _____

6. a movie with great stunt scenes _____
7. a movie that's a true story _____
8. a movie with great special effects _____
9. a movie that's subtitled _____
10. a movie with a sad ending _____

2 Make a list of different types of movies. Link each one to a specific movie you have seen. Then write a sentence saying what the movie is about.

	Type of movie	Name of movie	What is it about?
1.			
2.			
3.			
4.			

3 **Word builder** Find out what kinds of movies these are. Put them in a chart like the one above. Can you think of the name of a movie for each one and say what it's about?

detective movie   fantasy film   historical drama   teen movie
documentary   gangster movie   martial arts movie   western

 On your own

Read a review in English of a new movie. Then write a paragraph about the movie.

It's an animated film about robots. It takes place in the future. It's pretty funny.

Can Do! Now I can . . .

✓ I can . . .   ? I need to review how to . . .

- ☐ catch up with friends and tell them my news.
- ☐ say how long things have been happening.
- ☐ describe different kinds of movies.
- ☐ ask someone for a favor politely.
- ☐ use *All right*, *OK*, *Sure* to agree to requests.

- ☐ say *All right*, *OK*, and *So* to change topic.
- ☐ understand people asking for favors.
- ☐ understand people talking about going to see a show.
- ☐ read a movie review.
- ☐ write a review.

Impressions

✓ Can Do! In this unit, you learn how to . . .

Lesson A
- Speculate using *must, may, might, can't,* and *could*

Lesson B
- Describe situations and feelings with adjectives ending in *-ing* and *-ed*

Lesson C
- Show you understand another person's feelings or situation
- Use *you see* to explain a situation and *I see* to show you understand

Lesson D
- Read an article about *El Sistema*, a music education program
- Write an email to the founder of a charity

1

2

3

Before you begin . . .

What impressions do you get from each of these pictures? Make some guesses.

- What do you think is the relationship between the people in each picture?
- What do you think is happening?
- How do you think each person feels?

Getting started

A Make three guesses about the picture. Who do you think the people are?
How old are they? Where are they?

Emma	Hey, look. That girl over there must be graduating.
Lloyd	From college? Are you kidding? She can't be more than 12. She can't be graduating, surely?
Emma	Well, she's wearing a cap and gown.
Lloyd	Huh. She must be a genius.
Emma	Sure, but she must study a lot, too.
Lloyd	Yeah, probably all the time. She can't have too many close friends here. I mean, she's so much younger than everyone.
Emma	Well, the guy she's talking to might be one of her friends.
Lloyd	He could be. Or he may be one of her professors.
Emma	True. . . . Oh, look. Those must be her parents – the people with the cameras.
Lloyd	Yeah. They must be feeling pretty proud.

B ◀)) 4.12 Listen. Emma and Lloyd are speculating about the young girl. What guesses do they make?

Figure it out **C** Complete the second sentences so they mean the same as the first sentences.
Use the conversation above to help you. There may be more than one correct answer.

1. I'm sure that girl is smart. She _____ smart.

2. I'm sure she isn't older than 12. She _____ older than 12.

3. Maybe the guy she's talking to is her professor. The guy she's talking to _____ her professor.

4. I'm sure her parents are feeling proud. Her parents _____ proud.

2 **Speaking naturally** Linking and deletion with *must*

Before a vowel sound and / *h, l, r, w, y* /	Before most consonant sounds
She must enjoy school.	*She mus(t) be a genius.*
She must have some friends who are her age.	*She mus(t) study all the time.*
She must live with her parents.	*She mus(t) feel lonely sometimes.*

A ◀)) 4.13 Listen and repeat the sentences above. Practice linking the words as shown.

B Which of the speculations about the girl do you agree with? Can you add any more? Tell the class.

3 Grammar Modal verbs for speculating 🔊 4.14

Extra practice p. 150

She **must be** a genius.	= I bet she**'s** a genius.
She **must work** pretty hard.	= I bet she **works** pretty hard.
She **must not go out** much.	= I bet she **doesn't go out** much.
She **must be graduating** today.	= I bet she**'s graduating** today.
She **can't be** more than 12.	= It's not possible she**'s** more than 12.
He **could be** one of her friends.	= It's possible he**'s** one of her friends.
He **may be** her professor.	= Maybe he**'s** her professor.
They **might be feeling** sad.	= Maybe they**'re feeling** sad.

📃 **In conversation**

Most uses of *must* and *might* – over 90 percent – are in affirmative statements. In negative statements, people usually say *must not* and *might not* with no contractions

A Look at the pictures below. Rewrite the sentences with modal verbs. There may be more than one possible answer.

1. I'm 100 percent sure she's feeling cold.
   She must be feeling cold.

2. It's possible that she's training for a marathon.
   She could be training for a marathon

3. I'm sure she's taking a break.
   She must be taking a break

4. I'm sure she's exercising. She's not doing anything else.
   She must be excercising

5. I think she's definitely crazy to run in the snow.
   She must be crazy to run...

6. Maybe she's trying to get in shape.
   She might be trying to get...

1. Maybe she's lost.
   She could be lost

2. I bet her parents are looking for her.
   Her parents must be looking for her

3. It's possible she's in trouble.
   She might be in trouble

4. I bet she's scared. It's not possible she's on her own.
   She must be scared...

5. It's possible her mother is standing nearby.
   Maybe her mother is standing nearby

6. Maybe she's throwing a tantrum.
   She might be throwing a tantrum

B **Pair work** What other guesses can you make about each picture? Discuss with a partner. Explain your guesses.

"She must be pretty tough. It looks really cold."

1 Building vocabulary and grammar

A 🔊 **4.15** Look at the picture. What guesses can you make about the party? Then listen. Can you identify each guest Fred describes?

Yoshi looks **bored**. **Tom** must be telling one of his **boring** stories. His stories are never **interesting**. **Sophia** seems **fascinated**, though. She must be **interested** in Tom.

Oh, no. **John** just spilled juice all over **Amy**. I bet he's **embarrassed**. She looks a bit **annoyed**. She can't be too **pleased** about her dress.

David just did something **embarrassing**. He locked his keys inside the car, and now he can't get in. That's so **frustrating**. He wanted to leave an hour ago. I bet he's **disappointed**.

What was that scream? Oh, there's a spider in **Jennifer**'s glass. She looks **shocked**. I think she's **scared** of spiders. **Ahmad** seems **surprised** by her reaction.

Andrea seems **excited** to see **Alan**. She used to go out with him. Her new boyfriend, **Albert**, must be **jealous** and a little **anxious**. He may be **worried** that she'll go back to Alan.

Word sort B Look at the things people say below. How are they feeling? Make guesses. Use the adjectives in bold above. Then compare with a partner.

1. "This movie's too long."
   He must be bored.
2. "I lost my house keys."
3. "Oh no! He has a girlfriend!"
4. "My vacation starts on Friday."
5. "This show is interesting."
6. "I fell and broke my glasses!"
7. "I failed the test? No!"

📔 **Vocabulary notebook** p. 116

Figure it out C Can you complete the sentences with the adjectives given? Compare with a partner.

1. Yoshi isn't _____ in Tom's story. It's not an _____ story. (interesting, interested)
2. Sophia isn't _____ . She doesn't think Tom's story is _____ . (boring, bored)

2 Grammar Adjectives ending in -ed and -ing ◀)) 4.16

Extra practice p. 150

Adjectives ending in -ed can describe how you feel about someone or something.

I'm **bored** with my job.
I'm **interested** in astronomy.
I get **annoyed** with my sister.
I'm **excited** about my vacation.
I'm **scared** of spiders.

Adjectives ending in -ing can describe someone or something.

My job is very **boring**.
I think astronomy is **interesting**.
She does a lot of **annoying** things.
My vacation is going to be **exciting**.
But: I think spiders are **scary**.

💬 In conversation

Interesting, interested, amazing, scary, surprised, worried, scared, excited, exciting, and *boring* are all in the top 2,000 words.

✖ Common errors

Don't confuse *boring* and *bored*.
*I often feel **bored** at work.*
(NOT *I often feel ~~boring~~ at work.*)

A Choose the correct words to complete the sentences.

1. I get really (**frustrated**)/ **frustrating** when I call somewhere and they put me on hold. It's very **annoyed / annoying**.

2. We watched a really **bored / boring** TV show last night. I actually fell asleep.

3. I'm really **excited / exciting** about my trip. I'm going to Hong Kong.

4. It's really **embarrassed / embarrassing** when you forget someone's name.

5. I get really **confused / confusing** when movie plots jump around.

6. I wasn't able to get tickets to see my favorite band. I was so **disappointed / disappointing**.

7. I heard something **surprised / surprising**. Coffee might actually be good for you.

8. We went whitewater rafting recently. It was **amazed / amazing**.

9. My sister forgot my birthday. I was **shocked / shocking**.

10. We went on a huge roller coaster last weekend. It was really **scared / scary**.

11. I think documentaries about space are really **fascinated / fascinating**.

12. All of my friends think golf is **interested / interesting** to watch. I have no idea why.

About you B Pair work Make the sentences above true for you. Tell your partner.

A I get really frustrated when I don't understand something.
B Like with your homework or something? I find that frustrating, too.

3 Talk about it Feelings

Group work Discuss the questions. Write down any interesting or unusual responses, and then tell the class.

▶ Do you know anyone who is annoying? Do you get annoyed with people often?
▶ What kinds of things do you find boring? Do get bored easily?
▶ Are you scared of things like spiders? heights? flying? What's most scary?
▶ What things make you feel anxious or worried? Do you worry a lot?
▶ Have you ever felt really disappointed? What happened?
▶ Are you excited about anything right now?
▶ What's the most exciting thing you've ever done?
▶ What subjects do you find fascinating? What are you most interested in?

"One of our neighbors is really annoying.
He's always borrowing things."

(((· Sounds right p. 139

1 Conversation strategy Showing you understand

A What impressions do you get about Hal and Debra from the picture?

B 4.17 Listen. Why hasn't Hal made much progress with his saxophone?

Debra Hey, what's this saxophone doing here?

Hal I have a lesson after work.

Debra So, how long have you been playing?

Hal Oh, a couple of years.

Debra You must be getting pretty good by now.

Hal I wish! I haven't made much progress lately.

Debra Huh. How come?

Hal Well, you see, I used to practice every morning. But then I started this job, and somehow I can't get myself to practice at night.

Debra Well, you must be tired after work.

Hal Yeah. But you know, I just joined a band.

Debra That must be fun.

Hal Yeah, it really is, and it keeps me motivated to practice. In fact, that's why I joined.

Debra I see. Well, let me know if your band performs anywhere. I want to hear you play!

C Notice how Debra uses *must* to show she understands Hal's situation or feelings. Find examples in the conversation.

"That must be fun."

D Think of two responses to each sentence. Use *That must be* and *You must be* and adjectives from the box. Then practice with a partner.

1. My computer keeps crashing.
   That must be annoying. You must be frustrated.
2. I've been taking archery lessons for two years now.
3. I just got a scholarship to a master's program in business.
4. I got up at 5:00 this morning to finish some work.
5. I'm taking an ethics class. It's tough, but I'm going to finish it.
6. I'm going skydiving next week.
7. I've finished all my work, so I'm leaving early today.
8. I'm reading a long report about data security.

annoying	hard
bored	interesting
boring	irritating
difficult	motivated
excited	nervous
exciting	nice
fascinating	pleased
frustrated	scary
fun	thrilled
good	tired
happy	

About you E **Pair work** Write five true sentences like the ones above. Take turns saying your sentences and reacting to them.

2 Strategy plus *You see* and *I see*

You can use *you see* to explain something that the other person might not know.

> You see, I used to practice every morning.

You can use *I see* to show you understand something that you didn't know earlier.

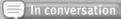

In conversation

I see and *you see* are in the top 900 words and expressions.

> It keeps me motivated. In fact, that's why I joined.

> I see.

About you Complete the conversations with *you see* or *I see*. Then practice with a partner. Practice again, this time giving your own answers.

1. A Is there a country you'd really like to go to?
   B Yeah, China. ___You see___ , my dad goes there a lot with his work, and it sounds fascinating.
   A ___I see___ . He must have a really interesting job.

2. A Would you like to have more free time?
   B I actually have a lot of free time at the moment. I've finished my final exams, ___you see___ .
   A ___I see___ . You must be pleased about that.

3. A What class would you like to take if you had the chance?
   B Actually, I'd really like to learn how to blow glass. My aunt does it, ___you see___ .
   A ___I see___ . That must be hard to do.

3 Listening and strategies People and situations

A 🔊 4.18 Listen to four conversations. Match each person with the situation he or she explains.

1. Mark _____
2. Angela _____
3. Linda _____
4. Dave _____

a. has always dreamed of going abroad to study art.
b. has been studying a lot recently.
c. doesn't have enough time to practice.
d. wants to be able to talk to people while on vacation.

B 🔊 4.18 Listen again. Show you understand. Write a response to each person using *must*.

1. _____
2. _____
3. _____
4. _____

About you **C** Pair work Discuss the questions below.

1. What have you always dreamed of doing?
2. What have you not been doing a lot this year?
3. What don't you have enough time to do?
4. What do you want to be able to do on vacation?

   A Well, I've always wanted to drive a race car. You see, I follow all the Formula One races.
   B That must be fun. Do you actually go to any of the races?

Free talk p. 135

113

Lesson D / **Making an impression**

1 Reading

A What kinds of cultural activities are available in your area? Have you ever participated in any of them? Tell the class.

B Read the article. How does El Sistema benefit young people?

 Reading tip

Before you read a factual piece, ask yourself questions like *What is it? Where is it? Who does it?* Then scan the text to see if you can find answers.

EL SISTEMA

Venezuela has a revolutionary and inspiring music education program, which aims to improve the lives of disadvantaged children and their families. *El Sistema* – meaning "the system" – is a total-immersion[1] program that brings children together to play music every day. Preschool children sit on their mothers' knees to sing, play rhythm games, or play with paper instruments that they make themselves. At age five, children start to play a real instrument, which is a thrilling experience for them. As soon as the children are good enough, they teach the younger ones. The program is highly successful. By high school, students are tackling some of the most difficult pieces of classical music. However, the program is demanding, and participants need to be committed; they practice after school every day and on weekends.

There are now some 500 or so orchestras throughout the country, some of which perform internationally. Many of the young musicians have even become professionals. El Sistema graduates include conductors of the Venice Opera and Los Angeles Philharmonic and the Berlin Philharmonic's youngest player ever. According to British conductor Sir Simon Rattle, "There is nothing more important in the world of music than what is happening in Venezuela." These young musicians must surely be motivating role models[2] for other young people in their home country.

However, music wasn't the primary goal when the program began in 1975 with just 11 students in a garage. El Sistema's founder, José Antonio Abreu, was interested in "human development," or social action through music. Abreu's slogan, "*Tocar y Luchar,*" (Play and Struggle) describes his hope that learning and playing music together helps children overcome academic, social, and economic obstacles. "If you put a violin in a child's hands, that child will never hold a gun," he is quoted as saying. Interestingly, 90 percent of the program's funding comes from social service agencies rather than cultural organizations. Since 1975, El Sistema has made an amazing difference in many lives. Two million graduates have become skilled musicians, and according to Abreu, they are resilient, flourishing citizens, as well. More than 25 countries, including the United States, Austria, and India, have since copied El Sistema's groundbreaking[3] model[4].

1 *total-immersion*: constant involvement in an activity
2 *role model*: someone that other people respect and copy
3 *groundbreaking*: completely new
4 *model*: type of program

C Read six people's comments about El Sistema. Are their impressions correct? Write *Yes* or *No*. Find evidence in the article to support your answer.

1. A program like that can't really work. I mean, they can't teach them to play advanced pieces. _____

2. The children must spend hours practicing. _____

3. Sir Simon Rattle must be really impressed with the program. _Y_

4. Some of the students may come from wealthy families. _N_

5. They must get a lot of their money from arts and music organizations. _____

6. Programs like that can't work in other countries, though. _____

Listening and speaking People making a difference

A Look at the people and the organizations they are involved with. Can you guess what the organizations do?

Janine Licare

Arn Chorn-Pond

Ardena Gojani

1. **Kids Saving the Rainforest**

2. **Cambodian Living Arts**

3. **The International Book Project**

_____

_____

_____

B 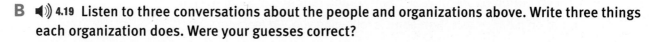 4.19 Listen to three conversations about the people and organizations above. Write three things each organization does. Were your guesses correct?

C 4.19 Listen again. How does each student plan to get involved with the organization? Take notes. Tell the class which program you would choose to get involved in.

About you **D** **Group work** Think of a volunteer project you could start. Who would it help? What would it do? Present your program to the class. Choose two programs to support.

Writing My impression is . . .

A Read the two emails and the Help note. Circle the expressions in the emails that show impressions, reactions, and opinions.

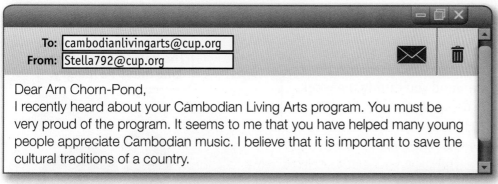

To: cambodianlivingarts@cup.org
From: Stella792@cup.org

Dear Arn Chorn-Pond,
I recently heard about your Cambodian Living Arts program. You must be very proud of the program. It seems to me that you have helped many young people appreciate Cambodian music. I believe that it is important to save the cultural traditions of a country.

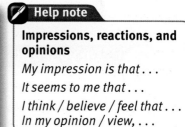
Help note

Impressions, reactions, and opinions
My impression is that . . .
It seems to me that . . .
I think / believe / feel that . . .
In my opinion / view, . . .

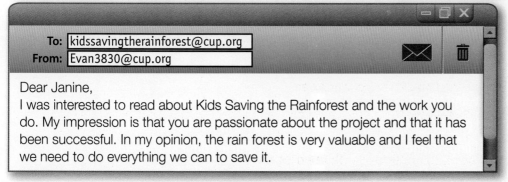

To: kidssavingtherainforest@cup.org
From: Evan3830@cup.org

Dear Janine,
I was interested to read about Kids Saving the Rainforest and the work you do. My impression is that you are passionate about the project and that it has been successful. In my opinion, the rain forest is very valuable and I feel that we need to do everything we can to save it.

About you **B** Which person in this lesson would you like to contact? Why? Tell a partner. Then choose one, and write an email.

C **Group work** Read your classmates' emails. Who did most people write to?

Learning tip *Linking situations and feelings*

When you learn words for feelings, link them to different situations where you might experience each one.

1 Complete the sentences. Use the adjectives in the box or other words you know.

annoyed   bored   disappointed   scared

1. In class, you've finished your work. There's nothing else to do. *I'd probably feel* _____ .
2. You are waiting for a friend, and she calls to say she can't meet you. *I think I'd be* _____ .
3. A friend borrowed one of your sweaters and returned it stained. *I'd feel* _____ .
4. You're on a dark street. Someone is following you. *I'd feel* _____ .

2 Think of situations for these different emotions. Complete the sentences.

1. I feel very motivated to practice my English when _____ .
2. I think it's annoying when _____ .
3. I was really shocked once when _____ .
4. Sometimes I get frustrated when _____ .
5. I think it's embarrassing when _____ .
6. Sometimes I get confused when _____ .

3 Word builder Can you make sentences with each pair of adjectives?

astonished / astonishing   terrified / terrifying   thrilled / thrilling   upset / upsetting

 **On your own**

Observe the people around you during the week. Notice what they are doing, and guess how they feel. Write sentences in your notebook.

The baby's screaming. She must be hungry.

Can Do! Now I can . . .

✓ I can . . .   ? I need to review how to . . .

- [ ] speculate about people and things.
- [ ] describe situations and people's feelings.
- [ ] use *must* to show that I understand.
- [ ] use *you see* to explain something and *I see* to show that I understand.

- [ ] understand people talking about their situations.
- [ ] understand conversations about charities.
- [ ] read an article about *El Sistema*.
- [ ] write an email to the founder of a charity.

In the news

UNIT

12

✓ **Can Do!** In this unit, you learn how to . . .

Lesson A
- Talk about news events using the simple past passive

Lesson B
- Talk about natural disasters using the simple past passive + *by*

Lesson C
- Use expressions like *Guess what?* to tell news
- Use expressions like *The thing is . . .* to introduce ideas

Lesson D
- Read an interview with a foreign correspondent, Christiane Amanpour
- Write a survey and report statistics

1

2

voda AU 🔋 11:46 AM

Sign In

Twitter is a rich source of instant information. Stay updated. Keep others updated. It's a whole thing.

SIGN UP

🔍 Search for topic or name

Suggested Users 〉

MileyCyrus Just got myself an early b-day present :) how cute is this little black diamond "L" necklace! Reminds me of my bo...

3

4

WORLD NEWS

Business Opportunities:

LES EXTRÊMES DROITE

diplo

CHOSES VUES À PYONGYANG

n Corée du No
a société s'évol

Before you begin . . .

- How do you find out about what's going on in the world?
- Which aspects of the news are you most interested in?
- What major events are in the news right now?

117

Ruth Anything interesting in the paper?

Jack Oh, not much. Let's see. Uh, $10,000 was found in a bag on a city bus.

Ruth $10,000? I should ride the bus more often!

Jack Yeah, and listen to this. Two large bears were seen last night in someone's yard.

Ruth Huh. That's kind of scary.

Jack Oh, and a jewelry store was broken into, and some diamonds were stolen. Um, what else? The city airport was closed yesterday because of strong winds.

Ruth Really? Well, it was pretty windy.

Jack Yeah. All the flights were delayed. Oh, and a bus was hit by a falling tree. Fortunately, the passengers weren't hurt.

Ruth Is that all? Nothing exciting, I guess.

1 Getting started

A How often do you read local news? What local news have you read recently?

B 🔊 4.20 Listen. Jack is telling Ruth some local news. Complete the sentences.

1. Someone found _____ on a city bus.
2. There were two bears in a _____ .
3. A thief broke into a _____ .
4. The airport had to close because of _____ .
5. A falling tree hit a _____ .

Figure it out **C** Complete the second sentence so it means the same as the first. Use the conversation above to help you. What do you notice about the verbs?

1. Someone broke into a jewelry store.   A jewelry store _____ .
2. A falling tree hit a bus.   A bus _____ by a falling tree.
3. Someone saw two bears last night.   Two bears _____ last night.
4. Someone stole some diamonds.   Some diamonds _____ .
5. The accident didn't hurt the passengers.   The passengers _____ in the accident.

2 **Grammar** Simple past passive 🔊 4.21

Extra practice p. 151

In sentences with active verbs, the subject is the "doer" and the object is the "receiver" of an action. Use active verbs to focus on the "doer" or cause.

A student **found** a bag on a bus.
The authorities **closed** the airport.
A teenager **saw** two bears in a yard.
The accident **didn't injure** the passengers.

In sentences with passive verbs, the subject is the "receiver" of the action. Use passive verbs to focus on the "receiver" or when the "doer" or cause is not known or not important.

A bag **was found** on a bus.
The airport **was closed**.
Two bears **were seen** in a yard.
The passengers **weren't injured**.

💬 **In conversation**

The passive is approximately 5 times more common in written news than in conversation.

A Complete the sentences. Use the simple past passive.

1. A 500-pound bear _____ (find) asleep in a basement on Tuesday morning. The bear _____ (wake up) by a workman, who said he "freaked" when he realized it was a bear. Wildlife officers _____ (call), and the bear _____ (take) to a state park.

2. A sporting goods store _____ (break into) yesterday, and 50 bicycles _____ (steal). A white truck _____ (see) outside the store around 5:00 a.m. However, security cameras _____ (damage) during the break-in, so the thieves _____ (not catch) on camera.

3. Millions of stolen banknotes _____ (find) in a police raid this morning. Police believe the money _____ (steal) from a city bank two years ago.

4. The highway _____ (close) for several hours last night after a car _____ (hit) by an oil truck. Hundreds of gallons of oil _____ (spill) onto the highway. Two passengers in the car _____ (take) to the hospital. The driver of the truck _____ (not injure).

B Pair work Take turns retelling the stories above without looking at your books. Then prepare a story about a recent news event to tell your partner.

A *A bear was discovered in a basement last week.*

B *Right. I guess it was found after a workman went in there.*

3 **Speaking naturally** Breaking sentences into parts

*Ten thousand **dollars** / was found in a **bag** / on a city **bus**.*
*Two large **bears** / were **seen** last night / in someone's **yard**.*
*A **jewelry** store / was broken **into**, / and some **diamonds** were stolen.*
*The city **airport** / was **closed** yesterday / because of strong **winds**.*

A 🔊 4.22 Listen and repeat the sentences above. Notice how long sentences are broken into shorter parts. The word with the new information in each part is stressed.

B Pair work Take turns saying the sentences above. How many times can you change the information?

"A suspicious suitcase was found in the airport terminal."

Lesson B / Natural disasters

1 Building vocabulary and grammar

A 🔊 **4.23** Listen. Which picture goes with each news item? Number the pictures.

1 The island of Puerto Rico was **hit** by **Hurricane** Calvin late this morning. Electric power was temporarily **disrupted** throughout the island, and many homes were **damaged** by **heavy rains** and **strong winds.**

2 Quebec was hit by **severe thunderstorms** yesterday. Flights at several airports were delayed by heavy rains, **thunder,** and **lightning**. Last night, three families were **rescued** by emergency workers after their homes were damaged by **flash floods** resulting from the rains.

3 Firefighters in Australia say over 10,000 acres of forest were completely **destroyed** by **catastrophic wildfires** this year. Investigators suspect some fires were caused by careless campers. They believe other fires started when trees were **struck** by lightning.

4 A shopping mall in Kansas was badly damaged by a **tornado** last night. A nearby town was later hit by a **freak hailstorm**. Cars were struck by **hailstones** the size of golf balls. Amazingly, no one was seriously **injured** by the tornado or the storm.

5 A small town in Italy was struck by a **minor earthquake** this morning. The quake measured 4.9 on the Richter scale. **Aftershocks** were felt in several towns. Some homes were partially destroyed, but no serious injuries were reported.

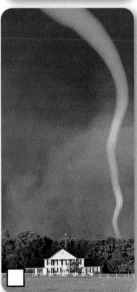

Word sort **B** Write words and expressions from the news stories in the chart below. Add your own ideas. Then compare with a partner.

Weather problems	Other natural disasters	Verbs for damage and help
hurricane	(catastrophic) wildfires	hit
typhoon		

Figure it out **C** Can you put these statements in the correct order?

1. firefighters / rescued / two families / by / were
2. was / hailstones / struck / a car / by
3. injured / was / seriously / no one
4. completely / a mall / destroyed / was / by / a fire

Vocabulary notebook p. 126

120

2 **Grammar** Simple past passive + *by* + agent ◀)) 4.24

Extra practice p. 151

When the "doer" of the action – the agent – is important, you can use *by* to introduce it.	**Adverbs with the passive**
Three families were rescued **by** emergency workers. The fires were caused **by** careless campers. A shopping mall was damaged **by** a tornado.	A mall was **badly** damaged. No one was **seriously** injured. The forest was **completely** destroyed. Power was **temporarily** disrupted. Homes were **partially** destroyed.

A Rewrite the extracts from news stories. Use the simple past passive with *by* + agent. Add the adverb where given in parentheses.

1. A fire destroyed an old warehouse. (partially)

   _____

2. A minor earthquake disrupted power supplies. (temporarily)

   _____

3. A hurricane damaged a high school. (badly)

   _____

4. A tornado destroyed a police station. (completely)

   _____

5. Lightning injured two golfers. (seriously)

   _____

6. Catastrophic wildfires destroyed three homes. (totally)

   _____

7. Emergency workers rescued two injured hikers in a state park. (finally)

   _____

8. High winds blew down a 500-year-old tree yesterday.

   _____

B **Pair work** Choose one of the news extracts above. Add details to make it into a short news report. Then read your report to the class. Which story is the most interesting?

3 **Listening and speaking** News update

A ◀)) 4.25 Listen to two news stories. Answer the questions.

1. What kinds of weather does the reporter talk about? _____
2. What problems did the weather cause? _____
3. Who were the people rescued by? _____
4. Why was the wedding canceled? _____
5. What happened to the groom? _____
6. What update on the story does the reporter give? _____

B **Pair work** Create your own news story. Role-play a TV news anchor and a reporter. Practice your story, and then act it out for the class.

(((**Sounds right** p. 139

1 Conversation strategy Telling news

A What kinds of car-related crime is there in your city? Are cars broken into or stolen? How often do you hear car alarms?

B ◀)) 4.26 Listen. What happened in Joey and Paula's neighborhood last night?

Joey	Did you hear about all the trouble here last night?
Paula	No, but I heard some police sirens.
Joey	Well, you know that older guy on the first floor of my building?
Paula	Yeah. . . .
Joey	Guess what? His car was stolen.
Paula	That's terrible.
Joey	And you know what? He heard his car alarm and called the police, but they came way too late.
Paula	I'm not surprised. The thing is, they just don't have enough police on duty at night.
Joey	Exactly.
Paula	Oh, and did I tell you? My car was broken into last Thursday night.
Joey	No. Really? Was anything stolen?
Paula	No. The only thing was, they damaged the ignition trying to start the car . . . but the funny thing was, they couldn't start it because the battery was dead!

C **Notice** how Joey and Paula introduce news with expressions like these. Find examples in the conversation.

Did you hear (about) . . . ?	*Guess what?*
Have you heard (about) . . . ?	*You know what?*
Did I tell you?	*You know . . . ?*

D ◀)) 4.27 Listen. Write the expressions you hear. Then practice with a partner.

1. *You know what* ? I got caught in a storm last night. My new shoes are completely ruined.
2. _____ ? The traffic is getting bad around here. We were stuck in traffic for an hour last night.
3. _____ ? They're going to open a new organic food store near here.
4. _____ ? My cousin is coming to stay with us this summer. I'm really excited about it.
5. _____ the guy I used to sit next to in class? The one with dark hair? He bought a new car.
6. _____ ? I'm getting married next spring!
7. _____ that high school principal? He crashed his car into the front of the school.
8. _____ the plans for a new skate park in the city? It's opening next spring.

About you **E** **Pair work** Are any of the stories above similar to stories you know? Take turns telling a partner. Can you continue the conversations?

2 Strategy plus *The . . . thing is / was*

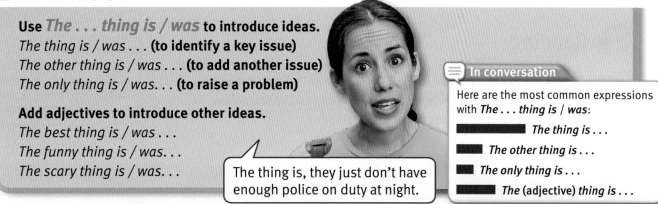

Use ***The . . . thing is / was*** **to introduce ideas.**
The thing is / was . . . **(to identify a key issue)**
The other thing is / was . . . **(to add another issue)**
The only thing is / was. . . **(to raise a problem)**

Add adjectives to introduce other ideas.
The best thing is / was . . .
The funny thing is / was. . .
The scary thing is / was. . .

> The thing is, they just don't have enough police on duty at night.

💬 **In conversation**

Here are the most common expressions with ***The . . . thing is / was***:

▬▬▬▬ *The thing is . . .*
▬▬▬ *The other thing is . . .*
▬▬ *The only thing is . . .*
▬▬▬▬ *The (adjective) thing is . . .*

A Circle the most appropriate expressions to complete the sentences. Then compare with a partner.

1. I loved everything about my vacation, but **the best thing was / the thing is** the food.

2. I like my college but **the other thing was / the only thing is**, it's too far away from everything.

3. My car was broken into once. **The funny thing was / The worst thing was**, they didn't take anything.

4. I was in an earthquake one time. **The worst thing was / The nice thing was**, I was on the twentieth floor of a building. I guess **the other thing was / the good thing was**, I wasn't alone.

5. My friends want me to go skiing with them this winter. **The only thing is / The exciting thing is**, I can't ski.

6. I get along with my brother. **The only thing is / The scary thing is**, he gossips too much. And I guess **the great thing is / the other thing is**, he's always borrowing my stuff without asking.

About you **B** **Pair work** Change the sentences above to make them true for you.

"I loved everything about my trip to Boston. The only thing was, it was very cold."

3 Listening and strategies What do they say next?

A 🔊 4.28 Listen to four people tell some news. How do you think they started their stories? Number the sentences 1 to 4. There is one extra.

☐ You know what? There's a big hurricane coming.
☐ Did you hear the news about my sister?
☐ Have you heard about the picnic by the river next week?

☐ Guess what? The strangest thing happened last night.
☐ Did I tell you? My purse was stolen.

B 🔊 4.28 Listen again. What comments do the speakers make? Complete the sentences.

1. The thing was, I wasn't _____ .
2. The weird thing is, _____ .
3. The thing is, _____ .
4. The funny thing was, _____ .

C 🔊 4.29 Now listen to the complete conversations, and check your answers.

Free talk p. 136

1 Reading

A What qualities do you need to be a foreign correspondent for a news organization? Make a list. Then read the interview. How many of your ideas are mentioned?

 Reading tip

After you read, ask yourself questions, for example, *What did I learn? Do I agree? What can I take away from this article?*

LIFE'S WORK:
Christiane Amanpour

An Interview with Christiane Amanpour, by Alison Beard

Christiane Amanpour gained global fame in the 1990s as a war correspondent for CNN. After a short time in the studio, she returned to foreign news reporting because "there simply aren't enough people doing it."

How did you get started in journalism?

My first job was at a local television station in Providence [Rhode Island]. They took a leap of faith with me, I think because they saw a young woman who was very serious about her career path and knew exactly what she wanted to do with her life. I was committed to journalism; I wanted to be a foreign correspondent. Today I think that's quite unusual. So I think it was the ambition I showed, the sense of mission, the desire to improve myself, and also the willingness to do anything, go anywhere.

You've said covering the war in Bosnia for CNN was a turning point in your career. Why?

That's where I really started my professional journey. I was questioned early on about my objectivity. And I was very upset about it because objectivity is our golden rule, and I take it very seriously. But I was forced to examine what objectivity actually means, and I realized it means giving all sides a fair hearing.

Has being a woman been an advantage or a disadvantage for you?

It's been nothing but an advantage. It's allowed me to get my foot into places where men have not been able to.

Your father is Persian, your mother is British, and you grew up in Iran and the UK. How did that cross-cultural experience help you in your career?

It simply made me aware, from the moment I was born, of different cultures. I've lived in a completely multicultural, multiethnic, multireligious environment, in some of the most difficult places in the world. I've seen firsthand that you can bridge differences; you can have tolerance between groups. The trick is to minimize the extremes and to stick to the sensible center.

Would you ever want to take on more of a leadership role in a news organization?

I don't know. I hope I'm fulfilling my responsibility to lead when it's necessary and to follow when it's necessary, and to encourage young people who come to me.

What advice do you give them?

Have a dream. Have a passion. Know that there's no such thing as overnight success, that success comes only with enormous hard work. And know that the only way to be good at something is to love what you do.

Source: *Harvard Business Review Magazine*

B Find these expressions in the interview. What do you think they mean? Compare with a partner.

1. take a leap of faith
2. objectivity is our golden rule
3. give all sides a fair hearing
4. see firsthand
5. bridge differences
6. overnight success

C Read the interview again. Are these sentences about Christiane Amanpour true or false? Check *T* or *F*. Correct the false sentences.

	T	F
1. She was unsure about what job she wanted to do.	☐	☐
2. She started her career in Bosnia.	☐	☐
3. She wants people to believe she is objective.	☐	☐
4. She believes that being a woman makes her job more difficult.	☐	☐
5. Her family background has helped her understand different cultures.	☐	☐
6. She believes you have to love your work to be successful.	☐	☐

2 Speaking and writing Are you up on the news?

A **Class activity** Survey your classmates, and find out their news habits. Keep a record of their answers, and then tally (卌) the results.

News Survey

1 How often do you keep up with the news?

every day   once or twice a week   less than once a week   never

2 Where do you usually get the news?

TV   newspapers   Internet
radio   magazines   smartphone   other _____

3 What news are you most interested in?

local / regional   national   international

4 What three topics are you most interested in?

politics / current events   sports   business   science / technology
celebrities   arts / culture   the weather   other _____

B Use the information from your survey to write a report about the class's interest in the news. Use the Help note to make sure you use the correct forms of verbs.

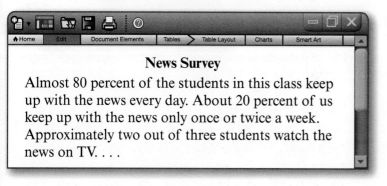

News Survey

Almost 80 percent of the students in this class keep up with the news every day. About 20 percent of us keep up with the news only once or twice a week. Approximately two out of three students watch the news on TV. . . .

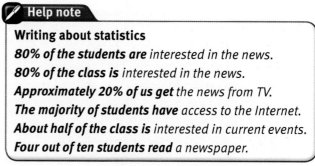

Help note

Writing about statistics
80% of the students are interested in the news.
80% of the class is interested in the news.
Approximately 20% of us get the news from TV.
The majority of students have access to the Internet.
About half of the class is interested in current events.
Four out of ten students read a newspaper.

About you **C** **Pair work** Read a partner's report. Do you agree on your findings? What information from the survey is most surprising? Why?

Vocabulary notebook / Forces of nature

Learning tip *Collocations*

When you learn a new word, use a dictionary to find out what other words are typically used with it. For example, you can say *flash floods,* but not usually *quick floods.* Or you can say *seriously injured,* but not usually *completely injured.*

1 **Look at the adjectives on the left. Circle the word that is typically used with each one.**

1. **freak**   rain   hailstorm   earthquake
2. **heavy**   wildfire   tornado   rain
3. **minor**   earthquake   rain   wind
4. **flash**   tornado   earthquake   flood
5. **catastrophic**   thunder   wildfire   hailstones

2 **Word builder** For each sentence below, cross out the one word that *cannot* be used to complete it.

1. A building was _____ by lightning.
   a. damaged   b. destroyed   c. injured   d. struck   e. hit
2. _____ was disrupted by an ice storm yesterday.
   a. Electrical power b. A shopping mall   c. Traffic   d. Telephone service   e. Train service
3. Two people were _____ injured.
   a. seriously   b. critically   c. severely   d. partially   e. slightly
4. The village was struck by _____ .
   a. an earthquake   b. lightning   c. a hurricane   d. hailstones   e. rain

3 **Word builder** Look at the expressions below. Can you figure out their meanings?

freak accident   heavy traffic   major earthquake   minor injuries

 On your own

Think of three places in different parts of the world. Go online and find out what the weather is like today.

Weather Report: Honolulu 92°F 33°C

Can Do! Now I can . . .

✓ I can . . .   ? I need to review how to . . .

- talk about news events.
- talk about natural disasters.
- use expressions like *Guess what?* to tell news.
- introduce ideas with expressions like *The thing is . . . .*

- understand news stories.
- listen to people telling personal news.
- read an interview with a journalist.
- write a report including statistics.

1 What can you guess about Suki?

A Look at the pictures of Suki's apartment. What has she been doing? What has she finished? Complete each sentence with the present perfect or present perfect continuous.

There are two pots on the stove, so she _'s been cooking_ (cook). She _____ already _____ (bake) some cookies. She _____ (write) a letter, but she _____ (not finish) it yet. There's a whole pizza, so I bet she _____ (not eat) lunch. Her headphones are on the table, so she _____ probably _____ (listen) to music. Her paints and brushes are out, so it looks like she _____ (paint). She _____ already _____ (paint) a vase of flowers.

B Pair work Make more guesses about Suki and the pictures. Use _must_, _may_, _might_, _can't_, or _could_.

"She must like pizza." *"She might be an art teacher."*

2 That must be interesting!

Complete A's statements with _since_, _for_, or _in_, and add an adjective to B's responses. Practice with a partner. Then practice again, making the sentences true for you.

1. A I've been taking dance lessons _____ I was a kid.   B You must be _____ .
2. A I haven't heard from my boyfriend _____ ages.   B You must be _____ .
3. A I've been going out with someone _____ several months now.   B That must be _____ .
4. A I've been working hard _____ May. I haven't had a vacation.   B That must be _____ .

"I've been taking piano lessons since I was five."   *"You must be really good."*

3 Have you seen any good movies lately?

Complete the chart with three movies you've seen. Discuss with a partner.

Name of movie	Type of movie	What was it like?
The Hunger Games	science fiction / drama	The suspense was unbearable.
1.		
2.		
3.		

A *Have you seen any good movies lately?*

B *Yeah. I saw* The Hunger Games. *It was so good!*

A *I read the book, but I haven't seen the movie yet.*

Can you complete this conversation?

Complete the conversation with the words and expressions in the box. Use capital letters where necessary.

all right	✓guess what	I was wondering	the only thing is	yet
already	I see	that must be	the thing is	you know what

Ana *Guess what* ? We have a new boss – Abigail Freeman. And _____ ? Things are going to change around here!

Nat Really? So, have you met her _____ ?

Ana No, but I've _____ heard lots of stories about her. _____ , she's a "clean freak." She hates clutter. So everyone is busy cleaning and putting things away.

Nat _____ . So I guess we're going to have to clean up this mailroom.

Ana Actually, _____ if we could start now because she might come by later.

Nat Yeah. We need to make a good first impression. _____ , every time I clean up, I lose something!

Ana Really? _____ frustrating! So let's be careful when we throw things away!

Nat Good idea. _____ , let's get started!

5 I was wondering . . .

Pair work Think of two more favors to add to the list below. Then think of a way to ask politely for each favor. Role-play conversations.

1. Ask a teacher for more time to finish an assignment.
2. Ask a friend to give you a ride to the airport.
3. _____
4. _____

A *Excuse me. I was wondering if I could have more time to finish my assignment.*

B *Well, can you tell me why you need more time?*

6 Here's the news.

A Complete the news report. Use the simple past passive.

Four cars _____ (involve) in an accident on the highway this morning. The accident _____ (cause) by a truck that spilled hundreds of tomatoes onto the road. Fortunately, the drivers _____ seriously _____ (not injure). Two people _____ (take) to the hospital with minor injuries. The truck driver _____ (interview) by police. The highway _____ (open) again two hours later.

B **Pair work** Brainstorm words and expressions describing extreme weather and natural disasters. Then write five sentences to create a news report. Read your report to the class.

> severe thunderstorm   heavy rains

128

UNIT 1 What are we like?

1 Class activity What new things can you find out about your classmates?
Ask questions and take notes.

Find someone who . . .	Name	Notes
eats extremely slowly.	Kenji	Friends say, "Hurry up."
reads very fast.		
gets impatient easily.		
is incredibly organized.		
can do math in his or her head quickly.		
thinks it's important to dress properly.		
automatically turns on the TV when he or she gets home.		
plays several sports really well.		
remembers dates and numbers very easily.		
likes to do things absolutely perfectly.		

"So do you eat extremely slowly?"   *"Yes, I do. My friends are always saying 'Hurry up.'"*

2 Class work Tell the class something new and interesting that you learned about two classmates.

UNIT 2 I've never done that!

1 Are there things you've *never* done that you think people in your group *have* done? Complete the chart with things that you have *never* done. Try to think of surprising things.

Think of . . .	I've never . . .	Points
a sport you've never done.	I've never been snowboarding.	2
a tourist attraction in your town or city you've never visited.		
something you've never understood.		
a food you've never eaten.		
a well-known movie you've never seen.		
a TV show you've never watched.		
something you've never drunk.		
something else you've never done.		
	Total points	

2 Group game Now ask your classmates questions. Score a point for every person who *has* done the thing you haven't done. The person with the most points wins.

A I've never been snowboarding. Have you?

B Yeah. I've been snowboarding a lot. I love it.

C Me too!

A OK. So, that gives me two points

^{UNIT} **3** **Where's the best place to . . . ?**

1 **Pair work** What advice would you give to someone visiting your country for the first time? Discuss the categories below, and agree on one idea for each category.

MY COUNTRY **ADVICE FOR FIRST-TIME VISITORS**

The most famous attraction

The most beautiful natural feature

The cheapest way to travel around the country

The most comfortable place to stay

The best souvenir

The nicest shopping area

The most unusual food to try

The worst thing to do

The city with the most things to see

The most interesting thing to do in the evening

The least interesting place to visit

A *Well, everyone should go see Tokyo Sky Tree. It's probably the most famous attraction. It's definitely popular.*

B *It sure is. But what about Osaka Castle?*

2 **Group work** Join another pair. Compare your ideas. Did you have any of the same ideas?

UNIT 4 Family histories

1 Prepare a short history of your family. Use these ideas to help you.

> **Think about . . .**
> - where your grandparents are from.
> - interesting facts about your aunts and uncles.
> - how your parents met.
> - where your parents used to live when they were younger.
> - how your family life has changed.
> - any special memories you have.

_____
_____
_____
_____

2 **Group work** Present your family history to the group. Listen to your classmates' histories. Take notes, and ask them questions for more information.

"My father's parents are from Guadalajara. They moved to Mexico City in 1965. My father grew up there. . . . My mother's parents . . . "

UNIT 5 Whichever is easier

1 **Group work** Imagine you and your classmates are going to have a "potluck" dinner tonight. Everyone must bring food – but only what you already have at home. Decide on the following:

1. Are you going to go to someone's home? Whose?
2. What time do you want to arrive?
3. Do you have enough plates?
4. Do you need to bring silverware (knives, forks, spoons, etc.)? Do you have enough?
5. What drinks are you going to have?
6. What dishes do you want to cook?
7. What food does each person need to bring?
8. Is someone going to bring music?
9. Are you going to play any games?

> A *Well, there are five of us. The table in my apartment isn't big enough, but we could sit on the floor.*
> B *Why don't we eat at the park?*
> A *Either way for me. How about you, Melly?*

2 **Class activity** Tell the class about your potluck dinner. Decide which dinner you would like to go to. Which is the most popular?

Free talk

UNIT 6 Who's going to do what?

1 Group work Imagine you are going to hold a community event in your school or neighborhood. The event should have a theme, food, and entertainment.

Discuss the following:

1. When is the event going to be? Where? What time?
2. What theme will the event have? (for example, a holiday theme, a "green" theme?)
3. What kinds of attractions or entertainment will you have at the event?
4. How much will it cost to run the event?
5. What are you going to do to get ready for the event? Who's going to do what?

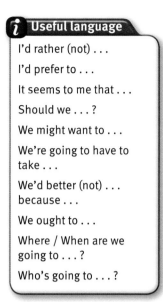

i **Useful language**

I'd rather (not) . . .

I'd prefer to . . .

It seems to me that . . .

Should we . . . ?

We might want to . . .

We're going to have to take . . .

We'd better (not) . . . because . . .

We ought to . . .

Where / When are we going to . . . ?

Who's going to . . . ?

A Well, we ought to hold the event right away because the weather's good.

B I agree, though we might want to wait a month – there's a lot to prepare.

2 Class activity Take turns telling the class about your event. After you have heard about all the events, vote on the one that you'd like to go to. Which event do most people want to go to?

UNIT 7 Your ideal partner

1 Group work What do you think people look for in an ideal life partner? Discuss the ideas below and add your own. Which of these things matter most to you?

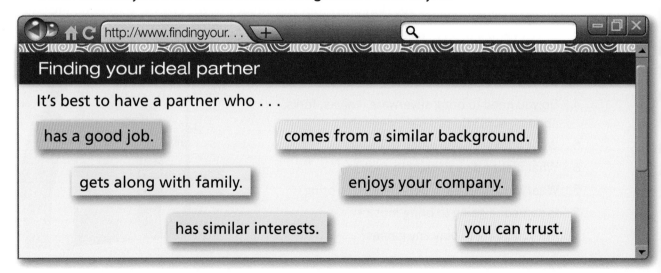

Finding your ideal partner

It's best to have a partner who . . .

has a good job.

comes from a similar background.

gets along with family.

enjoys your company.

has similar interests.

you can trust.

A I guess it's good to choose someone who has a good job.

B Well, you probably don't want a partner who's only interested in work, though.

2 Group work What ten questions should people always ask their partner before they decide to get married? Discuss your ideas and give reasons. Decide on the ten most important questions.

"You should ask, 'How many times have you broken up with someone?'"

UNIT **8** **What would you do?**

Group work Discuss the questions. How are you alike? How are you different?

1. If you had an hour to spare right now, what would you do?

2. If you had one month of free time, what would you do?

3. If you had to choose one thing to keep throughout your life, what would it be?

4. If you had to choose one electronic gadget to live without, what would it be?

5. If you could invite a famous person to a party, who would you invite?

6. If you could be like one person, who would you want to be like?

7. If you could have any job, what kind of work would you do?

8. If you could have one special talent, what would it be?

9. If you had to give up one habit, what would it be?

10. If you could do one thing over, what would you do?

A *If you had an hour to spare right now, what would you do?*
B *I'd play computer games!*
C *Really? I wouldn't. I'd go and hang out with my friends.*

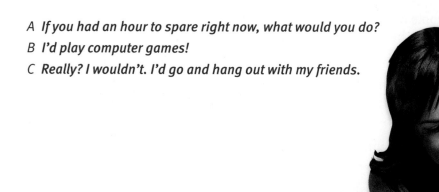

133

Technology etiquette

Pair work Read the opposite opinions in the chart below. Debate each pair of arguments.
Do you agree?

1.

| It's perfectly fine to have a long conversation on your phone when you're out with a friend. | **OR** | You should turn your phone to vibrate when you're out with friends and only take urgent calls. |

2.

| It's OK to play loud music on a beach or in a public place. | **OR** | You should always listen to your music with your headphones on. |

3.

| You don't need to return voice-mail or text messages right away. | **OR** | It's important to return a message immediately. |

4.

| Microblogging is fun. It's a great way to keep up with what's going on with your friends. | **OR** | Microblogging is a complete waste of time. Who wants to know all those silly details about people's lives? |

5.

| It's OK to "unfriend" people on your social networking site and not tell them. | **OR** | You shouldn't unfriend people – it can hurt their feelings. |

6.

| It's OK to post photos of your friends online. | **OR** | You shouldn't do that. You should always ask permission first. |

A *Well, I don't see why you should turn your phone off or put it onto vibrate when you're out with friends. I don't really see what the problem is with taking calls. You know?*

B *I know what you mean. But it can be annoying when you're trying to have a conversation with someone and their phone keeps ringing.*

10 Who's been doing what?

Class activity Find classmates who answer yes to the questions. Write their names in the chart.
Write notes about each person. Tell the class two interesting things you learned.

Find someone who's been . . .	Name	Notes
planning something special.	_Ana_	_has been planning a birthday party_
helping a friend with something.		
working or studying too much lately.		
taking a fun class or learning something new.		
going to the movies a lot.		
hanging out with their friends a lot.		
watching a series on TV.		
thinking about taking a trip.		
trying to give up a bad habit.		
eating out a lot.		

A *Ana, have you been planning anything special?*

B *Actually, yeah, I have. I've been planning a birthday party for my sister.*
   OR *No, I haven't. I haven't planned anything special for ages.*

11 That must be fun!

1 Write true sentences for each conversation below. Make sure your sentences make sense with the
   responses given.

1. **You** _____ B That must be fun.	2. **You** _____ B You must be excited.	3. **You** _____ B That must be interesting.
4. **You** _____ B That must be annoying.	5. **You** _____ B You must be nervous.	6. **You** _____ B That must be scary.

2 **Pair work** Take turns sharing your sentences. Continue conversations with your classmates.
   Ask questions and speculate about the things they say.

   A *I just started working at a museum. I'm helping them set up some displays.*

   B *Wow, that must be fun. You must like your job.*

Free talk

1 **Pair work** Make up a short TV news report about each picture. Think of three facts for each story.

2 **Group work** Join another pair. Take turns telling your news stories.

Sounds right

UNIT 1

🔊 **4.30 Listen and repeat the words. Is the stress in each word like the stress in *fairly*, *admire*, *arrogant*, or *correctly*? Write the words from the list in the correct columns below.**

1. complain	4. generous	7. reckless	10. politely
2. dishonest	5. helpful	8. wonderful	11. relaxed
3. forget	6. impatient	9. borrow	12. patiently

● · **fairly**	· ● **admire**	● · · **arrogant**	· ● · **correctly**
	complain		

UNIT 2

🔊 **4.31 Listen and repeat the words. Notice the different ways the letter *o* is pronounced. Match the words with the same underlined sounds.**

1. d<u>o</u> ____   a. forg<u>o</u>t
2. d<u>o</u>ne ____   b. l<u>o</u>se
3. g<u>o</u> ____   c. sp<u>o</u>ken
4. g<u>o</u>tten ____   d. w<u>o</u>n

UNIT 3

🔊 **4.32 Listen and repeat the words. Notice the underlined sounds. Which sound in each group is different? Circle the odd one out.**

1. h<u>igh</u>   <u>i</u>sland   r<u>i</u>ver   w<u>i</u>de
2. c<u>o</u>ntinent   m<u>o</u>st   <u>o</u>cean   volcan<u>o</u>
3. airp<u>o</u>rt   sp<u>o</u>rts   st<u>o</u>re   w<u>o</u>rst
4. ab<u>ou</u>t   c<u>ou</u>ntry   m<u>ou</u>ntain   s<u>ou</u>th
5. b<u>ea</u>ch   d<u>ee</u>p   m<u>e</u>ter   <u>o</u>c<u>ea</u>n

UNIT 4

🔊 **4.33 Listen and repeat the words. Notice the underlined sounds. Are the sounds like the sounds in *clean*, *great*, *law*, *uncle*, or *wife*? Write the words from the list in the correct columns below. There is one extra word.**

1. c<u>ou</u>sin   2. d<u>au</u>ghter   3. f<u>igh</u>t   4. n<u>ie</u>ce   5. n<u>e</u>phew   6. st<u>ay</u>

clean	great	law	uncle	wife
			cousin	

137

Sounds right

UNIT 5

🔊 **4.34** Listen and repeat the pairs of words. Notice the underlined sounds. Are the sounds the same (S) or different (D)? Write *S* or *D*.

1. th<u>ir</u>sty / dess<u>er</u>t _<u>S</u>_
2. r<u>aw</u> / s<u>au</u>ce _____
3. br<u>o</u>ccoli / b<u>oi</u>led _____
4. fr<u>ie</u>s / p<u>ie</u> _____
5. sh<u>ou</u>ld / p<u>ou</u>nd _____
6. t<u>oo</u> / s<u>ou</u>p _____
7. g<u>oo</u>d / f<u>oo</u>d _____
8. m<u>u</u>ch / l<u>o</u>ve _____
9. f<u>u</u>ll / h<u>u</u>ngry _____

UNIT 6

🔊 **4.35** Listen and repeat the words. Notice the underlined sounds. Are the sounds like the sounds in *home*, *good*, *math*, *worse*, or *ought*? Write the words from the list in the correct columns below.

1. b<u>ou</u>ght
2. b<u>u</u>lly
3. t<u>o</u>tal
4. fab<u>u</u>lous
5. g<u>ir</u>lfriend
6. r<u>a</u>ther
7. rese<u>ar</u>ch
8. sh<u>ou</u>ld
9. th<u>ou</u>ght
10. c<u>oa</u>ch

h<u>o</u>me	g<u>oo</u>d	m<u>a</u>th	w<u>or</u>se	<u>ough</u>t
				bought

UNIT 7

🔊 **4.36** Listen and repeat the words. Notice the underlined sounds. Which sound in each group is different? Circle the odd one out.

1. <u>h</u>ot | <u>h</u>ung | <u>wh</u>ich | <u>wh</u>o
2. ano<u>th</u>er | <u>th</u>at | <u>th</u>ere | <u>th</u>rough
3. <u>o</u>ne | w<u>e</u>nt | w<u>o</u>rk | wr<u>o</u>te
4. alo<u>ng</u> | goi<u>ng</u> | si<u>gn</u> | weddi<u>ng</u>
5. play<u>s</u> | sit<u>s</u> | there'<u>s</u> | turn<u>s</u>
6. a<u>c</u>ross | <u>c</u>ircle | <u>c</u>ollege | ro<u>ck</u>

UNIT 8

🔊 **4.37** Listen and repeat the pairs of words. Notice the underlined sounds. Are the sounds the same (S) or different (D)? Write *S* or *D*.

1. pla<u>ce</u> / ex<u>c</u>iting _<u>S</u>_
2. b<u>o</u>rrow / w<u>o</u>rk _____
3. en<u>g</u>ineering / for<u>g</u>et _____
4. <u>E</u>gypt / apolo<u>g</u>ize _____
5. c<u>ou</u>ld / w<u>ou</u>ld _____
6. sh<u>are</u> / anyw<u>here</u> _____
7. enou<u>gh</u> / a<u>ff</u>ord _____
8. bu<u>s</u>y / choo<u>se</u> _____
9. i<u>f</u> / o<u>f</u> _____

UNIT 9

🔊 **4.38** Listen and repeat the words. Notice that one or more syllables in each word are unstressed. They have a weak vowel sound like the /ə/ sound in _around_ or the /ər/ sound in _battery_. Circle the unstressed syllables.

1. (a)round   3. computer   5. remember   7. problem   9. support

2. batt(er)y   4. idea   6. controller   8. tablet   10. virus

UNIT 10

🔊 **4.39** Listen and repeat the words. Notice the underlined sounds. Are the sounds like the sounds in _again_, _bought_, _eat_, _made_, _there_, or _true_? Write the words from the list in the correct columns below.

1. alien   5. hilarious   9. scene

2. cartoon   6. place   10. seen

3. costume   7. saw   11. serious

4. fall   8. scary   12. suspense

again	**bought**	**eat**	**made**	**there**	**true**
			alien		

UNIT 11

🔊 **4.40** Listen and repeat the adjectives. Do the -ed endings sound like /t/, /d/, or /ɪd/? Write t, d, or ɪd.

1. annoyed _d_   5. excited _id_   9. scared _d_

2. bored _d_   6. fascinated _id_   10. shocked _t_

3. disappointed _id_   7. interested _id_   11. surprised _~~d~~ t_

4. embarrassed _t_   8. pleased _d_   12. worried _d_

UNIT 12

🔊 **4.41** Listen and repeat the words. Match the words with the same underlined sounds.

1. bus _c_   a. amazingly

2. closed ____   b. catastrophic

3. flash ____   c. city

4. fortunately ____   d. damage

5. injure ____   e. much

6. shock ____   f. partially

Lesson A Adjectives vs. manner adverbs

A Choose the correct words to complete the sentences.

1. I know this sounds **bad** / **badly**, but I love to drive really **quick** / **fast.** I think I drive really **good** / **well**, though. I don't get **reckless** / **recklessly** when I get behind the wheel or anything.

2. I try **hard** / **hardly** to be neat and tidy. Like, I always put my keys on the shelf **automatic** / **automatically** when I get home. You can lose your keys so **easy** / **easily**.

3. I think it's **important** / **importantly** to take work **serious** / **seriously.** I mean, it only seems right. If you do a job **good** / **well** you feel **good** / **well** about yourself, too.

4. I guess I can get **impatient** / **impatiently** sometimes. Like, I want **instant** / **instantly** replies to my texts and emails. I just don't like to wait when I need an answer **quick** / **quickly.**

5. I love sports, but I don't really play for fun. I feel pretty **strong** / **strongly** that you should play to win. I feel **terrible** / **terribly** if I lose. My friends see things **different** / **differently** and say that I'm too **serious** / **seriously** about sports and that I should relax.

6. I hate it when people don't write texts **proper** / **properly** and don't use **correct** / **correctly** grammar and punctuation. It's not because they're writing **quick** / **quickly** – they just don't care about it. I always check over my texts very **careful** / **carefully** before I send them.

About you **B Pair work** Are any of the sentences above true for you or someone you know? Tell your partner.

Lesson B Adverbs before adjectives and adverbs

A Complete the statements about people's personalities with words from the box.

absolutely crazy	extremely talented	pretty laid-back
arrogant at all	incredibly generous	really reliable

1. My sister's _extremely talented_. She's just good at everything she does.
2. My brother's _absolutely crazy_. He does that extreme biking thing, jumping upside down on his bike and everything.
3. My parents are _incredibly generous_. They bought me a new car when my old one broke down.
4. My best friend is _really reliable_. I can count on her for absolutely anything.
5. I'm _pretty laid-back_. I don't get stressed very often.
6. My brother isn't _arrogant at all_. He doesn't think he's better than everyone else.

> **✗ Common errors**
>
> Don't use *very* with extreme adjectives like *wonderful*.
>
> She's **absolutely** wonderful. (NOT She's ~~very~~ wonderful.)

About you **B Pair work** Make sentences like the ones above about people you know. Tell your partner.

UNIT
2 **Lesson A** Present perfect statements

A Use the underlined words to write sentences about travel experiences. Use the present perfect.

1. I / always / do a lot of traveling. I guess it / always / be my main interest in life.
   I've always done a lot of traveling. I guess it's always been my main interest in life.

2. I travel with an old school friend and she / be to lots of places.
   _____

3. She and I / travel around Asia three or four times. We / always / enjoy traveling together.
   _____

4. We / walk on the Great Wall of China twice. It's so amazing.
   _____

5. We / be so lucky. We / visit some amazing places and I / try all kinds of food.
   _____

6. We're always talking about places we would like to go. We / think about going to Australia or India.
   _____

7. My friend / not be to India because she / not have the chance, and I / never be to Australia.
   _____

8. We / not make a decision about where to go next, but I'd really like to go to Sydney.
   _____

About you **B** **Pair work** Tell a partner five true things about travel. Use the sentences above to help you.

UNIT
2 **Lesson B** Present perfect vs. simple past

A Complete the conversations about unusual experiences. Use the present perfect or simple past.

1. A *Have you ever done* (you / ever / do) anything scary?
   B Yes, I _____ . I _____ (play) the piano in a big concert last year.
   A Really? _____ (you / play) a solo?
   B No, I _____ . Thank goodness! There _____ (be) an orchestra, too.

2. A _____ (you / ever / see) the Northern Lights?
   B No, I _____ , but I _____ (always / want) to see them. We _____ (go) to Alaska last year, but we _____ (not / see) them.

3. A _____ (you / ever / try) kickboxing?
   B Yes, I _____ . I _____ (take) a class last semester. But I _____ (not / like) it.

4. A _____ (you / ever / cook) a meal for a big group of people?
   B Yes, I _____ . It _____ (be) my sister's birthday last weekend.
   She _____ (invite) 25 of her friends, and we _____ (make) Moroccan food.
   A Really? I _____ (never / eat) Moroccan food before. _____ (it / be) good?
   B Oh, yeah. Everybody _____ (love) it!

About you **B** **Pair work** Ask and answer the questions above. Give your own answers.

UNIT
3 **Lesson A** Superlatives

A Complete the facts and tips about different places in the world. Use the superlative forms of the adjectives or *the most / the least* with the nouns.

1. _____ (big) national park in the world is in Greenland.
2. _____ (fast) roller coaster in Europe is in Spain.
3. Canada has _____ (long) coastline in the world. It's great for sightseeing.
4. _____ (expensive) hotel in the world is in Dubai. The rooms cost over $10,000 a night.
5. _____ (good) time to visit Thailand is from November to February. These are the months with _____ (good) weather because there is _____ (rain).
6. Summer is _____ (bad) time to visit Venice because that's when there are _____ (tourists).
7. The city that has _____ (people) in the United States is New York City.
8. The city with _____ (large) population in the world is Shanghai.
9. _____ (deep) lake in the world is Lake Baikal in Siberia.
10. _____ (small) country in the world is Vatican City in Rome. It's also _____ populated country with only 500 inhabitants.

About you **B** **Pair work** Can you think of similar facts and tips for visitors to your country?

UNIT
3 **Lesson B** Questions with *How* + adjective . . . ?

A Complete the questions and answers about Spain. Use the words from the box. If you don't need a word to complete the answers, write a dash (–). Some words are used more than once.

big deep high hot long

1. Q: How _____ is Mount Teide in Tenerife, Spain?
   A: It's 4,964 meters (16,286 feet) _____ .
2. Q: How _____ is the coastline?
   A: It's 7,517 kilometers (4,671 miles) _____ .
3. Q: How _____ is the population of Spain?
   A: It's almost 47 million people _____ .
4. Q: What is the largest natural lake in Spain? How _____ is it?
   A: Lake Sanabria is 51 meters (167 feet) _____ .
5. Q: How _____ is it in southern Spain in August?
   A: It is usually around 35°C (90°F) _____ .

About you **B** **Pair work** What do you know about *your* country? Take turns asking questions similar to the ones above. Do you know the answers?

A OK. So how high is Mount Aconcagua?
B Well, I'm guessing, but I think it's almost 7,000 meters (23,000 feet) high.

Lesson A Verbs *let, make, help, have, get, want, ask, tell*

A Complete the sentences. Use the correct forms of the verbs given.
Sometimes there is more than one correct answer.

1. I want my children _____ (make) good decisions for themselves.

2. I don't let my kids _____ (play) computer games before bedtime.
   It makes them _____ (sleep) badly.

3. I usually make my teenagers _____ (clean up) the kitchen after meals.

4. I want to get my kids _____ (eat) well. They're always eating junk food.

5. I usually tell my kids _____ (do) their homework before dinner, but I don't help
   them _____ (do) it.

6. I'm always asking them _____ (turn off) the lights in the house.

7. I have them _____ (shut down) their computers at night.

8. I'm always telling my kids _____ (be) careful when they go out.

9. I always have my kids _____ (write) thank-you letters when they get a gift.

10. We often help our sons _____ (study) for exams. We make up games for them.

About you **B** **Pair work** Read the sentences above again. Did your parents say similar
things about you when you were growing up? Discuss with a partner.

"My parents wanted me to do well in school. They made me study every night."

Lesson B *used to* and *would*

A Read this person's memories about her summer vacations. Rewrite eight sentences using *used to*
or *would*. Sometimes both are correct.

When I was younger, we had long school vacations in the summer – about 10 weeks. I saw a lot of
my extended family in those days. They lived about 30 miles away. My cousins came to stay
every summer. We didn't have a big house like we do now, so we always camped in the backyard.
There was a stream near our house, and we swam in it. One of my little cousins didn't like
swimming. She was really scared of water, and my brother always teased her about it. He made her
go into the water. He wasn't very nice to her. Thank goodness he's not like that now!

_____

_____

_____

_____

_____

_____

About you **B** **Pair work** Ask and answer questions about your elementary school summer breaks, using
Did you use to . . . ?

A *Did you use to spend your summers with your family?*
B *Not really. I used to play with the kids in the neighborhood. We'd go off and . . .*

143

Extra practice

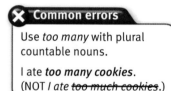

UNIT 5 Lesson A Talking about quantities of food

A Complete the sentences about shopping and eating habits. Use the words in the box.

a few	cartons	few	fewer	less	less	little	loaves	many

1. I don't eat _____ fruits or vegetables. I really should eat more healthy food.
2. We have a small freezer so we buy very _____ frozen meals.
3. I prefer to go shopping at the local store. I'm trying to buy _____ food from the big supermarkets than I used to.
4. My family buys about six _____ of bread a week and eight _____ of fruit juice.
5. I don't fry food anymore. It means I eat _____ calories and _____ fat. But I have to say, I like a _____ butter on my potatoes.
6. When I go out to eat, I like to try _____ different things that I don't normally eat.

About you **B** **Pair work** Are any of the sentences above true for you? What other shopping and eating habits do you have?

UNIT 5 Lesson B *too, too much, too many,* and *enough*

> **✗ Common errors**
>
> Use *too many* with plural countable nouns.
>
> I ate *too many cookies*.
> (NOT I ate ~~too much cookies~~.)

A Complete the online forum conversation with *too, too many, too much,* and *enough*.

A few months ago, I completely changed my eating habits. I used to eat ___*too much*___ sugar, _____ processed fat, and _____ take-out meals. I also didn't eat my meals slowly _____ because I was always rushing out somewhere. My mother was always saying 'You eat _____ quickly.' or 'You're not eating _____ protein,' and as for fast food, I know I definitely ate _____ . I really thought my mom complained _____ , but actually I guess I didn't pay _____ attention to her. I got sick! The doctor said my diet wasn't healthy _____ and said I needed to change it. He also told me that I needed more vitamins and that I wasn't getting _____ . No surprise there! So I changed my diet. In the end, it was simple _____ to do. Now I'm eating a lot of raw vegetables – I guess you can't eat _____ of those! I feel great. And guess what? My mom can't say I don't eat well _____ . Not now!

COMMENTS:

> Good for you! You should never be _____ busy to look after your health! _____ junk food and _____ sweets are not good for you.

About you **B** Write your own comment to add to the forum. Then compare with a partner.

> *"I eat very little healthy food, too. I guess I should eat less fast food."*

UNIT 6 Lesson A Talking about the future

A A man is telling a friend about his plans for the evening. Circle the correct phrases to complete the sentences. Sometimes both are correct.

Well, tonight **I'm going to stop** / **I stop** by the store on my way home. I need to get some stuff for dinner. I think **I'll buy** / **I'm buying** some pasta, and **I'll make** / **I make** some garlic bread. That sounds good. So, yeah, **we eat** / **we're eating** late tonight because **I have** / **I'll have** a gym class at 6:00. I think **I'll go** / **I'm going to go** home straight after class, because **my roommate's having** / **my roommate has** dinner with me tonight. I guess **he's not getting** / **he won't get** home until 7:30, so maybe **we'll eat** / **we're eating** at about 8:00. I think **we're going to go** / **we go** out later. There's a movie I want to see. It **starts** / **will start** at 10:00.

About you B **Pair work** What plans do you have for tonight? Tell your partner.

> **⊗ Common errors**
>
> Use *have to*, not *'d better*, for general advice. Use *'d better* for a particular situation.
>
> *You have to get* a visa to travel to some countries. (NOT ~~You'd better get~~ a visa to travel to some countries.)

UNIT 6 Lesson B What's *advisable, necessary, preferable*

A Rewrite these sentences about making changes in life. Use the words given.

1. I'd prefer not to move out of my apartment. ('d rather not)
   I'd rather not move out of my apartment.

2. I should really learn to drive. (be going to have to)
   _____

3. I should save some money to buy a car. (ought to)
   _____

4. I think you should talk to your boss about a promotion. (might want to)
   _____

5. My brother should get a job soon, or he won't be able to pay his rent. (had better)
   _____

6. My classmates shouldn't go out tonight, or they won't pass the exam tomorrow. (had better not)
   _____

7. My sister wants to go to Europe. She should learn some English before she goes. ('d better)
   _____

8. My friend has to choose her major soon, but she says she prefers not to think about it. ('d rather not)
   _____

9. My parents are going to have to retire soon, but they say they prefer to work. (would rather)
   _____

10. I should get more exercise – I spend too much time at my desk. (ought to)
    _____

About you B **Pair work** Make the sentences you wrote true for you. Then compare.

"I'd rather not stay in my apartment. It's too small!"

Extra practice

UNIT 7 Lesson A Relative clauses

A Complete the questions about your circle of friends. Use *who*, *that*, or a preposition, or write a dash (–) if no word is needed. Sometimes more than one answer is possible.

Who's . . .

1. a friend ___*that*___ you often go out ___*with*___ ?
2. the person in your family _____ you most often talk _____ ?
3. the classmate _____ is always interrupting other people _____ ?
4. the friend _____ you like to spend time _____ ?
5. a friend _____ you went to elementary school _____ ?
6. the co-worker _____ has the most impeccable taste in clothes _____ ?
7. the friend _____ has the best sense of humor _____ ?
8. someone _____ always makes a good impression on people?
9. a friend with a car _____ you'd like to own _____ ?
10. the friend _____ you can always rely _____ when you have problems?
11. a person _____ you sometimes have arguments _____ ?
12. the co-worker _____ you're always apologizing _____ ?

> **Note**
>
> Some relative clauses end with a **preposition**.
>
> *Yuya is a guy that Jen introduced me to.* (= Jen introduced me **to Yuya**.)
>
> *Mike is the guy I run with.* (= I run **with Mike**.)
>
> *Charlie is someone I grew up with.* (= I grew up **with Charlie**.)

> **Common errors**
>
> Don't leave out *who*, *that*, or *which* in a subject relative clause.
>
> *She works for a company that / which makes computers.* (NOT ~~She works for a company makes computers.~~)

About you **B** Pair work Ask and answer the questions above.

UNIT 7 Lesson B Phrasal verbs

A Complete the questions with the correct particle.

1. Did you have any friends who had to move ___*away*___ when you were young?
2. Did you hang _____ with a big crowd when you were growing _____ ?
3. Have you ever gone _____ to your elementary school to visit?
4. Can you think of someone who you get _____ with but don't see often enough?
5. Have any of your friends ever had a relationship that didn't work _____ ?
6. What's the most recent class you signed _____ for?
7. Why would you come _____ early from a vacation?
8. Can you think of a situation that started _____ badly but turned _____ well?
9. Have any of your friends gotten married and settled _____ ?
10. How long should you go _____ with someone before you introduce him or her to your parents?

About you **B** Pair work Ask and answer the questions above. Give as much information as you can.

"I had one friend who had to move away. Her dad got a job in another city."

146

Lesson A   Wishes and imaginary situations or events

A   Use the information to complete the sentences about people's behavior.

1. I'm so disorganized. I lose things all the time.

   I wish _I were less disorganized_ .

   If I _were less disorganized, I wouldn't lose things all the time_ .

2. My sister never pays attention in school. She doesn't get good grades.

   I wish _____ .

   If she _____ .

3. I can't take a vacation this year. I feel so stressed all the time.

   I wish _____ .

   If I _____ .

4. My parents never let me use their car. They have to drive me everywhere.

   I wish _____ .

   If my parents _____ .

5. My brother never helps clean up the house. I don't have time to do other things.

   I wish _____ .

   If he _____ .

About you   B   Pair work   Do you have similar wishes? Make the wishes true for you. Tell a partner.

Lesson B   Asking about imaginary situations or events

> **✗ Common error**
>
> Use *would* when asking about imaginary situations.
>
> *What **would** you do if you missed an appointment?* (NOT *What ~~will you do~~ if you missed an appointment?*)

A   Make questions about these imaginary situations using the words given.

1. A friend talks about you behind your back. / You say something.

   What would you do if a friend talked about you behind your back (what / you / do)? Would you _say something_ ?

2. You forget an important homework assignment. / You give your teacher an excuse.

   _____ (how / you react)? Would you _____ ?

3. You don't meet a big deadline. / You apologize to your boss.

   _____ (what / you / do)? Would you _____ ?

4. Your parents buy you a present that you don't like. / You tell them the truth.

   _____ (what / you / say)? Would you _____ ?

5. A friend invites you to a party that you don't want to go to. / You say you're busy.

   _____ (how / you / react)? Would you _____ ?

6. You lend some money to a friend, and she forgets about it. / You remind her about it.

   _____ (what / you / do)? Would you _____ ?

About you   B   Pair work   Ask and answer the questions above. Add other reactions and solutions to the problems.

"What would you do if a friend talked about you behind your back? Would you be very upset?"

Lesson A Questions within sentences

A Unscramble the questions, and complete the answers with your own information.

1. you know / has / your computer / do / how much memory
   Q: *Do you know how much memory your computer has*_____ ?
   A: No, actually, I can't remember _____ .

2. how many hours / do / you / online each week / spend / you have any idea
   Q: _____ ?
   A: A lot! I don't know exactly _____ .

3. you know / do / is / a good wireless Internet connection in your classroom / there / if
   Q: _____ ?
   A: Well, I don't know _____ .

4. every week / you know / do / how many text messages / you / send
   Q: _____ ?
   A: Not really. I don't really know _____ .

5. you remember / sent / can / who / you / emails to yesterday
   Q: _____ ?
   A: Yes, I can remember exactly _____ .

About you **B** **Pair work** Ask and answer the questions. Give your own answers.

Lesson B Separable phrasal verbs; *how to, where to, what to*

> ❌ **Common errors**
>
> Don't put object pronouns like *it*, *them*, etc. after the particle (*on, up,* etc.).
>
> *Can you **turn it off**?*
> (NOT *Can you ~~turn off it~~?*)

A Complete the first questions using the words given. There are two correct answers. Then complete the second questions using pronouns.

1. How often do you ___*turn off your cell phone*___ OR
   ___*turn your cell phone off*___ ? (your cell phone / turn off)
   When do you have to _____*turn it off*_____ ?

2. Did you know how to _____ ? (your computer / set up)
   Did you _____ yourself?

3. Has anyone ever asked you _____ ? (your music / turn down)
   Did you _____ ?

4. Do you _____ to listen to music? (your headphones / put on)
   Did you _____ yesterday?

5. Do you know how to _____ on your computer? (the spell check / turn on)
   Do you usually _____ ?

6. Do you know how to _____ in your home? (wireless Internet / set up)
   Did you _____ ?

About you **B** **Pair work** Ask and answer the questions with a partner. Give your own answers.

Lesson A Present perfect continuous

A Complete the questions with the verbs given. Use the present perfect continuous.

1. _____have_____ you and your friends _been eating out_ (eat out) a lot recently?

2. What _are_ you _doing_ (do) today? _Have_ you _been doing_ (do) anything interesting?

3. How long _____have_____ you _been working_ (work) in your current job?

4. _Have_ you _been going out_ (go out) a lot during the week?

5. How long _____have_____ you and your friends _been hanging out_ (hang out) together?

6. _____has_____ your best friend _been taking_ (take) other classes this year?

7. _Have_ you _been following_ (follow) any sports teams this year?

8. How long _____have_____ you and your family _been living_ (live) in your apartment or house?

9. How long _____has_____ your best friend _been learning_ (learn) English?

10. How long _____have_____ you _been studying_ (study) today? _____Have_____ you _been studying_ (study) all day?

About you **B** Write your own true answers to the questions above. Write at least one sentence using the present perfect continuous, and one sentence using the present perfect.

1. Actually, we've been eating out every Friday. We've been to a couple of nice restaurants.

About you **C** **Pair work** Ask and answer the questions above. Ask follow-up questions for more information.

> **Common errors**
>
> Don't use the present with *for* or *since* to talk about past time.
>
> ***I've been taking*** this class for nine months, since September. (NOT *I'm taking* this class . . .)

Lesson B *already*, *still*, and *yet* with present perfect

A Write the title of a TV show, two movies, a book, a singer, and a place in the conversations. Then complete the conversations with *already*, *yet*, or *still*.

1. A You know, there's a new show on TV – _____ . I haven't seen it _____ . Have you?

   B No. I've heard about it, but I haven't seen it _____ , either. It looks good.

2. A You know that new movie, _____ ? Have you seen it _____ ?

   B Yes, I've _____ seen it. It was good. But I _____ haven't seen _____ . I'd like to see that, too. Actually, there are a few movies that I _____ want to see.

3. A Have you read any good books recently? I just read _____ . Have you read it?

   B No, I haven't read it _____ . I've been busy. I _____ haven't read the book assignment for my English class.

4. A Have you heard _____ 's new song _____ ?

   B No. I haven't downloaded it _____ . I _____ haven't heard the other songs on the album, either.

5. A There are a lot of great places to visit in the city, but I've never been to _____ . Have you?

   B No, I haven't been there _____ . I _____ haven't been to some of the museums or art galleries either.

About you **B** **Pair work** Practice the conversations above. Then practice again, giving your own answers.

Extra practice

UNIT **11**

Lesson A Modal verbs for speculating

Common errors

Don't use *can* to speculate.

*It's snowing, and she's not wearing a coat. She **must** be cold.* (NOT ~~She can be cold~~.)

A Make guesses about the situations below. Complete the sentences with modal verbs and the verbs given. Sometimes there is more than one correct answer.

1. You hear the sound of breaking glass at your neighbor's house next door, and then a siren.
   a. It _must be_ (be) a burglar for sure.
   b. The neighbors _____ (be) away, perhaps.
   c. The police _____ (come).
   d. The burglar _____ (be) in the house.

2. You see a young woman and young man talking outside a cinema. They look upset.
   a. They _might be having_ (have) an argument.
   b. They _can't_ (feel) very happy.
   c. He _could / might / may_ (be) her date, perhaps.
   d. He _must_ (try) to comfort her.   _may / might (must)_

3. You're in a cab that is going too fast.
   a. The driver _must_ (be) in a hurry, for sure.
   b. He _might_ (be) a very safe driver.   _negative can't_
   c. He _could_ (break) the speed limit.
   d. He _might_ (want) to get off work early.

4. You see a cyclist sitting on the ground next to his bike.
   a. He _might_ (be) hurt, perhaps.
   b. He _might_ (take) a rest.
   c. He _might_ (take part) in a bicycle race.
   d. His bicycle _might_ (be) damaged.

B Pair work What other guesses can you make about each situation? Discuss with a partner. Explain your guesses.

UNIT **11**

Lesson B Adjectives ending in *-ed* and *-ing*

A Complete the sentences. Write the correct adjective forms of the words given.

1. I hate it when I'm out with a group of friends and we can't decide what to do. It can be incredibly _frustrating_ (frustrate). I guess we're all _interested_ (interest) in different things.   _frustrated_

2. I get really _annoyed_ (annoy) when people say they'll meet me and then they're half an hour late. It's _surprised_ (surprise) how selfish people can be.   _surprising_

3. My parents are very _pleased_ (please) that I have nice friends. I think parents get _worried_ (worry) about things like that.   _describing feeling?_

4. I'm always really _shocked_ (shock) when friends get into fights with each other. _boring_

5. It's always _exciting_ (excite) to see my friends. Not one of them is _bored_ (bore).

6. It's _disappointing_ (disappoint) when friends don't keep in touch. But it happens.

7. I feel _di(ed)_ (disappoint) when friends don't call when they promised.

8. Some people post really mean comments online. They can be pretty _scare_ (scare).   _scary_

9. It's always _fascinating_ (fascinate) to find out about other people's jobs.

About you B Pair work Discuss the sentences above. Do you agree?

"It's very frustrating when I'm out with friends and we can't decide what to do. I think we all just have a hard time choosing something interesting."

150

Lesson A Simple past passive

A **Write sentences using the prompts given and the simple past passive.**

1. A dinosaur bone / find / in a storage box at a Boston museum this week.

   _____

   The bone / identify / as a new species of dinosaur.

   _____

2. Two main subway lines / close / yesterday for a second day.

   _____

   Repairs to the lines / not complete / on time.

   _____

3. A live show in New York City / cancel / last night after the lead singer fell off the stage.

   _____

   Ticket holders / not refund.

   _____

4. Police / call / to an apartment after neighbors heard strange sounds.

   _____

   A raccoon / trap / inside the apartment. It / remove / by animal services.

   _____

About
you **B** **Pair work** How many more ideas can you add to the news reports above? Take turns
making suggestions.

"The dinosaur bone was found by a student who was working at the museum."

Lesson B Simple past passive + *by* + agent

A **Rewrite the two news stories using the prompts given. Use the simple past passive and an adverb.
Use *by* where needed.**

1. A thief broke in through the roof of a police station late last night – thinking it was a local business.
   The roof (partial / damage) when the thief fell through and landed on the floor of the police station.
   The man (quick / arrest / an officer on duty). Although the man (serious / not injure), he (immediate /
   take to the emergency room / ambulance). Police say the burglar alarms at the station (temporary /
   disconnect).

   _____

   _____

   _____

2. Dozens of cars (bad / damage) yesterday after a freak hailstorm. The cars (hit / large hailstones) in the
   parking lot of a local supermarket. One driver said her windshield (complete / shatter). The store
   (partial / flood) in the storm.

   _____

   _____

   _____

B **Pair work** Take turns retelling the two news stories without looking at your books.

Illustration credits

Photography credits

Text credits

Answers

Unit 3, Lesson A

1 Getting started, Exercise B, page 22

1. b Taipei. Taipei 101 is the tallest office building in the world.
2. a Japan. The Akashi-Kaikyo Bridge is the longest suspension bridge.
3. b China. The New South China Mall is the largest shopping mall.
4. b Moscow. McDonald's is the world's busiest restaurant.
5. c Barcelona. Camp Nou is the largest soccer stadium in Europe.
6. c France.

1 Getting started, Exercise C, page 22

1. What's the <u>biggest</u> train station in the world?
   Grand Central Station in New York City. It has the most platforms.
2. What's the <u>busiest</u> airport in the world?
   Harsfield-Jackson Atlanta International Airport in Georgia, U.S.A. It has the most passengers.
3. Where is the <u>largest</u> building in the world?
   Boeing Everett Factory in Washington, U.S.A. It has the most usable space.
4. What's the <u>most expensive</u> city in the world?
   Tokyo.

SECOND EDITION

TOUCHSTONE

WORKBOOK 3

MICHAEL MCCARTHY

JEANNE MCCARTEN

HELEN SANDIFORD

CAMBRIDGE
UNIVERSITY PRESS

Contents

The way we are

Lesson A / People in a hurry

1 Opposites

Grammar and vocabulary | **Look at the pictures. Correct the sentences to match the pictures.**

1. Craig is a careful driver.
   Craig is a reckless driver.

2. Lucia always arrives early.
   _____

3. Carlos is waiting impatiently.
   _____

4. Emily walks slowly.
   _____

5. Laila is talking loudly.
   _____

6. Tom seems polite.
   _____

7. Tamara plays tennis badly.
   _____

8. Joe and Kay are dressed informally.
   _____

2 My new job!

Grammar and vocabulary | Circle the correct words to complete Cleo's email.

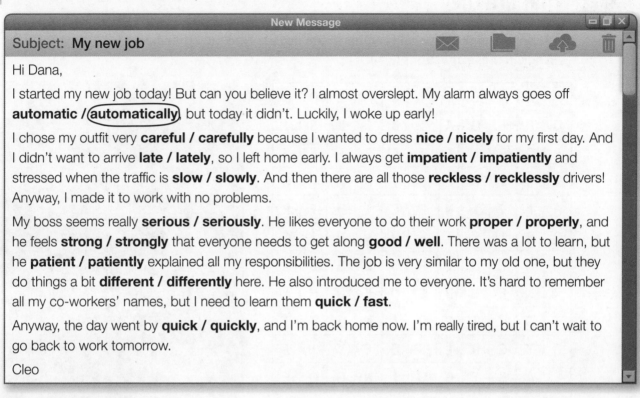

New Message

Subject: **My new job**

Hi Dana,

I started my new job today! But can you believe it? I almost overslept. My alarm always goes off **automatic /(automatically)**, but today it didn't. Luckily, I woke up early!

I chose my outfit very **careful / carefully** because I wanted to dress **nice / nicely** for my first day. And I didn't want to arrive **late / lately**, so I left home early. I always get **impatient / impatiently** and stressed when the traffic is **slow / slowly**. And then there are all those **reckless / recklessly** drivers! Anyway, I made it to work with no problems.

My boss seems really **serious / seriously**. He likes everyone to do their work **proper / properly**, and he feels **strong / strongly** that everyone needs to get along **good / well**. There was a lot to learn, but he **patient / patiently** explained all my responsibilities. The job is very similar to my old one, but they do things a bit **different / differently** here. He also introduced me to everyone. It's hard to remember all my co-workers' names, but I need to learn them **quick / fast**.

Anyway, the day went by **quick / quickly**, and I'm back home now. I'm really tired, but I can't wait to go back to work tomorrow.

Cleo

3 Are you fast?

Grammar and vocabulary | **A** Complete the answers with an adjective or adverb. Sometimes more than one answer is possible.

1. A Are you a fast reader?

    B No, actually, I read very _____*slowly*_____ .

2. A Do you think you're lazy?

    B No, actually, I'm a _____ worker.

3. A Do you have difficulty remembering names?

    B I don't think so. I remember names very _____ .

4. A Do you eat your meals quickly?

    B Yes, I'm a _____ eater.

5. A Are you a careful driver?

    B Actually, yes. I drive very _____ .

6. A Are you good at sports?

    B Yes, I play most sports _____ .

B Write true answers to the questions in part A.

1. *Yes, I am. I read everything very quickly.*

2. _____

3. _____

4. _____

5. _____

6. _____

3

Lesson B — Personality and character

1 What are they like?

Vocabulary | **A** There are eight personality words in the puzzle. Find the other seven. Look in these directions (→ ↓).

P	R	A	C	T	I	C	A	L	O	D
D	P	L	O	A	T	B	F	K	S	I
L	O	R	E	L	I	A	B	L	E	S
T	G	T	P	E	B	M	D	W	L	O
A	F	V	J	N	P	C	I	H	F	R
Q	B	I	E	T	S	H	V	N	I	G
H	G	E	N	E	R	O	U	S	S	A
R	K	E	L	D	G	O	K	D	H	N
U	O	U	T	G	O	I	N	G	T	I
O	Y	C	R	L	S	Q	E	Y	I	Z
E	A	S	Y	G	O	I	N	G	Q	E
X	B	A	I	H	P	N	T	A	Z	D

B Complete the sentences with the words from part A.

1. My aunt likes to paint. She has creative ideas and is incredibly __talented__ .
2. My sister is totally _____ . She can never find her car keys and is always losing her cell phone.
3. My friend Steve is extremely down-to-earth and _____ . He gives useful advice.
4. My brother is really _____ . He isn't shy at all.
5. My dad bought me a laptop computer for college. He's very kind and _____ like that.
6. My co-workers are usually good about completing their work. They're fairly _____ .
7. My mom is pretty laid-back and _____ . She never gets upset about anything.
8. My little sister never shares anything. She's so _____ !

2 About you 1

Grammar and vocabulary | Complete each question with the opposite of the adjective given. Then write true answers.

1. Are you honest or __dishonest__ ? _I'm honest. I always tell the truth._
2. Is your doctor friendly or _____ ? _____
3. Is your best friend reliable or _____ ? _____
4. Are you organized or _____ ? _____
5. Are you patient or _____ ? _____
6. Are your neighbors considerate or _____ ? _____

4

3 All or nothing

Grammar and vocabulary | **What's the best next sentence? Circle *a* or *b*.**

1. My brother's not talented at all.
   a. He sings, dances, and acts.
   b. (He can't sing, dance, or act!)

2. My parents are extremely generous.
   a. (They give a lot of money to charity.)
   b. They give a little money to charity.

3. My sister is incredibly smart.
   a. She's the best student in her class.
   b. (She does fairly well in school.)

4. My best friend is so funny.
   a. His jokes don't make me laugh at all.
   b. His jokes always make me laugh.

5. My cousin is fairly outgoing.
   a. She never goes to parties.
   b. She sometimes goes to parties.

6. My math teacher is really helpful.
   a. She explains things really well.
   b. She can't explain things clearly.

7. My dad is pretty laid-back.
   a. He gets upset about everything.
   b. He doesn't get upset about most things.

8. My brother is completely inconsiderate.
   a. He never helps around the house.
   b. He sometimes helps me around the house.

4 About you 2

Grammar and vocabulary | **Use the expressions in the box to write true sentences about someone you know. Then add a second sentence about yourself.**

fairly easygoing	not impatient at all	really practical
incredibly friendly	✓ pretty reliable	very honest

1. *My older brother's pretty reliable. I think I'm pretty unreliable.*
2. My younger sister is very easygoing. And I am too.
3. My brother is incredibly friendly, I think I am not incredibly friendly.
4. It is really practical, I think them really impractical.
5. My best friend is very honest. I'm honest too.
6. My younger sister is not impatient at all, Sometimes I am patient.

1 They're always . . .

Conversation strategies | The people in this office don't work very hard. Look at the picture, and write what each person is always doing.

1. Jedd _is always leaving work early_ .
2. Reba _is always listening to music_ .
3. John _is always sleeping_ .
4. Kayo _is always eating_ .
5. Yasmin _is always talking on the phone_ .
6. Chad _is always reading_ .

2 Individual habits

Conversation strategies | Write a response to each statement with *always* and a continuous verb. Use the expressions in the box.

| buy things | ✓cancel plans | help people | lose stuff | tell jokes |

1. Beth is so unreliable. | I know. _She's always canceling plans!_

2. Matt is incredibly disorganized. | That's for sure. _he's always losing stuff._

3. Elizabeth is very funny. | That's true. _She's always telling jokes._

4. Theresa isn't practical with money. | You're right. _She's always buying things._

5. Kenny is generous with his time. | Yeah, he is. _He's always helping people._

3 Complaints, complaints

Conversation
strategies Complete each conversation with *always* and a continuous verb. Then add *at least*
to the response when appropriate. Write *X* if *at least* is not appropriate.

1.   Sam   My sister hardly ever talks to my friends when
            they come over. She *'s always doing*____ (do)
            something else. I mean, she says "Hi," but that's all.

    Fatema   Well, __*at least*__ she isn't rude to them.

2.   Jody   Last year, my roommate in college
            __*always borrowing*__ (borrow) my books
            and stuff without asking.

    Pam   That's too bad – __*at least*__ it sounds
            like she was really inconsiderate.

3.   Sandy   My last boss was really nice but completely
            disorganized. She *'s always canceling* (cancel)
            meetings at the last minute.

    Natsuko   Yeah, __*at least*__ it's hard to work for
            somebody like that.

4.   Daniel   My brother __*always listening*__ (listen)
            to music. He's always got his
            headphones on.

    Sarah   Well, __*at least*__ his music isn't loud.

5. Alejandro   I never see my kids these days. They
            __*always going*__ (go) to their friends'
            houses to play basketball or baseball or
            something.

    Diana   Well, you know, *at least*____ they're
            interested in sports. A lot of kids just play
            computer games all the time.

4 About you

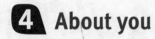

Conversation
strategies Complete each sentence with true information. Use *always* and a continuous verb.

1. When I was little, *I was always eating candy*_____.
2. My friends and I _____.
3. I have some bad habits. I _____.
4. My best friend _____.
5. My parents _____.
6. My favorite teacher in high school _____.
7. My neighbor _____.

Lesson D   Is that a fact?

1 Star qualities

Reading **A** Read the article. Circle the two adjectives that describe actor Aishwarya Rai in each column.

famous	accomplished	inconsiderate	generous
arrogant	influential	down-to-earth	unfriendly
talented	selfish	beautiful	nice

Aishwarya Rai   THE QUEEN OF BOLLYWOOD

Aishwarya Rai is the Queen of Bollywood, India's version of Hollywood and the film capital of the world. With over 18,000 websites devoted to her, she is India's, and possibly the world's, best-known actor.

Aishwarya Rai was born in Mangalore, India, on November 1, 1973. She was raised in a traditional, middle-class family. When she was four, her family moved to Mumbai (Bombay), where she still lives today with her husband, actor Abhishek Bachchan, and their daughter, Aaradhya.

Rai started modeling for fun when she was in college studying architecture. She also received many offers to act. However, her first priority was school, so she said no to all movie offers. Then in 1994, at the age of 21, Rai won the title of Miss World. Soon after that, she accepted her first movie role.

Now an accomplished actor, Rai won Filmfare's Award for Best Actress for her role in *Hum Dil De Chuke Sanam* in 2000. She also starred in Bollywood's most successful international blockbuster, *Devdas*.

Rai acts in five different languages: Hindi, Telugu, Tamil, Bengali, and English.

She is the first Bollywood star to be a juror at the Cannes Film Festival in France, to appear in *Rolling Stone* magazine, and to be on *The Oprah Winfrey Show*. Rai is also the first Indian woman to have a statue in London's wax museum, Madame Tussaud's. In 2012, she received the second highest Order of France.

Aishwarya Rai is one of the most beautiful women in the world, but when Oprah Winfrey asked her about her beauty, she simply said, "Beauty is as beauty does," meaning that what you do is more important than how you look. This is perhaps why Rai created a charitable organization called the Aishwarya Rai Foundation, which helps women, children, the elderly, and animals. She was also named the Goodwill Ambassador for a United Nations program on AIDS in 2012. Her philosophy is very simple: "It's nice to be important, but it's important to be nice."

B Read Rai's biography again. Then correct these false sentences.

with her husband and daughter

1. Aishwarya Rai lives ~~by herself~~ in Mumbai.
2. Rai was born in Mumbai.
3. Rai started modeling in high school.
4. Rai studied acting in college.
5. Rai won the title of Miss World when she was 19.
6. Rai makes movies in four languages.
7. Rai has a statue in Cannes, France.
8. Rai feels that it's important to be beautiful.

8

2 She's admirable.

Writing **A** Use the words and expressions in the box to complete the profile of Midori Goto.

accomplished	called	started
at the age of	can be	✓ was born and raised

Midori Goto

Midori Goto is an incredibly talented violinist. She _was born and raised_ in Osaka, Japan. She _started_ studying the violin with her mother, and _at the age of_ seven, she gave her first public performance in Osaka.

Studying music _can be_ very demanding, as well as rewarding. When she was only 10, Midori moved to New York City to study music at the Juilliard School. She also attended the Professional Children's School for her academic studies. By the time Midori turned 11, she was already an _accomplished_ artist and had performed with the New York Philharmonic.

Midori is also very generous. In 1992, she created an organization _called_ Midori & Friends that provides free music education for children in city schools.

Midori is now a professor of music at the University of Southern California.

B Write a short profile about someone you admire.

Unit 1 Progress chart

What can you do? Mark the boxes. ✓ = I can . . . ? = I need to review how to . . .	To review, go back to these pages in the Student's Book.
☐ use manner adverbs and adjectives correctly.	2 and 3
☐ use regular and irregular adverbs.	3
☐ use adverbs to make adjectives and adverbs stronger.	5
☐ add prefixes to adjectives to make opposites.	5
☐ name at least 12 adverbs.	2, 3, 4, and 5
☐ name at least 15 personality adjectives.	4 and 5
☐ use *always* and a continuous verb to describe individual habits.	6
☐ use *at least* to point out the positive side of a situation.	7
☐ write a short profile about someone.	9

Grammar

Vocabulary

Conversation strategies

Writing

Lesson A / Hopes and dreams

1 Have you or haven't you?

Grammar **A** Read the "to do" list. What things have you done? What things haven't you done?
Write true sentences using the present perfect.

Things I want to do

1. drive a sports car
2. go skiing
3. learn a second language
4. see the Taj Mahal
5. study photography
6. travel to Europe
7. try windsurfing
8. surf in Hawai'i

1. _I haven't driven a sports car._
2. _I haven't gone skiing_
3. _I have learned a second language._
4. _I haven't seen the Taj Mahal._
5. _I have studied photography._
6. _I haven't traveled to Europe._
7. _I haven't tried windsurfing_
8. _I haven't surfed in Hawai'i_

B Complete the sentences using the present perfect and the expressions in the
"to do" list in part A. Use the negative form where necessary.

1. My cousin _has driven a sports car_ once or twice. He loves to drive.
2. My sister and I _have gone skiing_ many times. We love the snow.
3. Each of my brothers _has learned a second language_ . One speaks Mandarin and one
   speaks Cantonese.
4. We _haven't seen the Taj Mahal_ , but I really want to go to India one day.
5. My teacher _has studied photography_ . She takes beautiful travel photos.
6. My parents _haven't traveled to Europe_ before, but they hope to go next year.
7. My older brother _haven't tried windsurfing_ . He's afraid of the water.
8. My best friend _hasn't surfed in Hawai'i_ , but she wants to go this summer.

2 I've tried . . .

Grammar | **Write sentences with the present perfect.**

1. My teacher (go / many times) to the United States.
   My teacher's been to the United States many times.
   or *My teacher's gone to the United States many times.*

2. My boss (ski / several times) in the Swiss Alps.
   My boss's skied in the Swiss Alps several times.

3. I (always / want) to go on a roller coaster.
   I've always wanted to go on a roller coaster.

4. My neighbor (never / go / before) to Canada.
   My neighbor's never gone to Canada before.

5. My parents (see / five times) the movie *Titanic*.
   My parents have seen the movie Titanic five times.

6. My brothers (try / once or twice) Vietnamese food.
   My brothers have tried Vietnamese food once or twice.

7. My best friend (never / see) the ocean.
   My best friend has never seen the ocean.

8. I (never / have) the money to take a vacation.
   I never had the money to take a vacation.
      have

3 About you

Grammar | **Answer the questions with true information. Add a frequency expression where necessary.**

1. What's something exciting you've done?
   I've gone hang gliding once.

2. What's something scary you've done?

3. What's something boring you've done in the last month?

4. How many times have you been late to class recently?

5. What country have you always wanted to visit?

6. What kind of food have you never tried before?

7. What movie have you seen several times?

8. What's something you've never done, but always wanted to do?

| **Unusual experiences**

1 Have you ever . . . ?

Grammar | **Complete the conversations with the simple past or present perfect.**

1. A ___Have___ you ever ___gone___ (go) cliff diving?

    B No, I _____ . It sounds too scary!
    _____ you _____ (do) it?

    A Yeah, I _____ (go) last weekend.

    B Wow! You're brave. How _____ (be) it?

    A It was incredible! I _____ (love) it.

2. A I _____ never _____ (travel) alone.
    How about you?

    B No, but I _____ always _____ (want) to. I'm
    sure it's exciting.

    A I think so, too. Do you know my friend Jill?
    She _____ (take) a hiking trip alone last year.

    B I know. I _____ (speak) to her about it last week.

3. A _____ you ever _____ (try) horseback riding?

    B Yeah. I actually _____ (do) it once several years
    ago.

    A Really? _____ you _____ (like) it?

    B No, not really. It _____ (be) very scary.

    A Oh, too bad. I go all the time. I _____ (get) really
    good at it.

4. A _____ you _____ (do) anything special
    last weekend?

    B Yes. My family and I _____ (take) a ride in a hot-air
    balloon! _____ you ever _____ (be) up
    in one?

    A No, I _____ . _____ you _____ (enjoy) it?

    B Yeah, we _____ (love) every minute! It was amazing!

2 Yes or no?

Grammar and vocabulary Complete the questions with the simple past or present perfect form of the verbs in the box. Then answer the questions with true information.

break	eat	✓go	have	lose	ride	visit	win

1. ___*Did*___ you ___*go*___ to the zoo yesterday? _*No, I didn't go to the zoo yesterday.*_
2. _____ you ever _____ your leg? _____
3. _____ you ever _____ a spelling contest? _____
4. _____ you _____ a bike to class yesterday? _____
5. _____ you _____ your grandparents last summer? _____
6. _____ you ever _____ a bad cold? _____
7. _____ you _____ a big breakfast this morning? _____
8. _____ you ever _____ your wallet? _____

3 About you

Grammar Use the cues to write questions in the simple past or present perfect. Then write true answers.

1. (try any new foods on your last vacation)
   Did you try any new foods on your last vacation?
   Yes, I did. I tried oysters. They're delicious.

2. (ever / hike in the mountains)
   _____
   _____

3. (see a lot of movies last summer)
   _____
   _____

4. (ever / walk across a tightrope)
   _____
   _____

5. (ever / find a lost wallet or cell phone)
   _____
   _____

6. (ever / forget an important appointment)
   _____
   _____

Lesson C / I've heard good things . . .

1 Tell me more!

Conversation strategies | Complete the conversations with the responses in the box.

Cool. Do you have a favorite place?   That sounds great. How do you get there?
I've heard her tests are hard. How did you do?   That's too bad. Did you study for it?
Oh, that sounds hard. Did you finish?   ✓Yeah, I am. Do you want to come?

1. **Jake** Hey, Alex! Are you going surfing this weekend?

   Alex *Yeah, I am. Do you want to come?*

   Jake Well, I'm working this weekend. And, actually, I've never surfed before.

   Alex Really? I started surfing three years ago, and now I can't stop.

   Jake _____

   Alex Yeah, I like to go to Cove Beach. Have you heard of it?

   Jake Yeah, I have, but I've never been there.

   Alex You should come sometime. I can teach you the basics.

   Jake _____

   Alex I usually drive. You can ride your bike there, but it's a little far.

   Jake All right. Tell me the next time you're planning to go.

2. **Ki-Won** Hi, Erin. You look upset. What's wrong?

   Erin I just took Mrs. Chen's English test.

   Ki-Won _____

   Erin I don't think I did too well.

   Ki-Won _____

   Erin Yeah, I studied really hard.

   Ki-Won Was it an essay or a multiple-choice test?

   Erin Well, it was both. There were 30 multiple-choice questions *and* an essay question!

   Ki-Won _____

   Erin Yeah, I finished it, but I didn't have time to check my answers.

   Ki-Won Well, maybe you did better than you think!

14

2 Did you?

Conversation strategies | Complete each conversation with a response question to show interest.

1. A I went on an amazing roller coaster last weekend.
   B _Did you?_ That sounds like fun.

2. A I love going to the movies!
   B _Do you?_ Let's go sometime!

3. A I won first prize in the art contest!
   B _Did you?_ That's wonderful!

4. A I'm scared of snakes and spiders.
   B _Are you?_ I am too.

5. A I ride my motorcycle on the weekends.
   B _Do you?_ I've never ridden a motorcycle.

6. A I've broken my arm twice.
   B _Have you?_ That's too bad.

7. A It's my birthday today. I'm 18!
   B _Are you?_ Happy birthday!

8. A I've seen that documentary about fast food four times.
   B _Have you?_ What's it about exactly?

3 Extreme sports

Conversation strategies | Respond to these statements with a response question. Then add a follow-up question to ask for more information.

1. In the summer, I love to go hang gliding. | _Do you? Is it scary?_

2. I've gone scuba diving several times. |

3. Last spring, I went deep-sea fishing. |

4. I'm a pretty good windsurfer. |

5. I absolutely love sailing. |

6. I started surfing last year. |

1 Finally here!

Reading **A** Read Gisele's travel blog about her trip to China. What is one thing she has always wanted to do?

Gisele's Blog

Finally here!

We arrived in Chengdu, the capital of Sichuan province, the day before yesterday. Exhausted, we went straight to bed, but got up early yesterday. We took a bus to Mount Emei. Fortunately, it's close to Chengdu, so we had a full day to explore. Mount Emei is beautiful, and it has lots of temples and monasteries.

Today we went to Leshan to see the giant Buddha statue. It's the largest stone Buddha in the world and was cut into a cliff. It took 90 years to make. It's huge—233 feet (71 meters) high!

Our hotel in Chengdu is inexpensive and very nice. We met some people from Canada last night. We all went out for some delicious Sichuan food.

We're going to the Giant Panda Nature Reserve tomorrow. I've always wanted to see a baby panda. I'm so excited. Have any of you been there? What's the best way to get there?

Posted January 25 at 7:57 p.m.

JOE TRIP Re: Finally here!

I went to see the pandas last year. It was pretty cool. You're going to love it. There are regular buses from Chengdu, and the bus ride usually takes three hours. But go early to see the pandas when they're awake.

Posted January 25 at 9 p.m.

Last day in Chengdu

We went to the Panda Reserve yesterday. I was able to see some baby pandas. They are so cute. They do amazing things at the Reserve to save these animals.

Posted January 27 at 10 a.m.

Wow!

We just spent a few days in western Sichuan. It was really interesting. Tonight we head to Beijing. I really want to see the Forbidden City, Tiananmen Square, and the Bird's Nest Stadium. This really is a fantastic trip.

Posted February 2 at 4:45 p.m.

B Read the blog again. Then answer the questions.

1. When did Gisele arrive in Chengdu? _She arrived in Chengdu on January 23._

2. What did she see first? _____

3. Who did she meet at the hotel? _____

4. When does Joe Trip think Gisele should go to see the pandas? _____

5. Where did Gisele go after Chengdu? _____

6. Where is Gisele going tonight? _____

2 Fortunately, . . .

Writing **A** Read Ian's blog entry about his trip to Belize. Complete the sentences with *fortunately*, *unfortunately*, or *amazingly*. Sometimes more than one answer is possible.

Ian's Blog ▢ ▣ ☒

We were very tired when we got off the plane in Belize City, but ___*fortunately*___ , our host was there to meet us. _____ , the airline lost my luggage, so I left the airport without it. We got on a bus and headed for Maya Mountain Lodge. _____ , when we got to the lodge, the airline called to say my luggage was on its way. The next morning, we set out on our first day trip. The mountain road was narrow and winding. _____ , we had a careful driver. Our first stop was at a big waterfall. _____ , it was raining when we got there, so we just took pictures from the bus. Our next stop was at a river called Rio on Pools. By then it was sunny, so everyone went swimming. _____ , I didn't have my bathing suit with me, so I couldn't swim. The views were beautiful, and I took a lot of photos. I'm not usually a very good photographer, but _____ , my pictures turned out really well.

B Write a blog entry about one of the following experiences. Use adverbs like *fortunately* and *amazingly* to show your feelings about what happened.

- Competing in a contest
- Having a fun picnic
- Taking an exciting trip
- Trying a new activity

Blog ▢ ▣ ☒

_____

_____

_____

_____

Unit 2 Progress chart

What can you do? Mark the boxes. ☑ = I can . . . ? = I need to review how to . . .	To review, go back to these pages in the Student's Book.
☐ use the present perfect with regular and irregular verbs.	12 and 13
☐ use the present perfect to say what I have and haven't done.	13, 14, and 15
☐ ask and answer questions beginning with *Have you ever . . . ?*	14 and 15
☐ use the simple past to answer questions in the present perfect.	14 and 15
☐ name at least 12 irregular past participles.	13, 14, and 15
☐ keep a conversation going by showing interest.	16
☐ use *Do you?*, *Did you?*, *Are you?*, or *Have you?* to show interest.	17
☐ use adverbs to show my feelings about something.	19

Grammar

Vocabulary

Conversation strategies

Writing

1 That's expensive!

Grammar and vocabulary | Complete the questions with superlatives. Then match the questions with the correct pictures and information below.

1. What's _the most expensive_ (expensive) musical instrument ever sold? _h_
2. Which country has _____ (long) school year? ____
3. What sport has _____ (fans) in the world? ____
4. Who was _____ (young) number-one classical artist? ____
5. Where's _____ (narrow) house in the world? ____
6. What's _____ (famous) statue in the United States? ____
7. What's one of _____ (tall) hotels in the world? ____
8. What's _____ (fast) car in the world? ____

a

The Burj al-Arab Hotel in Dubai is 321 meters (1,060 feet) tall.

b

Almost 4 million people visit the Statue of Liberty each year.

c

Millions of fans around the world watch soccer.

d

The Thrust SSC went up to 1,227 kilometers (763 miles) per hour.

e

Welsh soprano Charlotte Church was only 12 years old when her album, *Voice of an Angel*, sold over 2 million copies in the UK.

f

Chinese children go to school 251 days a year.

g

The Keret House in Warsaw, Poland, is less than 1.5 meters (5 feet) at its widest point.

h

"The Lady Tennant" violin by Antonio Stradivari sold at auction for over $2 million.

2 ▶ It's the best.

Complete the conversations. Use superlative adjectives.

1. A That's a really big airplane.

   B Yeah. It's _the biggest_ airplane I've ever seen.

2. A It's really easy to get to the airport by subway.

   B Right. It's definitely _____ way to get there.

3. A This restaurant isn't expensive at all.

   B I know. It's _____ place to eat around here.

4. A This subway is really crowded.

   B Yeah, it is. Actually, it's always _____ subway line.

5. A Look at that cruise ship. It's so big!

   B It's the *Oasis of the Seas*. It's one of _____ cruise ships in the world.

6. A Wow. I like your watch. It's so thin.

   B I know. It's _____ watch I've ever seen.

7. A This is a pretty good price for these pants.

   B Yes, it is. Actually, I think this store has _____ prices in the mall.

8. A This is a nice gallery, but the new exhibition has some really bad paintings.

   B Yeah. They're some of _____ paintings I've ever seen.

3 ▶ About you

Complete the questions with superlatives. Then write true answers.

1. Where's _the cheapest_ (cheap) place to go shopping around here?
   The cheapest place to go shopping is downtown.

2. And where's _____ (bad) place to go shopping?
   _____

3. Which neighborhood has _____ (many) restaurants?
   _____

4. What's _____ (quiet) neighborhood in your city?
   _____

5. What's _____ (amazing) building you've ever seen?
   _____

6. Which neighborhood has _____ (a lot of) traffic?
   _____

7. What's _____ (wonderful) city you've ever visited?
   _____

8. Where can you buy _____ (delicious) pastries in your city?
   _____

1 Wonders of the earth

Vocabulary | **A** Look at the pictures and complete the puzzle. Then write the answer to the question below.

1. <u>v</u> <u>o</u> <u>l</u> <u>c</u> <u>a</u> [n] <u>o</u>
2. ___ ___ [ ] ___ ___ ___ ___
3. ___ ___ ___ [ ] ___ ___ ___
4. ___ ___ ___ [ ] ___ ___ ___ ___ ___ ___
5. ___ ___ ___ ___ ___ [ ] ___ ___ ___
6. ___ ___ [ ] ___ ___

What is the most powerful force on the planet? Mother <u>N</u> ___ ___ ___ ___ ___ .

B Complete these sentences with the words from part A.

1. The Grand <u>Canyon</u> in Arizona is 1,600 meters (5,249 feet) deep in some parts.
2. The Pacific _____ is about ten times larger than the Arctic.
3. K2, the second highest _____ in the world, is 8,610 meters (28,250 feet) high.
4. In the Sahara _____ , temperatures can reach 54 degrees Celsius (130 degrees Fahrenheit).
5. The Siachen, with more than 57 billion cubic meters of ice, is one of the world's largest _____ .
6. Mt. Pinatubo in the Philippines is an active _____ . It last erupted in 1991.

2 How wide?

Grammar | Look at the pictures. Complete each question with *How* + adjective. Then write the answers.

1. Q _How wide_ are the Khone Falls on the Mekong River?
   A _They're 10.8 kilometers wide._

2. Q _____ is the Amazon Rain Forest?
   A _____

3. Q _____ can it get in Antarctica?
   A _____

4. Q _____ is the Mississippi River?
   A _____

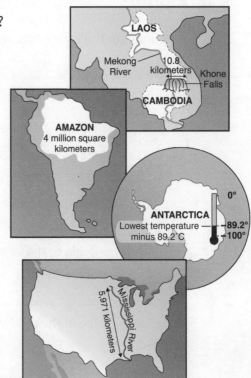

3 Discover New Zealand!

Grammar | Write *How* questions based on the guidebook page. Then answer the questions.

1. Q _How big is the North Island?_
   A _It's 115,777 square kilometers._

2. Q _____
   A _____

3. Q _____
   A _____

4. Q _____
   A _____

5. Q _____
   A _____

6. Q _____
   A _____

7. Q _____
   A _____

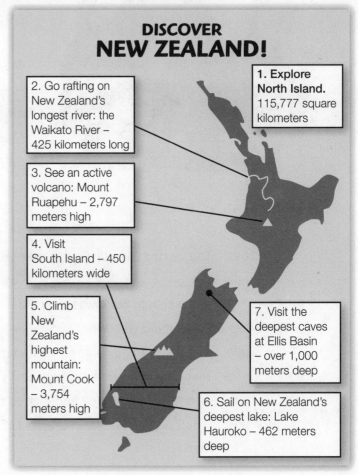

DISCOVER **NEW ZEALAND!**

1. Explore North Island. 115,777 square kilometers

2. Go rafting on New Zealand's longest river: the Waikato River – 425 kilometers long

3. See an active volcano: Mount Ruapehu – 2,797 meters high

4. Visit South Island – 450 kilometers wide

5. Climb New Zealand's highest mountain: Mount Cook – 3,754 meters high

7. Visit the deepest caves at Ellis Basin – over 1,000 meters deep

6. Sail on New Zealand's deepest lake: Lake Hauroko – 462 meters deep

I had the best time.

1 Really?

A Complete the conversations with the sentences in the box.

It really was.	It sure is.	They really are. ✓Yeah, it really is.
It sure does.	Really? I didn't know that.	We really should.

1. **Danielle** I think Hawai'i is one of the most interesting
   states in the U.S.

   Mark _Yeah, it really is._____ You know, more
   than one-third of the world's pineapples
   are from Hawai'i.

   Danielle Really? I didn't know that. I know it has some
   of the best surfing in the world, though.

   Mark _____ They get some of
   the highest waves there. And did you know all eight islands are volcanoes? . . .

2. **Mee** Mount Sorak in South Korea is so beautiful,
   especially in the fall.

   Kyong _____ I love it there.
   Have you ever gone hiking there?

   Mee Uh-huh, I've hiked there several
   times with my friends.

   Kyong _____

   Mee Yeah. The waterfalls are the best.

   Kyong Yeah. _____

3. **Chika** The weather was terrible last weekend.

   Kacie _____ I wanted to go
   to the beach, but it was too cold.

   Chika So what did you do?

   Kacie Well, I stayed home and watched movies.

   Chika Yeah? Well, I heard next weekend's going to be
   warm and sunny. We should go to the beach then.

   Kacie _____ Let's plan on going
   then.

2 The best and the worst!

Conversation strategies | **Complete the conversations with superlative adjectives for emphasis.**

1. A Chichén Itzá in Mexico has ___the coolest___ (cool)
       Mayan ruins. Have you ever been there?

    B Yeah, I had _____ (good) time at the pyramids.

2. A The food at that restaurant was _____ (bad)!

    B I know, but at least the waiter was nice.

3. A How was your weekend?

    B Wonderful! We went to _____ (incredible) lake and
       rented a boat. We just sailed around for hours!

4. A Have you ever hiked the Appalachian Trail?

    B No, I haven't. But I hear it has _____ (amazing) scenery.

3 It really is the best!

Conversation strategies | **You're camping with your friend. Write responses with *really* or *sure* to show you are a supportive listener. Then add a sentence using a superlative adjective for emphasis.**

1. It feels really good to be on vacation.
    It sure does! And camping was the coolest idea!

2. Our hike yesterday was great.
    _____

3. We should go swimming in the lake today.
    _____

4. It's so nice to be in the country.
    _____

4 About you

Conversation strategies | **Write true sentences about your last vacation or trip. Use superlative adjectives for emphasis.**

1. I went *to Costa Rica last year. They have the most amazing beaches* .
2. I stayed _____ .
3. I saw _____ .
4. I met _____ .
5. I ate _____ .
6. I visited _____ .

1 The coldest continent

Reading | **A** Look at the topics below. Then read the article and write the number of the paragraph where the topic is explained in detail.

- _3_ the driest weather
- ____ the most time zones
- ____ the smallest population
- ____ the farthest south
- ____ the strongest winds
- ____ the most ice
- ____ the most daylight
- ____ the coldest temperature

AMAZING ANTARCTICA

Vostok Station

1 Antarctica is the coldest, windiest, and driest continent on Earth. It's the fifth largest of the world's seven continents. A layer of ice almost 5 kilometers (3 miles) thick covers the island in some places. In fact, 90% of the world's ice is in Antarctica.

2 The weather in Antarctica is the coldest on Earth. The lowest temperature ever recorded, –89.2 degrees Celsius (–128.6 degrees Fahrenheit), was in 1983 at the Vostok Station, an old Russian research base. At the South Pole, the temperature varies from –35 degrees Celsius (–31 degrees Fahrenheit) in the midsummer to –70 degrees Celsius (–94 degrees Fahrenheit) in the midwinter.

3 Antarctica is not only the world's coldest continent but also the driest place on Earth. Sometimes called the world's largest desert, it gets about the same amount of rain each year as the Sahara. Antarctic winds are the strongest on the planet, reaching up to 320 kilometers (199 miles) per hour.

4 Located at the South Pole, Antarctica is the farthest south of any continent. The South Pole gets six months of nonstop daylight from September through March. Then it gets six months of nonstop darkness. And because it's so far south, Antarctica covers the most time zones – all of them!

5 Explorers first visited Antarctica in 1821. Then in 1899, a Norwegian explorer set up a research station on Antarctica, and for the first time, people could live there. Now there are about 60 research bases there, set up by many different countries. The population of Antarctica grows from about 1,000 in the winter to about 4,000 during the summer. It has the smallest population of any continent.

B Read the article again. Write *T* (true) or *F* (false) for each sentence. Then correct the false sentences.

1. Antarctica is the world's ~~seventh~~ *fifth* largest continent. _F_

2. Antarctica has 90% of the world's ice. ____

3. Antarctica gets more rain than the Sahara Desert. ____

4. Antarctica's six months of nonstop daylight begins in March. ____

5. About 1,000 people live in Antarctica during the summer. ____

2 The dry facts

Writing | **A** Read the facts about the Sahara. Combine each pair of sentences to form one sentence.

1	2	3	4
The Sahara is the largest hot desert in the world. It covers 9.1 million square kilometers of land in North Africa.	The sand dunes are the highest dunes in the world. They are the biggest tourist attraction in the Sahara.	The Qattara Depression in Egypt's Sahara is one of the lowest points in Africa. It is 133 meters below sea level.	The Libyan Sahara is the driest place in the desert. It has the least amount of animal or plant life.

1. *The Sahara, the largest hot desert in the world, covers 9.1 million square kilometers of land in North Africa.*

2. _____

    _____

3. _____

    _____

4. _____

    _____

B Write four to six pieces of information about your favorite place. Then combine the facts to make sentences.

Unit 3 Progress chart

What can you do? Mark the boxes. ☑ = I can . . . ? = I need to review how to . . .	To review, go back to these pages in the Student's Book.
☐ use the superlative form of adjectives. ☐ use the superlative with nouns. ☐ ask and answer questions using *how* + adjective.	22 and 23 22 and 23 24 and 25
☐ name 5 human wonders. ☐ name 5 natural wonders.	21, 22, and 23 21, 24, and 25
☐ use short responses with *really* and *sure* to show I'm a supportive listener. ☐ use superlative adjectives to emphasize my opinions or feelings.	26 27
☐ add information about a place or thing in sentences.	29

Grammar

Vocabulary

Conversation strategies

Writing

25

Family life

Lesson A / Family gripes

1 Family obligations

Grammar | Complete the conversations with the correct form of the verbs in the box.

change	do	help	read	think
clean	do	play	stay	✓watch

1. **Jeff**   When I was young, my parents never let me __watch__ TV.

   Paul   Really? Why not?

   Jeff   They wanted me _____ books and _____ about the stories, not just watch TV.

   Paul   My parents were pretty easygoing about watching TV.

   Jeff   What do you mean?

   Paul   Well, they just made me _____ my homework first. Then I could watch all the TV I wanted.

2. **Liz**   I heard you broke your arm. What happened?

   Kaya   My grandmother asked me _____ a lightbulb in the ceiling fan. I lost my balance and fell off a ladder.

   Liz   Ouch! What did your doctor say?

   Kaya   He told me _____ home for a week.

   Liz   Yeah. And you should get someone _____ you next time.

3. **Kyle**   I hate Mondays!

   Naomi   Me too. They're the worst.

   Kyle   Yeah, Monday is when my mom has me _____ the entire house.

   Naomi   Really? By yourself? My brother always helps me _____ my chores.

   Kyle   Well, my little sister never helps. My mom just lets her _____ video games all day!

   Naomi   That's not fair!

2 Gripes and grumbles

Grammar and vocabulary | **Complete the sentences using the words given.**

1. My brother loves anchovies.
   He can't _get me to try one_ .
   (get / try one)

2. My father is pretty strict.
   He always _____ .
   (have / come home early)

3. My parents want me to be a pianist.
   They _____ .
   (make / practice every day)

4. My sister is always watching TV.
   She never _____ .
   (let / have the remote)

5. My daughter is always on her cell phone.
   She always _____ .
   (want / pay the bill)

6. My parents never have enough time to cook.
   They often _____ .
   (ask / prepare dinner)

7. My kids don't like to clean.
   They rarely _____ .
   (help / wash the dishes)

8. My grandfather can't hear very well.
   He always _____ .
   (tell / speak louder)

3 About you

Grammar | **Complete these sentences with true information.**

1. My parents want me _to go to a really competitive college_ .

2. My best friend often asks me _____ .

3. Our English teacher sometimes has us _____ .

4. I always tell my friend _____ .

5. I can't get my family members _____ .

6. Parents shouldn't let their kids _____ .

7. My friends sometimes help me _____ .

8. I can't make my parents _____ .

9. My mom always has me _____ .

10. I'm always telling my friend _____ .

Lesson B — Family memories

1 My family tree

Vocabulary Look at Kelly's family tree. Then complete the sentences with the words in the box.

aunt	brother-in-law	great-grandmother	✓immediate	niece	stepmother
blended	cousin	half brothers	nephew	stepdaughter	uncle

1. My sister, Melissa, is the most talented member of my _____immediate_____ family. She's a great musician.

2. My mother's sister, Jessica, is my _____ . I'm Jessica's favorite _____ .

3. Jessica's husband, Max, is my mother's _____ and my _____ .

4. Max and Jessica's son, Evan, is my _____ .

5. Evan is my mother's only _____ .

6. My parents got divorced when I was 12. My father later married Helena. She's my _____ .

7. My father and his second wife had twin boys, Keith and Noah. They're my _____ .

8. With Helena, Keith, and Noah, I grew up in a _____ family.

9. Helena has a daughter from her first marriage. Her name is Kristen. She's my father's _____ .

10. My _____ , Irene, is the oldest member of my extended family. She's my grandmother's mother.

28

2 When I was a kid, . . .

Grammar and vocabulary | Complete the conversation with *used to* or *would* and the verbs given. Sometimes more than one answer is possible.

Tia   Hi, Mom. What are you looking at?

Mom   I'm looking at some old pictures from when I was a kid.

Tia   Cool. Who's this boy?

Mom   That's my friend Jay. He _used to live_ next door to me.
(live)

We _'d spend / used to spend_ every day together in the summer.
(spend)

Tia   Really? Doing what?

Mom   We _____ to ride bikes.
(love)

We _____ our lunches and spend the whole day riding in the woods.
(bring)

Tia   Cool. What else?

Mom   Well, we _____ fishing, and my mom _____ whatever
(go)   (always cook)

fish we caught.

Tia   It sounds like you had a lot of fun.

Mom   We did. We _____ an old black-and-white TV, and we _____
(have)   (watch)

horror movies all the time.

Tia   Black-and-white TV? You mean you didn't have a color TV?

Mom   No, we didn't. And we didn't have remotes, either.

Tia   Wow. I can't even imagine!

3 About you

Grammar | Are these sentences true or false for you? Write *T* (true) or *F* (false). Then correct the false sentences.

1. _F_   When I was a kid, I used to go to the movies on Saturdays.
      I didn't use to go to the movies on Saturdays. I would play with my brother.

2. ____   Our neighbors used to have a pet rabbit.
      _____

3. ____   I used to hate pizza.
      _____

4. ____   My parents used to make me go to bed before 9:00.
      _____

5. ____   I used to ride my bike to school every day.
      _____

6. ____   My family used to live in a small house in the country.
      _____

Lesson C / If you ask me, . . .

1 What's your opinion?

Conversation strategies | Read the news items. Then write your opinions using the expressions in the box.

| I don't think | If you ask me, | It seems to me (that) |
| I think | It seems like | |

The percentage of obese children and adolescents has tripled in the last 30 years.

1. *If you ask me, children and adolescents don't exercise enough these days.*

Learning a language after age 14 is not required in British schools.

2. _____

Surveys show South Korean teens get a new cell phone every year.

3. _____

Most Japanese high schools don't allow their students to hold part-time jobs.

4. _____

Russia has one of the world's highest divorce rates.

5. _____

North American children are spending more time on their computers than they do outside.

6. _____

2 I agree.

Conversation strategies **Follow the instructions and complete the conversations. Use the expressions in the box.**

Absolutely.	✓I agree with you.	That's true.
Definitely.	Oh, I know.	You're right.

1. **Bruno** I think there's a lot of pressure on young couples these days.

   You _I agree with you._
   (Tell Bruno you agree.)

   Bruno They work longer hours and still don't make much money.

   You _____
   (Tell Bruno you're in definite agreement.)

2. **Salma** If you ask me, our teachers give us too much homework.

   You _____ I never have any time to spend with my family.
   (Tell Salma you're in absolute agreement.)

   Salma And we never get a break. We even get homework over school vacations.

   You _____
   (Tell Salma she's right.)

3. **Ciara** It seems like a lot of elderly people live alone.

   You _____
   (Tell Ciara her information is true.)

   Ciara It's terrible when families don't spend time with their elderly relatives.

   You _____
   (Tell Ciara you know.)

3 Don't you agree?

Conversation strategies **Your friend is telling you his or her opinion. Agree and give an appropriate response.**

1. I think even little kids need cell phones these days.

   Definitely. I think they're good in an emergency.

2. If you ask me, movie tickets cost too much.

   _____

3. It seems to me that people eat too much fast food.

   _____

4. I think everyone should learn a second language.

   _____

5. I don't think people take enough vacation time.

   _____

1 Gripes from a stay-at-home dad

Reading | **A** Read the posts on a social network. What kind of thread is it?

☐ academic   ☐ news   ☐ personal   ☐ travel

Mark's Page

Mark Santos

What a day! I'm exhausted. I had to nag the kids to get them to help me around the house and clean up because their five cousins are coming for dinner. My brother and sister-in-law are going out for their anniversary. Can you imagine – eight kids for dinner? Also, my aunt wants to come over to see all her great-nieces and -nephews. To top it all off, my wife, Laura, is away on a business trip, so I have to do all the cooking myself. Any ideas for what to make?

One hour ago

Mei-ling Lee   Why don't you ask Laura? She's the best cook! Can you get in touch with her?

One hour ago

Mark Santos   Right, Mei-ling. Well, right now she's on a flight to Beijing. Before she got this new job, we used to make dinner together most nights. Now that she's working longer hours and traveling more, I guess it's more up to me.

45 minutes ago

Ann Wilkerson   Here's an idea: when our kids were younger, we used to make tacos. The kids can help you get everything ready, and then they can make their own. You just need to get everyone to help.

30 minutes ago

Mark Santos   Thanks, Ann. That's a great idea. I'll call my brother and have him do some shopping on the way here. I'll get the hang of being a stay-at-home dad pretty soon. Laura's happy traveling, and I'm more of a homebody, so I think it'll work out.

20 minutes ago

B Look at the words and expressions. Find them in the posts, and choose the correct meaning.

1. nag __b__   a. talk loudly   b. ask a lot of times   c. laugh quietly
2. great-niece ____   a. your favorite niece   b. your niece's mother   c. your niece's daughter
3. to top it all off ____   a. the last problem is   b. fortunately   c. one good thing is
4. get the hang of ____   a. stop   b. understand   c. dislike
5. homebody ____   a. someone who doesn't   b. a housekeeper   c. a personal chef
                       like to go out

C Read the posts again. Then answer the questions.

1. How many children does Mark have?
2. How many kids are coming for dinner?
3. Why is his aunt coming over?

4. Who used to do the cooking?
5. What is Mark going to make?

32

2 Lessons learned

A Read the journal entry. Then complete the sentences with the expressions in the box.

| In those days | Nowadays | Today | When I was a kid |

> *March 8*
>
> *I just bought some lemonade from some kids on the corner near my apartment. It brought back so many memories! _____ , I used to make lemonade with my brother. We'd set up a stand in front of our house and sell the lemonade to people walking down the street. _____ , we didn't worry about money, and we drank more lemonade than we sold. _____ , I still remember the lesson that experience taught me – don't drink your profits! I don't think we ever made any money, but it sure was a lot of fun. _____ we have air conditioning, but I still like a cold cup of lemonade on a hot day.*

**B Write a journal entry about a childhood memory you remember clearly.
Use the expressions from part A.**

_____
_____
_____
_____
_____
_____
_____
_____
_____

Unit 4 Progress chart

What can you do? Mark the boxes. ☑ = I can . . . ? = I need to review how to . . .	To review, go back to these pages in the Student's Book.
Grammar ☐ use *let*, *make*, *have*, *get*, *want*, *ask*, *tell*, and *help*.	34 and 35
☐ use *used to* and *would* to talk about memories.	36 and 37
Vocabulary ☐ name at least 15 family members.	36
Conversation strategies ☐ give opinions with expressions like *I think* and *It seems to me*.	38
☐ use expressions like *absolutely*, *exactly*, and *you're right* to agree.	39
Writing ☐ use time markers to write about the past and the present.	41

Food choices

Lesson A / **Healthy food**

1 A bag and a can

Vocabulary | **Look at the pictures. Complete the sentences with the expressions in the box. Some expressions are used more than once.**

a bag of	a box of	a carton of	a package of
a bottle of	a can of	a jar of	

1. In the United States, you can buy
   _a bottle of___ milk or _____ milk.

2. In Thailand, you can buy _____
   curry paste or _____ curry paste.

3. In Japan, you can buy _____
   crackers or _____ crackers.

4. In Australia, you can buy _____
   asparagus or _____ asparagus.

5. In Colombia, you can buy _____
   coffee or _____ coffee.

6. In France, you can buy _____
   soup or _____ soup.

2 What did Selena buy?

Vocabulary | Look at the picture. Write what Selena bought at the grocery store.

1. _a jar of olives_
2. _____
3. _____
4. _____
5. _____
6. _____
7. _____
8. _____

3 A lot or a little?

Grammar | Carl is doing his weekly grocery shopping. Circle the best quantifier to complete each of his thoughts.

Hmm . . . we only have **a few** / (**a little**) cheese left in the refrigerator. I guess I'll get some more. And there's **not many** / **not much** butter left, either, so I'll get some of that, too. I don't think that there are **many** / **much** oranges left in the fruit bowl, and I know my roommate likes bananas, so I'll get both. He's such a picky eater. He eats **very few** / **very little** vegetables, but I should get **a few** / **a little** peppers, at least. Um . . . the ice-cream section . . . I really want to eat **fewer** / **less** ice cream, but maybe I can buy a light, fat-free kind with **fewer** / **less** calories in it. Well, I think that's all I need. . . .

4 About you

Grammar and vocabulary | Complete each sentence with true information. Use a quantifier from the box and a food word. The quantifiers may be used more than once.

a few	fewer	very few
a little	less	very little

1. There are _very few apples_ in my refrigerator.
2. I try to eat _____ every day.
3. I had _____ yesterday.
4. I'm eating _____ these days.
5. There's _____ in my cupboard.
6. I eat _____ than I used to.

1 Prepared foods

Vocabulary | There are ten ways to serve foods in the puzzle. Find the other nine.
Look in these directions (→↓).

B	A	K	E	D	X	L	Y	Q	B
A	B	L	M	A	R	R	T	E	G
R	O	A	S	T	P	A	I	P	R
B	I	C	M	R	Z	W	Y	I	I
E	L	S	M	O	K	E	D	C	L
C	E	D	C	J	E	L	M	K	L
U	D	F	R	I	E	D	P	L	E
E	Z	T	S	T	E	A	M	E	D
D	M	U	X	P	Y	R	I	D	P

2 Smoked bread?

Vocabulary | Cross out the food that is the least likely to go with the preparation.
Then replace it with an appropriate food.

1. smoked ⌐ cheese
          ⊣ turkey
          ∟ ~~bread~~ *fish*

2. raw ⌐ fish
       ⊣ ice cream
       ∟ vegetables

3. boiled ⌐ grapes
          ⊣ eggs
          ∟ potatoes

4. steamed ⌐ rice
           ⊣ milk
           ∟ pizza

5. fried ⌐ noodles
         ⊣ yogurt
         ∟ chicken

6. barbecued ⌐ noodles
             ⊣ beef
             ∟ lamb

7. pickled ⌐ cabbage
           ⊣ cucumbers
           ∟ cheese

3 Too much rice

Grammar | What's the problem? Complete the sentences with *too*, *too much*, *too many*, or *enough*.

1. Martha got <u>*too much*</u> rice and not <u>*enough*</u> meat.

2. Sheila ate _____ cupcakes!
   She often eats _____ dessert.

3. This coffee costs _____ !
   It's _____ expensive.

4. Taro drank the lemonade
   _____ fast.

5. The soup's not hot _____ .
   And there's _____ salt in it.

6. Alice didn't take the turkey out early
   _____ . Now she won't have
   _____ food for dinner.

About you

Grammar and vocabulary | Complete the questions with *too*, *too much*, *too many*, or *enough*.
Then write true answers.

1. Do you eat a lot of snacks? Do you eat <u>*too many*</u> ? <u>*I eat three snacks a day.*</u>

2. Do you eat _____ vegetables every day? _____

3. Do you ever feel _____ full after eating a meal? _____

4. Do you exercise _____ – at least twice a week? _____

5. Do you eat _____ for lunch so you don't need a snack later? _____

6. Do you ever eat meals _____ quickly and feel sick? _____

7. Do you drink _____ water – at least two liters every day? _____

8. Do you think you eat _____ fried foods? _____

1 Either way is fine.

Conversation strategies | Complete the conversation with the expressions in the box.

> either one is fine   whatever you're having
> either way is fine   ✓whichever is easier for you

Brent I'm going to cook dinner tonight, so what would you like? Chicken or steak?

Imani Well, you're the cook, so _whichever is easier for you_ .

Brent No, I want you to choose. I got to decide last night's dinner menu.

Imani Well, you know, I really like both, so _____ .

Brent OK. I'll cook the chicken. How do you want it tonight? Fried or grilled?

Imani Oh, _____ . I'm sure whatever you cook will be delicious.

Brent OK, I'll grill it. Now, what do you want to drink?

Imani Oh, _____ . You know me, anything is fine.

Brent Well, you're certainly easy to please!

Imani I try.

2 Whatever you want.

Conversation strategies | Imagine you are at a friend's house. Respond to each question appropriately to let your friend decide.

Friend Do you want to eat out or get takeout later tonight?

You _Oh, I don't care. Whatever you prefer._

Friend OK, let's go out. Do you prefer Mexican or Indian food?

You _____

Friend Well, I know this great Mexican restaurant. I'll make reservations. 7:00 or 8:00?

You _____

Friend Oh, let's make it 7:30. Now, should we drive or take the subway?

You _____

Friend Well, driving is easier, so should we take your car or mine?

You _____

Friend All right. I'll drive. Now, would you like something to drink? Tea? Coffee?

You _____

3 ▸ I'm OK for now.

Conversation strategies | **Use polite refusal expressions to complete the conversation.**

Peggy Would you like some more iced tea?

Nora _No, thanks. Maybe later._ I've got enough here.

Peggy Gosh, there were a lot of fries here. I still have some left. Would you like a few?

Nora _____ I'm trying to cut down on things like fries. You didn't have much salad. Take some of my carrots.

Peggy _____ You know, they have the best chocolate cake here. You should try some.

Nora _____ I'm trying to eat less sugar, too.

Peggy Oh. Well, are you going to have coffee?

Nora _____

4 ▸ Let's have some . . .

Conversation strategies | **Respond to each question by politely refusing or letting the other person decide.**

1. Let's have some ice cream. Would you like vanilla or strawberry?

   Either one is fine. Whatever you're having.

2. I'm getting hungry. Do you want something to eat?

3. There's cake and cookies for dessert. Which would you like?

4. I'm going to bake a pie. Do you prefer apple or peach?

5. I'm taking you to lunch today! Would you like Italian or Thai?

1 Food alternatives

Reading | **A** Read the article. Circle the helpful foods and products that are mentioned.

DOUBLE DUTY

Did you know that you have a personal beauty spa right in your refrigerator? And did you know that for easy fix-it projects around your home, you simply need to look at your grocery list for help? Here are some ways to make your groceries do double duty.

Hair and face care

BRIGHTER EYES Were you up all night studying for a test, and now it's morning, and your eyes are tired and puffy? Take a few slices of a cold cucumber, and place them over your eyes. Leave them on for about 5 to 10 minutes. Good-bye puffiness, good morning bright eyes!

CLEARER SKIN Uh-oh. You've got a date this weekend, and you just woke up with a pimple! Take a little toothpaste – not too much – and put it on the pimple. Leave it on for at least 5 minutes. Repeat daily if necessary. By Saturday night, your date won't notice a thing!

LIGHTER HAIR Do you want some summer highlights and can't afford a hair salon? The next time you're going out in the sun, squeeze some fresh lemon juice into a bowl, and comb it through your hair.

Fix-it projects

WATER STAINS Did you leave a cold glass of water on a wooden table overnight, and now there's a ring on it? You can't make it disappear, but you can lighten it considerably – with

toothpaste. Mix equal parts toothpaste and baking soda, and then rub the mixture into the wood with a damp cloth. Wipe it off with a dry cloth.

CLOGGED DRAIN Is your shower drain clogged, and now the water's taking a long time to go down? Mix equal parts salt, baking soda, and cream of tartar, and then pour it down the drain. Follow with boiling water. Leave it overnight.

Pest remedy

INSECT BITES One thing about summer you can't control is the bugs. But you can stop them from biting you. White vinegar will deter some pests. Pour some vinegar onto a cloth, and wipe over your skin. The smell goes away after the vinegar has dried, but the bugs won't like the taste of the vinegar. Reapply often.

B Read the article again. Then match the two parts of each sentence.

1. For puffy eyes, ___d___
2. To get rid of pimples, _____
3. To lighten your hair, _____
4. To treat a water stain on wood, _____
5. To unclog a drain, _____
6. To deter biting pests, _____

a. wipe vinegar on your skin.
b. put baking soda, cream of tartar, and salt in it.
c. rub toothpaste and baking soda on it.
d. place cucumber slices on them.
e. comb lemon juice through it.
f. put a little toothpaste on them.

2 Ethnic eateries

Writing | **A** Read the article about healthy eating habits in Okinawa. Add *for example*, *like*, or *such as* to introduce examples. Often more than one is correct.

Food as the Secret to Good Health

If you want to live to be 100 years old, you may want to try the Okinawan diet. People on Okinawa live a very long time. Although Okinawa is part of Japan, the diet is a little different. _____ , people eat a lot of green vegetables, _____ broccoli and green beans. In fact, about three quarters of their diet is vegetables, fruit, and whole grains. Only about 3% comes from meat, poultry, and eggs. They also eat more soybean products, _____ tofu. They don't eat many foods that have a lot of fat, _____ , cheese.

B Write an article about healthy foods that people eat in your country. Give examples using *for example*, *like*, and *such as*.

_____
_____
_____
_____
_____
_____

Unit 5 Progress chart

What can you do? Mark the boxes. ✓ = I can . . . ? = I need to review how to . . .	To review, go back to these pages in the Student's Book.
Grammar □ use quantifiers like *a little*, *a few*, *very little*, *very few*, etc.	44 and 45
□ use *too*, *too much*, *too many*, and *enough*.	47
Vocabulary □ talk about food using expressions like *a jar of*, *a can of*, *a box of*, etc.	43 and 44
□ name at least 8 different ways of serving food.	46
Conversation strategies □ respond to questions by letting another person decide.	48
□ use expressions like *No, thanks. I'm fine* to refuse an offer politely.	49
Writing □ use *for example*, *like*, and *such as* to introduce examples.	51

1 What are you doing after work?

Grammar | Circle the best verb forms to complete the conversations.

1. Ahmed   Hey, Finn. What **do you do** / (**are you doing**) after work tonight?
   Finn   I have no plans. **I just go** / **I'm just going home**.
           Why? What are you up to?
   Ahmed   Well, **I go** / **I'm going** to the gym around 5:00,
           but after that, I have no plans.
   Finn   OK. Well, maybe **I'm stopping by** / **I'll stop by** later.
   Ahmed   Sure. **I make** / **I'll make** dinner.
   Finn   Oh, no. I just remembered. **I have** / **I'm having**
           a doctor's appointment at 6:00.
   Ahmed   That's OK. **I'm waiting** / **I'll wait** for you to eat.
           Just come right over when you're done.
   Finn   All right. **I'm going to be** / **I'll be** there by 7:30.
   Ahmed   Don't be late!

2. Leah   Hi, Mom. I was just calling to let you know
          that **I take** / **I'm going to take** a 5:30 train
          this Friday.
   Mom   Great, honey. **I'm meeting** / **I'll meet** you
          at the station.
   Leah   No, that's OK. **I won't need** / **I'm not needing** you to
          pick me up. **I get** / **I'll get** a taxi.
   Mom   OK. **Do you bring** / **Are you bringing** your friend?
   Leah   Yeah. Janice **will come** / **is coming** with me.
   Mom   Oh, how nice. I can't wait to meet her!
   Leah   I'm sure **you're going to like** / **you like** her. See you
          Friday!

2 **Let me check my schedule.**

Grammar Look at Millie's weekly planner, and complete the conversation. Use the verbs in parentheses and the information from the planner.

Monday	Thursday
~~art exhibit with Jenna~~	6:30 guitar lesson, as usual
Tuesday	**Friday**
6:30 guitar lesson	plans with Heidi?
Wednesday	**Saturday** dinner with Greg
5:45 eye doctor appointment	**Sunday** 7:00 flight

Raquel   Let's have dinner together this week.

Millie   Sounds good. I'd love to catch up with you.

Raquel   How about Saturday?

Millie   Hmm . . . I can't Saturday. I <u>'m meeting / 'm going to meet Greg for dinner</u> (meet).

Raquel   Well, then, what about Thursday?

Millie   That won't work, either. I _____ (have).

Raquel   Oh, yeah, I forgot. Well, I'm free next Sunday.

Millie   Sunday I'm leaving for Dallas. My flight _____ (leave).

Raquel   And Friday?

Millie   I may have plans with Heidi.

Raquel   Oh? What are you guys doing?

Millie   I don't know. I _____ (call) on Friday to see what's up.

Raquel   OK. Well, then why don't *you* pick a day?

Millie   Let's see . . . Oh, Wednesday, I _____ (have). Actually, you know what? Jenna canceled our plans to see an art exhibit tonight. Do you want to go?

Raquel   Sure. I _____ (go) with you!

3 **About you**

Grammar Answer the questions with true information.

1. What are you going to do tonight?

    _____

2. Are you doing anything special this weekend?

    _____

3. Do you have any appointments this month? If yes, who with?

    _____

4. Who are you having dinner with tomorrow night?

    _____

5. What do you think you'll do when you finish this exercise?

    _____

|

1 Make up your mind.

Vocabulary **A** Complete the *make* and *do* expressions. Use the definitions to help you.

1. make a ___living___ = work to earn money
2. make a good _____ = make someone think of you positively
3. make a _____ = make a positive change
4. do your _____ = try your hardest
5. make up your _____ = decide
6. make _____ of = make jokes about and laugh at
7. make _____ = make certain
8. make a _____ = get something wrong
9. do the _____ = figure out the numbers
10. make _____ = seem logical

B Complete the conversations with the *make* and *do* expressions from part A.

1. A Which computer are you going to get?
   Did you ___make up your mind___ ?

   B No. I can't decide. I like this one, but it's expensive.

   A Well, buy the best you can afford.
   It doesn't _____ to buy a cheap one.

   B Yeah, you're right. I need to _____
   and look at all the numbers before I decide.

2. A Are you all prepared for your interview? You look
   great. I'm sure you'll _____ .

   B Thanks. I really want this job with the children's
   charity. I've always wanted to _____
   in people's lives. I know it's not well paid, but it's how
   I want to _____ .

   A Well, good luck. You'd better leave now
   to _____ you get there on time.

3. A I have to give a presentation to the class today.
   I'm so afraid I'll _____ and say
   something wrong.

   B Well, just _____ , and I'm sure
   everything will be fine.

   A I know. I'm just scared that the other students
   will _____ me.

2 Let's ask Daphne.

Grammar | Circle the best expression to complete each sentence.

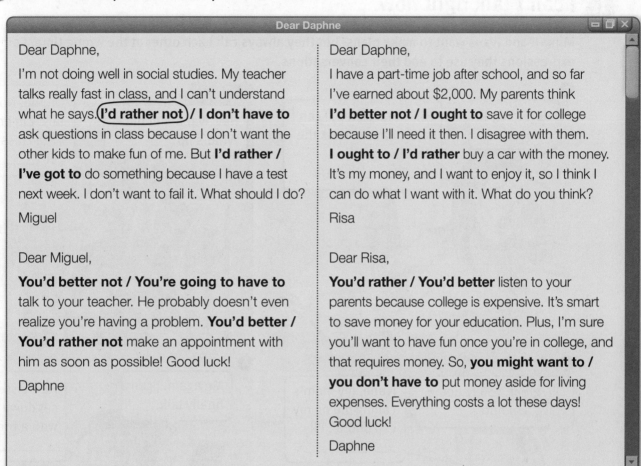

Dear Daphne

Dear Daphne,

I'm not doing well in social studies. My teacher talks really fast in class, and I can't understand what he says. (**I'd rather not**) / **I don't have to** ask questions in class because I don't want the other kids to make fun of me. But **I'd rather / I've got to** do something because I have a test next week. I don't want to fail it. What should I do?

Miguel

Dear Miguel,

You'd better not / You're going to have to talk to your teacher. He probably doesn't even realize you're having a problem. **You'd better / You'd rather not** make an appointment with him as soon as possible! Good luck!

Daphne

Dear Daphne,

I have a part-time job after school, and so far I've earned about $2,000. My parents think **I'd better not / I ought to** save it for college because I'll need it then. I disagree with them. **I ought to / I'd rather** buy a car with the money. It's my money, and I want to enjoy it, so I think I can do what I want with it. What do you think?

Risa

Dear Risa,

You'd rather / You'd better listen to your parents because college is expensive. It's smart to save money for your education. Plus, I'm sure you'll want to have fun once you're in college, and that requires money. So, **you might want to / you don't have to** put money aside for living expenses. Everything costs a lot these days! Good luck!

Daphne

3 About you

Grammar | Write true sentences about these topics.

1. something you've got to do this week
   I've got to make up my mind about a summer job.

2. something you'd better do before next week
   _____

3. two things you don't have to do this week
   _____

4. something you feel you ought to do this year
   _____

5. something you'd rather do now instead of homework
   _____

6. three things you're going to have to do tomorrow
   _____

1 I can't talk right now.

Conversation strategies | Ming-li and Ivana want to make plans, but they always call each other at the wrong time. Complete the expressions they use to end their conversations.

1 Hey, Ming-li. It's Ivana.

Hi, Ivana. Listen, I can't talk. I have to walk the dog. I've got _to go_ .

2 Hey, Ivana. I'm back. What's up?

Oh, no. Now I can't talk. I'm going to my yoga class. I've got to get _____ .

3 Oh, great, you're home. Have a minute?

Ivana, my mom's calling me on my cell phone. I'll _____ .

4 Me again. I can finally talk.

Hey. Listen, I just sat down to dinner with a friend. I'd _____ .

5 Hey. I just got back from dinner.

Ivana, it's midnight! Can I _____ tomorrow morning?

6 So, I got tickets to Friday's concert. Do you want to go?

Sure! Listen, call me Friday. I'm going _____ . I have a meeting.

2 Talk to you later!

Conversation strategies **Circle the best response. Then write the shorter form.**

1. A Oh, hi. Can I call you back later?
   B *Sure. Talk to you later.*
   a. Sure. I'd better go.
   (b.) Sure. I'll talk to you later.

2. A I'm really sorry. I've got to go out in two minutes.
   B _____
   a. No problem. I've got to go, too. Bye.
   b. No problem. I'm not busy.

3. A Let's talk tomorrow.
   B _____
   a. OK. Now's a good time.
   b. OK. I'll catch you later.

4. A Well, anyway, I'd better go.
   B _____
   a. OK. I'll see you later.
   b. OK. I can't talk right now.

5. A I'm so glad you called. It was fun to catch up.
   B _____
   a. Yeah, I'll call you later.
   b. Yeah, it was nice talking to you, too!

6. A I'd better go. I'm late.
   B _____
   a. That's OK. I'm free now.
   b. That's OK. I'd better go, too.

3 The end?

Conversation strategies **Imagine you're trying to leave your house to go to your English class, but four friends call you. Try to end each conversation. Then use a "friendly" good-bye.**

1. Liliana Hi, it's me. Listen, I have a problem. Do you have some time to talk?
   You *Not really. I've got to go to English class. Can I call you back?*
   Liliana OK.
   You *Talk to you later.*

2. Hans Hi, it's Hans. Are you busy right now? I need to ask you a question.
   You _____
   Hans No problem.
   You _____

3. Doug Hey! Guess what? I have some exciting news for you!
   You _____
   Doug Fine. Call me when you get home later.
   You _____

4. Louisa Hi! It's Louisa. I didn't understand the homework. Did you?
   You _____
   Louisa All right. Well, maybe we can meet in the library tomorrow.
   You _____

1 Getting organized

Reading | **A** Read the article. Then add the correct heading to each section.

Save money   Save space   Save time

$ $ $ $ $ $ $ $ $ Tips that $ave $ $ $ $ $ $ $ $ $ $

Whether your schedule is crazy, your apartment is cluttered, or your budget is mismanaged, here are some tips to get more organized.

[_____]

Do you find it difficult to find really good birthday presents because you wait until the last minute? And then do you spend hours in the stores because you can't find anything you like?

Whenever you're shopping and you see a gift at a great price, buy it and put it in your closet. When a special occasion comes up and you need a gift for someone, you'll have a selection of things to choose from. You won't have to make a special trip for last-minute shopping.

Do you ever pay bills late because you lose them in all the papers and clutter in your home? Well, if you need a system for paying your bills on time, the trick is to pay them online. You can arrange to pay your bills directly from your bank account. Once you have set up online bill pay, you can either set up a reminder for yourself to pay on a certain date, or you can have your bills paid automatically.

[_____]

Magazines can take over your home before you know it. Most magazines are also available online. Save space by reading the articles online.

Or, if you like to read a print magazine and want to save an article, go online and download the article to your computer. Then read it again whenever you want.

Buy brightly colored baskets or boxes for your shelves to store smaller items neatly. Label them with their contents. Your shelves will look neater, and you'll have more space for your larger items. Hang single shelves above doorways to store things you rarely use. Place low shelves in your closet to take advantage of unused space.

[_____]

Save for a rainy day, little by little. It's easy to make progress if you give yourself a weekly allowance. Try to spend less than your allowance each week. Put the remaining money in an envelope. At the end of each month, put the money in your bank account.

It's the little habits that count. Have you added up the cost of those cappuccinos you buy every morning? If you spend $3.50 on coffee five days a week, that adds up to $910 a year! By doing without fancy drinks and making your coffee at home, you can save a bundle. You might want to try packing a lunch instead of eating at the local café, too – this habit can also save you hundreds a year.

B Find these words and expressions in the article. Match them with the definitions.

1. clutter __e__
2. the trick ____
3. take advantage of ____
4. a rainy day ____
5. count ____
6. doing without ____
7. a bundle ____

a. make use of
b. a time when you need money
c. not having
d. a lot of money
e. mess
f. make a difference
g. best thing to do

C Read the article again. Then write *T* (true), *F* (false), or *D* (doesn't say).

1. __T__ Buy gifts cheaply when you see them; you can decide who they're for later.

2. ____ You can save money if you pay your bills late.

3. ____ Downloading articles to your computer is a good way to save time.

4. ____ You can save space on your shelves if you put lots of small things into boxes.

5. ____ It's better to keep your money in an envelope than a bank.

6. ____ You should make more food at home.

2 Making room

Writing **A Read the article. Add *as long as*, *provided that*, and *unless* to link ideas. Sometimes more than one answer is possible.**

Your closet is overflowing, and you need to make room for new clothes. How do you decide what to do with all your old clothes? First, get a box and put in everything you hardly ever wear, _____ they aren't clothes for special occasions.

Give them all to a charity store _____ you have some valuable clothes you can sell. Next, use the "two-season rule." Separate your remaining clothes by season. If it's winter, put your winter clothes back in the closet. Buy some under-the-bed boxes for your off-season clothes. If it's summer, store all your sweaters under your bed, _____ the space under your bed isn't already cluttered!

B Write a short article giving advice about how to reduce clutter, save money, or save time. Try to use *as long as*, *provided that*, and *unless* to link ideas.

Unit 6 Progress chart

What can you do? Mark the boxes. ✔ = I can . . . ❓ = I need to review how to . . .	To review, go back to these pages in the Student's Book.
Grammar ☐ talk about the future using *will*, *going to*, the present continuous, and the simple present.	54 and 55
☐ use *ought to*, *have got to*, *would rather*, *had better*, etc.	56 and 57
Vocabulary ☐ use at least 12 expressions with *do* or *make*.	56
Conversation strategies ☐ use at least 5 different expressions to end a phone conversation.	58
☐ say good-bye in an informal, friendly way.	59
Writing ☐ use *as long as*, *provided that*, and *unless* to link ideas.	61

1   He's the guy . . .

Grammar | Choose the correct relative pronoun to complete each sentence. If a relative pronoun is not needed, circle the dash (—).

1. This is Andrew. He's the guy **which** /(—) I met on vacation in Florida.

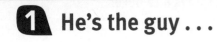

2. This is the dog **that / who** followed me on the beach one day. It turned out to be Andrew's dog. So I guess it was the dog **that / —** introduced us.

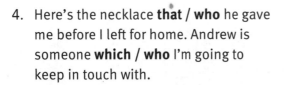

3. This is the amusement park **who / —** we went to on our first date. And this is the ticket for the first movie **that / who** we saw.

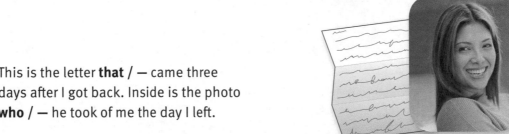

SUNSHINE CINEMA
SUMMER FUN
7:45 p.m.   Theater 8

4. Here's the necklace **that / who** he gave me before I left for home. Andrew is someone **which / who** I'm going to keep in touch with.

5. This is the letter **that / —** came three days after I got back. Inside is the photo **who / —** he took of me the day I left.

6. We talk every day. And this is the phone bill **who / that** I got yesterday!

cellular telecom   Phone Bill

EVA RODRIGUEZ

TOTAL DUE
$476.38

2 She's the girl . . .

Grammar | Complete the email with *who*, *that*, or *which*. Put the word in parentheses ( ) if the sentence is also complete without the relative pronoun. Sometimes more than one answer is possible.

New Message	▢ ▢ ☒

To: mel_bes@cup.com
From: camilleS@cup.com
Subject: Estella and Ramiro

Dear Melania,

I'm so excited about some news _(that / which)_ I just got from a friend. You know Estella, right? She's my friend from Peru _____ I met in college. Well, last year I introduced her to that cute guy, Ramiro, _____ I used to work with. He had the desk _____ was across from mine. Anyway, a group of us used to go out together sometimes after work. One day, I invited Estella along. (I knew Ramiro was exactly the kind of guy _____ she would like.) We went to the Caribbean restaurant _____ I love on Essex Street. To make a long story short, they met that night, and now they're getting married. I just got the invitation. I can't wait for the wedding!

Camille

3 I have a friend . . .

Grammar | Use the sentences in the box and *who*, *that*, or *which* to complete the sentences below. Put the relative pronoun in parentheses ( ) if the sentence is also complete without it. Sometimes more than one answer is possible.

Her family owns a store.	It served traditional Korean food.	The paper has rose petals in it.
I spoke to her in Korean.	✓ She lives in South Korea.	The shop sells handmade paper.

1. I have a friend, Seung-Li, _who / that lives in South Korea_____ .
2. I met her in Seoul at the store _____ .
3. It is a very special shop _____ .
4. I bought some paper _____ .
5. She was the only person _____ .
6. Later, she invited me to a restaurant _____ .

4 About you

Grammar | Complete the sentences with true information. Use relative pronouns where necessary.

1. I have a friend _who speaks three languages_____ .
2. My neighbor is someone _____ .
3. I like stores _____ .
4. I take a class _____ .
5. I don't like the food _____ .
6. I know someone _____ .

1 Which particle?

Grammar
and
vocabulary | **Circle the correct particle to complete each sentence.**

1. My sister's not home. She went **up /(away)/ along** for the weekend.
2. I grew **out / down / up** in Morocco, but now I live in California.
3. My brother isn't ready to settle **out / up / down**. He doesn't want to get married yet.
4. My mother's away on business now, but she plans to fly **away / along / back** next Tuesday.
5. I thought I had a doctor's appointment today, but it turns **out / up / down** that it's next week.
6. My best friend is moving **up / away / along** next month. I'm going to miss her.
7. I forgot to sign **back / out / up** for the class trip to the museum, so I can't go.
8. I sent my cousin an email last week, but he never wrote **back / away / out**.

2 Figure it out!

Grammar
and
vocabulary | **Complete the sentences with the phrasal verbs in the box. Then complete the puzzle and the sentence below.**

come back	go away	sign up	✓write back
get along	grow up	work out	

1. When a friend sends you an email, you should _write back_ immediately.
2. If a relationship doesn't _____ , don't worry about it. It may be for the best.
3. If you want to _____ well with someone, be a good friend!
4. It's good to take a break from your usual routine and _____ for a few days.
5. It's fun to go on vacation, but it's always good to _____ home, too!
6. A lot of kids _____ in blended families these days.
7. One way to meet new people is to _____ for a class.

1. _w_ _r_ _i_ _t_ _e_ | b | _a_ _c_ _k_
2. ___ ___ | | ___   ___ ___ ___
3. ___ | | ___   ___ ___ ___ ___ ___
4. ___ ___ | | ___ ___ ___
5. ___ ___ ___   ___ ___ | |
6. ___ ___ ___ | | ___
7. ___ ___ ___ ___ | | .

Some couples like to _____ _____ because they think it's fun to make up and get back together!

3 Breaking up is hard to do.

Grammar and vocabulary

Complete the conversation with the correct form of the phrasal verbs in the box. Sometimes more than one answer is possible.

✓break up	go out	turn out
get along	hang out	work out

Tina Hi, Jorge. You don't look so good. What's wrong?

Jorge Well, my girlfriend and I *broke up* last week.

Tina Oh, no. You did? That's too bad. How long were you ____________ with her?

Jorge About three months. I can't believe things didn't ____________. I mean, we ____________ really well. I thought everything was fine.

Tina Yeah, you guys were always ____________ together.

Jorge I know. We saw each other almost every day!

Tina Well, maybe that was the problem. Maybe she didn't want to spend every minute of every day with you.

Jorge Yeah, I guess you're right. Things didn't ____________ the way I thought.

Tina Why don't you talk to her? Ask her what she wants in a relationship.

4 About you

Grammar and vocabulary

Answer the questions with true information.

1. Who do you get along well with? Why?
   I get along well with my sister because we are very similar.
2. Do you like to go away for summer vacation?
   ____
3. Where do you and your friends like to hang out?
   ____
4. Do you always write back immediately when someone sends you an email?
   ____
5. Are there any classes you would like to sign up for?
   ____
6. Do you think you'll ever move far away from home?
   ____

1 I guess . . .

Conversation strategies | Rewrite each sentence with the two "softening" expressions in parentheses to complete the conversations.

1. A What's wrong with Jamil? He just yelled at me for turning on the TV.

   B _He's probably just tired._ He stayed
   He's tired. (probably / just)

   up all night. He had to finish a paper for school.

   A He always waits until the last minute to do his work.

   B I know. _____
   He's disorganized. (I guess / kind of)

   A Yeah, and he has so many activities at school.

   _____
   He's doing too much. (I think / a bit)

   B But it's good to be involved with your school.

   A That's true. _____
   He's stressed out. (I guess / sort of)

2. A Have you met Alissa yet? She's the new student in our class.

   B Yeah. I talked to her yesterday, but she didn't say much.

   A _____
   She's shy. (maybe / just)

   B Yeah, I'm sure she'll meet people soon.

   _____
   It takes time. (just / a little)

   A It's difficult when you don't know anyone.

   B I know. _____
   It's hard to fit in. (I think / sort of)

   A Yeah. _____
   Making friends is hard. (I guess / in a way)

2 It's spicy, though.

Complete the conversations with the responses in the box. Add *though* if appropriate.

He's pretty shy.	I'll find out when he's free.
He's here for two weeks.	It was a little spicy.
✓ I love Thai food.	It was really nice.

1. **Lee** How was your dinner date last night?

   Kyra Great. We went to a Thai restaurant that Wayne knows.

   Lee Cool. _I love Thai food._____ What did you have?

   Kyra Green curry with chicken and a vegetable dish.

   Lee Was it good?

   Kyra Yeah, the food was excellent. _____
   I don't usually like spicy food, but I really enjoyed it.

   Lee Was it expensive?

   Kyra Well, it was a little expensive. _____

2. **Becky** Brad, who's the new guy in your department?

   Brad Oh, that's Bart. He's just visiting from the Los Angeles office. _____

   Becky Only two weeks? That's too bad. He seems interesting.

   Brad Yeah. _____ He's probably kind of lonely.

   Becky Well, maybe we should invite him to dinner. Then we could show him around a little before he leaves.

   Brad That sounds like a great idea. _____

3 About you

Use true information to answer each set of questions. Respond to the first question using "softening" comments. Then respond to the second question using *though*.

1. What's something you're bad at? What's something you're good at?
   I guess I'm kind of bad at playing tennis. I'm really great at playing chess, though.

2. What's your worst quality? What's your best quality?
   _____

3. What's difficult about learning English? What do you like about learning English?
   _____

4. What annoying habit does one of your friends have? What's nice about him or her?
   _____

5. What's your least favorite kind of music? What's your favorite kind?
   _____

1 Interactive communities

Reading | **A** Read the article. What topics are discussed? Check (✓) all that apply.

☐ dating sites ☐ meeting people offline ☐ phone apps ☐ social networking

---

Using the online world to go offline

With our ability to connect to almost anyone in the world at any time, are we feeling more alone than ever? That's the question that critics of technology are asking. Some research suggests that people who use the Internet and social networks a lot often feel isolated and lonelier than people who don't. Supporters of online socializing disagree and point out that it's up to the user whether or not an online relationship becomes a meaningful, face-to-face one. After all, social networks, Internet companies, and app developers are merely doing their job – connecting users online. The next steps from online to offline are for us, the users, to take.

In fact, social networking websites often give us all the tools we need to move easily from an online relationship to an offline one. For example, there are websites that organize groups around particular interests. Perhaps you've just moved to a new city and want to meet people who have the same interests as you. You can sign up on websites that help you find others who enjoy the same hobbies. Many of these groups

plan face-to-face activities. It's a great way to connect with people you would never meet otherwise. There's no guarantee that you'll get along, but at least you'll have something in common.

Apps for cell phones or tablets can also help us connect with people offline in several ways. Some apps let you find friends nearby, find out what they are doing, and who's available to hang out. Other apps help you plan activities. You can send an invitation to friends electronically and include details about the activity, maps, and directions for how to get there. The people you invite can respond in the same way. There are also apps that recommend where you can meet people, for example, at restaurants or museums.

Technology doesn't have to isolate us. There are plenty of websites and phone apps that help us create social networks, both online and in real life. The trick is to make the effort. At some point, we have to pull our attention away from the screen in order to actually meet someone.

B Read the article again. Are the sentences true, false, or is the information not given? Write *T* (true), *F* (false), or *D* (doesn't say).

1. People who spend too much time online can feel lonely. ___T___

2. The writer suggests that social networks are to blame for people's loneliness. ___F___

3. Websites that are for people with similar interests connect people that get along. ___F___

4. If you sign up for a website that organizes face-to-face activities, you'll meet new people that you like. _____

5. Most people only want to use websites and apps to find dates, not to find friends. ___F___

6. Technology can improve your relationships with your circle of friends. ___F___

2 Common ground

Writing **A Read the email. Then complete the sentences with *both*, *both of us*, or *neither of us*.**

New Message

To: mitch_88@cup.com
From: PhilJ@cup.com
Subject: Your high school friend

Dear Mitch,

Remember me from high school? I'm the guy who sat behind you in world literature class. I got your email address from Kurt, the guy we ____*both*____ used to hang out with at lunchtime.

I'll always remember that class. _____ hated reading those short stories, but we had to take the class for some reason. And _____ liked our teacher, Mr. What's-his-name. He wasn't a very good teacher at all. It's amazing that we _____ passed the final exam. Good thing we _____ stayed up late studying the night before.

Anyway, I was talking to Kurt last week, and _____ would like to see you again. Maybe we can all meet and go out for dinner or something one day soon.

Take care,
Phil

B Write an email to an old friend you haven't seen in a long time. Include things you did and didn't have in common.

New Message

To: buddy1@cup.com
From: buddy2@cup.com
Subject: Long time no see!

_____

_____

_____

_____

Unit 7 Progress chart

What can you do? Mark the boxes. ✔ = I can . . . ? = I need to review how to . . .	To review, go back to these pages in the Student's Book.
Grammar ☐ write sentences with subject and object relative clauses.	66 and 67
☐ use phrasal verbs like *grow up*, *get along*, and *break up*.	68 and 69
Vocabulary ☐ use at least 12 phrasal verbs.	68 and 69
Conversation strategies ☐ use at least 6 expressions to soften comments.	70
☐ give a contrasting idea using *though*.	71
Writing ☐ use *both*, *both of us*, and *neither of us*.	73

What if?

Lesson A / Wishes

 When you wish . . .

Grammar **A** What are these people wishing for right now? Complete the sentences.

1. James _wishes he had a new car_ .

2. Emi and Sue _____ .

3. Joey _____ .

4. Esteban and Pilar _____ .

5. Al _____ .

6. Li-ming _____ .

B Complete the sentences about the people in part A.

1. If James ___had___ (have) more money, he ___would buy___ (buy) a new car.

2. If Emi and Sue _____ (live) in a bigger apartment, they _____ (have) more space.

3. If Joey _____ (be) taller, he _____ (score) more points.

4. If Esteban and Pilar _____ (have) two TVs, they _____ (not have) to watch the same TV shows.

5. If Al _____ (not be) a bad cook, he _____ (eat) better.

6. If Li-ming _____ (live) in the country, she _____ (be) much happier.

2 About you

Grammar | **Write true sentences about your wishes.**

=== **My Wish List** ===

1. I wish I _had more free time during the week_ . (have)
   If I _had more free time during the week, I'd exercise more_ . (have)

2. I wish I _____ . (be)
   If I _____ . (be)

3. I wish I _____ . (can)
   If I _____ . (can)

4. I wish I _____ . (not be)
   If I _____ . (not be)

5. I wish my parents _____ . (not be)
   If they _____ . (not be)

6. I wish my friend _____ . (be)
   If he or she _____ . (be)

7. I wish I _____ . (have)
   If I _____ . (have)

8. I wish I _____ . (not have to)
   If I _____ . (not have to)

9. I wish I _____ . (live)
   If I _____ . (live)

1 If I had a problem, . . .

Vocabulary | Circle the correct word to complete each sentence. Then decide if each sentence is true or false for you. Write *T* (true) or *F* (false). Correct the false statements.

1. __*F*__ If I had a problem, I would talk **for** / (**to**) / **about** my best friend.
   If I had a problem, I would talk to my Aunt Lisa.

2. _____ I always apologize **about** / **to** / **for** my mistakes.
   _____

3. _____ My friends never thank me **for** / **about** / **with** helping them.
   _____

4. _____ I always worry **for** / **about** / **from** taking tests!
   _____

5. _____ I often share books **to** / **with** / **about** my neighbors.
   _____

6. _____ If I forgot **with** / **from** / **about** a friend's birthday, I would feel bad.
   _____

2 Remind me about it.

Vocabulary | Complete the conversations with the words in the box.

ask for	✓ forget about	remind about	worry about
borrow from	lend to	talk to	
buy for	pay for	think about	

1. A Where's Marissa? I hope she didn't __*forget*__ __*about*__ our party.
   B I know. Let's call her and _____ her _____ it.

2. A Oh, no. I forgot my wallet. Can I _____ some money _____ you for lunch?
   B Oh, don't _____ _____ it. I'll get lunch. It's my treat!

3. A Do you think I should _____ this camera _____ my sister's birthday?
   B Why don't you _____ _____ her about it first?

4. A Can you _____ ten dollars _____ Lenny to buy a movie ticket?
   B I'm sorry. I can't. I have just enough to _____ _____ my own ticket.

5. A I think we're lost. Should we _____ someone _____ directions to the museum?
   B Not yet. I'm sure if I _____ _____ it for a minute, I'll remember how to get there.

3 Would you ask for an autograph?

Grammar | **Complete the questions with the correct form of the verbs.**

1. What _would you say_ (say) if you ___met___ (meet) a famous athlete?
   Would you ask (ask) for an autograph?

2. If you _____ (see) an accident, what _____ (do)?
   _____ (call) for an ambulance?

3. What _____ (do) if you _____ (have) a large spider
   on your leg? _____ (scream)?

4. If you _____ (break) your best friend's camera, how
   _____ (feel)? _____ (offer) to replace it?

5. How _____ (react) if your best friend _____ (win)
   a trip to Hawai'i? _____ (feel) jealous?

6. What _____ (say) to your neighbors if they
   _____ (complain) about your music? _____ (apologize)?

4 About you

Grammar | **Answer the questions in Exercise 3. Write true information.**

1. _If I met a famous athlete, I'd say, "I really admire you!"_
   I would definitely ask for an autograph.
   _____

2. _____
   _____
   _____

3. _____
   _____
   _____

4. _____
   _____
   _____

5. _____
   _____
   _____

6. _____
   _____
   _____

1 I'd choose . . .

Conversation strategies Complete the conversation with the expressions in the box. Sometimes more than one answer is possible.

✓ if I were you, I'd	I would	I wouldn't	you could	you might want to

Serge I really want to take a vacation this summer, but I need to work, too.

Nina Well, *if I were you, I'd* take a vacation first. You might not get another chance.

Serge Hmm. Maybe I should. Where's a good place to go – any ideas?

Nina Well, there are so many great places. I mean, _____ go anywhere. Have you been to Europe?

Serge No. I'd love to. It's kind of expensive, though.

Nina Well, _____ let that stop you! Seriously, you can always get a job there. There are programs for students who want to work abroad. _____ find out about them if I were you.

Serge I never thought of that.

Nina _____ look on the Internet and do a little research.

Serge Yeah. That's a great idea. So, I could work *and* take a vacation.

2 Good advice

Conversation strategies Grace is having a bad day. Respond to her statements with advice.

1. **Grace** I didn't do very well on my math exam.
   You *If I were you, I'd talk to the teacher.*

2. **Grace** Ouch! I just got a bad paper cut.
   You _____

3. **Grace** Oh, no! My car won't start.
   You _____

4. **Grace** I just stained my favorite sweater.
   You _____

3 You might want to . . .

Conversation strategies | Look at the pictures. Complete the advice.

1 You look tired. *I would get some coffee* .

2 The sun's really strong. I _____ .

3 It's very windy. If _____ .

4 It's very cold. You _____ .

4 That would be fun.

Conversation strategies | Respond to each sentence with *That would be* and an appropriate adjective.

1. I'd really like to hike in the Himalayas.   *Wow. That would be awesome!*

2. Maybe we could go to the mall this afternoon.   _____

3. It would be great to win a million dollars.   _____

4. One day, I'm going to learn to tango.   _____

1 What do you regret?

Reading **A** Read the article about regrets. According to the article, which of the following factors affect how people regret things in life?

☐ age   ☐ climate   ☐ culture   ☐ gender   ☐ health   ☐ income

Regrets? Too few to mention

Do you ever lie awake at night with regrets? Do you spend hours wishing you could change your life? _5_ If so, you're not alone. Regret – that negative feeling you have after a bad experience – is a fairly common human emotion. However, recent research suggests that while almost everyone experiences regret at some point or another, it is much more negative for some than for others.

What do we regret? According to research, we tend to regret decisions we made about our education, careers, romance, and parenting. We feel bad about things we did. ____ We wish we had different life opportunities, could make different choices, and relive moments with different outcomes. However, the nature and impact of regrets can vary across ages, sex, and cultures.

From the research, it would seem that the most striking difference in how regret affects people is between younger and older people. Younger people tend to regret the things they actually did, whereas older people regret the things they didn't do – their missed opportunities. Older people experience regret much more negatively. ____ Younger people are more likely to see a bad

experience as an important learning opportunity. They realize they made a mistake, and they use that to guide their decisions in the future. Older people don't feel they have the same chance to correct their actions and their outcomes.

Gender and culture can also affect what and how we regret. ____ According to some research, more women may regret lost romantic opportunities and family conflicts. More men may regret their decisions around career, money, and education. In cultures that put a high value on personal choice, such as the United States, people tend to have more regrets. In cultures where the family or the community makes more decisions, people have fewer regrets. Research suggests that the more choices we have, the more possibilities we have to regret.

So, if you find yourself staring at the ceiling at 3 a.m., what can you do to turn your regret into something positive? Use it to make better choices in the future. Realize that you couldn't control everything in the past situation. Take more chances in the future. ____ And be a little easier on yourself.

B Read the article again. Then add these missing sentences to the article by writing each number in the correct blank.

1. The differences between men and women are interesting.

2. We may feel worse about the things we didn't do.

3. Have more fun.

4. It can even lead to depression in some older people.

5. Do you torture yourself thinking about your mistakes?

C Choose the correct options to complete the sentences.

1. Feeling regret is **not common** / (**normal**).
2. The feeling of regret is **worse for some** / **the same for everyone**.
3. Older people mostly regret things they **did** / **didn't do**.
4. **Younger** / **Older** people feel they are in a better position to avoid the same mistakes.
5. Regret is **more** / **less** common when people make their own decisions.
6. The article suggests that in the end, regret is **useless** / **useful**.

2 If I won the lottery, . . .

Writing **A Read the journal entry. Complete the sentences with the adverbs given and the correct verb forms.**

If I won the lottery, I __'d definitely quit_____ (definitely / quit) my job, and I _____ (probably / not work) at all! If I were a millionaire, I _____ (definitely / buy) a house on the beach and one in the mountains. If I had two houses, I _____ (definitely / invite) my family and friends to visit, but I _____ (probably / not invite) them every weekend. I'd want some time for myself. If I had more time for myself, I'd write more, and I _____ (probably / try) to publish a book. What would the title of the book be? "How to Live Like a Millionaire," of course!

B Write a journal entry about what you would do if you were a millionaire. Use *definitely* and *probably* to show degrees of certainty.

_____
_____
_____

Unit 8 Progress chart

What can you do? Mark the boxes. ☑ = I can . . . ? = I need to review how to . . .	To review, go back to these pages in the Student's Book.
Grammar ☐ use *wish* + past form of verb for wishes about the present or future.	76 and 77
☐ use *If* + past form of verb, followed by *would* / *could* + verb to talk about imaginary situations in the present or future.	76, 77, and 79
Vocabulary ☐ use the correct preposition after at least 12 verbs.	78
Conversation strategies ☐ give advice using expressions like *If I were you* and *You could*.	80
☐ use *That would be* to comment on a possibility or a suggestion.	81
Writing ☐ use *definitely* and *probably* to show degrees of certainty.	83

Tech savvy?

Lesson A / Tech support

1 I have no idea why . . .

Grammar **A** Unscramble the questions.

1. which battery / Do you know / should / buy / I / ?
   Do you know which battery I should buy?

2. they / where / are / Can you tell me / ?
   _____

3. when / you / Can you remember / it / last changed / ?
   _____

4. it / Do you have any idea / how much / costs / ?
   _____

B Unscramble the statements.

1. why / isn't / I have no idea / working / it
   _____

2. last changed it / when / I don't know / I
   _____

3. two / I / if / I wonder / should / batteries / buy
   _____

C Complete the conversation with the questions and statements from parts A and B.

Woman Excuse me. Can you help me?
 Clerk Sure. What seems to be the problem?
Woman It's my camera. _I have no idea why it isn't working._
 Clerk Hmm. Let me look at it. It might be the battery. _____
Woman No, I can't. _____ I'm not sure if I've ever changed it.
 Clerk Well, you definitely need a new one.
Woman _____
 Clerk You need a 3.7 volt battery.
Woman _____
 Clerk They're $39.99 each.
Woman Great. _____
 Clerk Sure. They're at the back of the store. Here, let me show you.
Woman Thanks. _____ Maybe I should have an extra one.
 Clerk That might be a good idea.

66

2 I wonder . . .

Grammar **A** Tara wants to download some music from the Internet. Rewrite the questions she wants to ask her friend Kwang.

1. Can you download songs from this website?
2. How do you put them on your phone?
3. Is there a charge for each song?
4. Can you buy just one song?
5. How do you pay for the songs?
6. How do you make a playlist?
7. Are there any free songs?
8. Can I put the songs on my tablet, too?

1. I wonder *if you can download songs from this website* _____ .
2. Can you tell me _____ ?
3. Do you know _____ ?
4. Do you have any idea _____ ?
5. Do you know _____ ?
6. Can you remember _____ ?
7. I wonder _____ .
8. Do you know _____ ?

B Kwang doesn't know the answers to Tara's questions. Write his replies using the expressions in the box. Use each expression twice.

I don't know	I can't remember	I have no idea	I'm not sure

1. *I don't know if you can download songs from this website.* _____
2. _____
3. _____
4. _____
5. _____
6. _____
7. _____
8. _____

1 You should put it down.

Grammar and vocabulary | Complete the sentences with the phrasal verbs in the box. Add the correct pronouns.

look up	put away	put on	take apart	throw away
print out	✓ put down	set up	take off	turn off

1. Thanks for bringing in the box of groceries. Could you _put it down_ over here?
2. I did something awful to my computer. I tried to _____ , and now I can't get all the pieces back in it.
3. I hate those sticky price labels on things you buy. I can never _____ .
4. My game controller doesn't work anymore. I wonder if I should just _____ .
5. There's nothing good on TV. Do you mind if I _____ ?
6. I just bought these new headphones. Do you want to _____ and try them out?
7. I downloaded a video-chat app, but I can't _____ .
8. I don't know what this word means. Maybe I should _____ on the Internet.
9. My brother leaves his video games all over the floor. He should _____ , or they'll get damaged.
10. After you write documents, do you _____ to read them?

2 Step-by-step

Grammar and vocabulary | Complete the conversation with the words in the box.

hook up / the computer	✓ turn down / the air conditioning
pick up / the monitor	turn on / the radio
plug in / all the cables	turn up / the volume

Ruth We found this great apartment, but it's so cold in here.

Kate Oh, I'll _turn down the air conditioning_ .
There we go. So, what do you want to do first?

Ruth Let's put some music on.
Can you _____ ?

Kate Sure. Is that loud enough?

Ruth Not really. Can you _____ ? Thanks.

Kate I'd like to _____ , so I can check my email.

Ruth OK, let's put the computer over by the window.
I'll _____ .
You get the computer and the cables.

Kate OK. You know, I have no idea where to _____ .

Ruth I'm sure we can figure it out. Do you know where the manual is?

3 What to do?

Grammar and vocabulary | Complete the conversations using the given words. Write A's suggestions in two different ways. Then use the correct pronoun in B's response.

1. A Before you go out, _put on your hat and gloves_ .
   Before you go out, _put your hat and gloves on_ .
   (put on / your hat and gloves)

   B If I get too warm, can I _take them off_ ?
   (take off)

2. A _____ in a dictionary.
   _____ in a dictionary.
   (look up / the new words)

   B Can we _____ on the Internet?
   (look up)

3. A You have to _____ gently.
   You have to _____ gently.
   (put in / the DVD)

   B If it doesn't work, should I _____ ?
   (take out)

4. A The kitchen's so messy. We should _____ .
   The kitchen's so messy. We should _____ .
   (put away / the dishes)

   B Actually, why don't we _____ ?
   (throw away)

4 About you

Grammar | Complete the questions. Then fill in the survey with true answers.

	Yes	No
1. Can you explain to someone _how to set up voice mail on a phone_ ? (how / set up voice mail on a phone)	☐	☐
2. Do you have any idea _____ on your computer? (where / plug in the headphones)	☐	☐
3. Could you tell someone _____ ? (how / use your TV remote)	☐	☐
4. Do you know _____ on the Internet? (how / look up information)	☐	☐
5. Do you have any idea _____ when your computer crashes? (what / do)	☐	☐
6. Do you know _____ on your computer? (how / change the password)	☐	☐

Lesson C / On the other hand, . . .

1 Don't you think . . . ?

Conversation strategies

A Match Cameron's opinions with her friends' responses.

1. I think kids watch too much TV. _f_

2. I think video games are totally boring and stupid. ____

3. I don't think people should drive big cars. ____

4. It's a shame no one writes letters anymore. I used to love getting them. ____

5. Kids need to spend less time on the computer. ____

6. I don't like shopping on the Internet. You can't see what you're buying. ____

a. I know what you mean, but with email, you can get in touch with people more often and faster.

b. I'm not so sure. Don't you think they can learn a lot online, too? I mean, there are some good educational websites.

c. Maybe. People with large families need to have big cars, though.

d. I don't know. I find it saves me time because I don't have to go to the store and wait in line.

e. I know what you mean, but there are so many different kinds of games. You could probably find something you liked.

f. That's true. On the other hand, kids need to relax sometimes, and we all have our favorite shows.

B Write your own responses to Cameron's opinions in part A. Use the expressions in the box if you disagree with her.

I know what you mean, but . . .	I don't know.
I'm not (so) sure. Don't you think . . . ?	✓That's true. . . . , though.
Maybe.	On the other hand, . . .

1. _That's true. I think some TV shows_
   are educational, though.

2. _____
   _____

3. _____
   _____

4. _____
   _____

5. _____
   _____

6. _____
   _____

2 What's your opinion?

Conversation strategies Write opinions about the topics. Then add an expression from the box to get someone to agree with you. Use each expression twice.

> You know what I mean?   You know?   You know what I'm saying?

1. Texting is _really convenient. But it's really annoying when you're trying to have a_ _conversation with someone who's texting at the same time. You know what I mean?_

2. Video calling is _____
   _____

3. Blogging is _____
   _____

4. Online video clips are _____
   _____

5. Tablets are _____
   _____

6. Social networking is _____
   _____

3 I don't know.

Conversation strategies Respond to each statement with a different opinion. Try to convince the other person to agree with you.

1. Kids spend too much time on the Internet.

   I don't know. I think it's great they learn how to use computers _when they're so young. You know?_

2. Teens shouldn't go to school and work at the same time. It's too hard.

   _____
   _____

3. I think too many people are addicted to their computers and phones and everything.

   _____
   _____

4. You never know if things you see on the Internet are true.

   _____
   _____

1 Spam-a-lot

A Read the article. Then check (✓) the best title.

☐ How to Be a Successful Spammer   ☐ How Companies Avoid Spam
☐ Where to Send Spam   ☐ Don't Be a Victim – How You Can Avoid Spam

Are you fed up with junk email and spam that fills up your inbox every day? Spam isn't just annoying for home users of computers. It's becoming a serious problem for businesses, too. Getting rid of spam wastes employees' time. Spam takes up space on computers, and it can slow down – or even jam – normal email traffic.

Most people don't know how spammers get their email address, but in fact, it's very easy. Your email address may be on any number of Internet sites such as blogs, email newsletters, company directories, and many other lists on the Web. You can also become a spam victim if you've entered an online contest or responded to a survey using your email address.

Spammers also use software that generates email addresses automatically. This software makes up millions of email addresses by using common names and the addresses of well-known companies and Internet service providers. It then sends out messages to all the addresses it creates. Although some of them might not work and the messages "bounce back," many others will get through to real people. The spammers now have a valuable list of valid addresses, which they can sell to other spammers at high prices.

HOW TO PROTECT YOURSELF FROM SPAM

DO:

▶ Change your email address regularly. Create an address that is difficult to guess. For example, if your name is Kevin Smith and you love cycling, try an address like KSmith4biking@cup.org. Or if you live in Toronto, you could use KS_in_Toronto@cup.org.

▶ Have two email addresses – one for public use and a private one only for friends and family.

▶ Buy anti-spam software or use email filters. Many email programs have filters that automatically send spam to a junk-mail folder. Be sure to check the junk-mail folder periodically for any personal mail that goes there by mistake.

▶ Pay attention to typos and misspellings in email subject lines. These are warning signs of possible spam.

DON'T:

▶ Respond to spam – ever. When you respond, you confirm that your address is valid.

▶ Buy anything from a company that sent you spam. This supports their belief that spamming makes money.

B Find the underlined words in the article. Then circle the best meaning.

1. Spam can <u>jam</u> normal email traffic.   a. slow down   ⓑ stop or block
2. You can become a <u>spam victim</u>.   a. someone who gets spam b. someone who sends spam
3. The software <u>generates</u> addresses.   a. creates   b. gets rid of
4. Some messages "<u>bounce back</u>."   a. get to the people   b. go back to the spammers
5. They have a list of <u>valid</u> addresses.   a. real   b. false
6. Never <u>confirm</u> your address.   a. forget   b. say it's correct

2 Get rid of it!

Writing **A** Read the list of ideas, and add an idea of your own. Then use the ideas to complete the article.

Ways to prevent spam

- Get another email address. Use one email address for chat rooms and message boards.
- Tell friends and family how to prevent spam.
- Use spam-filtering software.
- Don't respond to spam.
- _____
  _____
  _____

How to get rid of spam

First of all, keep your personal email address private. If you want to participate in chat rooms or on _message boards_ , get a second _____ from a free email provider. Second, don't _____ to spam, even when it provides a link to "unsubscribe" from the list. Spammers see that your address is valid and sell it to other spammers. Third, use the _____ on your computer. Fourth, _____ .

Finally, tell _____ about these tips. If fewer people respond to spam, there will be less spam!

B Brainstorm ideas on one of these topics. Then plan and write a short article.

- How to avoid identity theft
- How to protect yourself from theft
- How to use the Internet safely
- How to get help with computer problems

Ideas

_____
_____
_____
_____

_____
_____
_____
_____
_____

Unit 9 Progress chart

What can you do? Mark the boxes. ☑ = I can . . . ? = I need to review how to . . .	To review, go back to these pages in the Student's Book.
Grammar ☐ use questions within questions and statements.	86 and 87
☐ use *how to*, *where to*, and *what to* + verb.	88
☐ use separable phrasal verbs like *turn on* and *plug in*.	88
Vocabulary ☐ use at least 12 phrasal verbs.	88 and 89
Conversation strategies ☐ use expressions to give a different opinion.	90
☐ use expressions to get someone to agree with me.	91
Writing ☐ brainstorm and organize ideas to plan an article.	93

1 What have they been doing?

Grammar **A** What have these people been doing? What have they done? Complete the sentences using the present perfect continuous and then the present perfect.

1. Kazuo _'s been doing yard work_ (do yard work). He _'s planted_ (plant) some flowers.

2. Sienna and Lynn _have been shoping_ (shop). They _have spent_ (spend) over $500 each!

3. Lola _has been running_ (run). She _has_ just _finished_ (finish) a marathon.

4. Carmen _has been cooking_ (cook) dinner. She _has grilled_ (grill) some fish.

5. Sal and Elena _have been skiing_ (ski). They _have had_ (have) one lesson.

6. Tony _has been doing_ (do) laundry all morning. He _has washed_ (wash) three loads.

B Circle the correct word to complete each sentence.

1. Kazuo's been doing yard work **since** / **(for)** a few hours.
2. Sienna and Lynn haven't shopped online **since** / **(in)** months.
3. Lola's been running **(since)** / **for** she was in college.
4. Carmen hasn't made unhealthy food **since** / **(in)** a long time.
5. Sal and Elena have been skiing **since** / **(for)** this morning.
6. Tony's been doing the laundry **(for)** / **in** over two hours.

2 Questions, questions . . .

Grammar | Read each situation. Then use the words to write questions and answers in the present perfect continuous or the present perfect.

1. You have a friend who has been taking Spanish lessons. You ask:

    A (how long / study / Spanish) _How long have you been studying Spanish?_

    B (seven months) _I've been studying Spanish for seven months._

    A (how many words / learn) _How many words have you learned?_

    B (about 250) _I have learned about 250._

2. You meet a famous baseball player. You ask:

    A (how long / play / baseball) _How long have you been playing baseball?_

    B (18 years) _I have been playing for 18 years._

    A (how many games / win this season) _How many games have you won this season?_

    B (12 out of 15) _I have won 12 out 15._

3 About you

Grammar | A Complete the questions. Use the present perfect continuous or the present perfect.

1. What _____have_____ you _____been doing_____ (do) lately after class?
2. How many times _____have_____ you _____gone_____ (go) to the movies this month?
3. Who _____have_____ you _been hanging out_ (hang out) with recently?
4. How many times _have_ you _eaten out_ (eat out) at a restaurant this week?
5. _____Why_____ you _have been studying_ (study) a lot lately?
6. How many phone calls _____have_____ you _____made_____ (make) this week?
7. How many times _____have_____ you _____overslept_____ (oversleep) in the last month?
8. What _____have_____ you _____been thinking_____ (think) about for the last hour?
9. How many books _____have_____ you _____read_____ (read) this year?
10. _____Why_____ you _have been exercising_ (exercise) lately?

B Answer the questions in part A with true information.

1. _I've been taking guitar lessons._ I've been sleeping early.
2. _I haven't gone to the movies this month._
3. _I have been hanging out with my daughter_
4. _I haven't eaten out this week._
5. _I have been study a lot I have a test._
6. _I have made 10 phone calls this week_
7. _I haven't overslept the last month_
8. _I have been thinking about what to cook tomorrow_
9. _I have read 1 book._
10. _I have been exercising because I need_

1 Crossword puzzle

Vocabulary | Complete the crossword puzzle.

Across

2. A movie with an exciting story and lots of suspense is a <u>thriller</u> .

3. A <u>war</u> movie is about soldiers.

5. In a romantic <u>comedy</u> , two people fall in love and funny things happen.

7. A movie about a real event is called a <u>true</u> story.

9. A movie that makes you cry is called a tear<u>jerker</u> .

10. An <u>action</u> movie has a fast-moving story and is often violent.

Down

1. A <u>science</u> -fiction movie often takes place in the future.

4. A movie with cartoon characters is an <u>animated</u> movie.

6. A movie that has singing and dancing is a <u>musical</u> .

8. <u>Horror</u> movies are often scary and have monsters in them.

2 Best of Bollywood

Vocabulary | Complete Daria's blog with the words in the box.

✓comedies	endings	love story	set in	subtitled
costumes	hilarious	play	stunts	take place

Daria's Blog

Daria 12:31 p.m.

Some of my favorite movies are musicals from Bollywood, especially the romantic <u>comedies</u> . The movies are usually <u>set in</u> India, and the actors often <u>play</u> characters who fall in love. I really enjoy a good <u>love story</u> . They can sometimes be tearjerkers, but the nice thing about Bollywood movies is that they often have happy <u>endings</u>, so you leave the movie theater feeling good. Some of them are also very funny – the last one I saw was just <u>hilarious</u> Some of them are historical and <u>takes place</u> in the past. These are my favorites because the colors and the <u>costumes</u> are wonderful. The movies aren't usually in English, but they're <u>subtitled</u> so you can read while you're watching. Sometimes the movies even have fight scenes with lots of special effects and <u>stunts</u> . They're really great!

dangerous act

very funny

3 About you

Vocabulary | Write reviews of movies you've seen. Complete each sentence with the title of a movie. Then write more about each one by answering the questions.

CHOOSE A MOVIE	What type of movie is it? What's it about? Who's in it? Did you like it? Why? Why not?
1. I really enjoyed _____ <u>Les Misérables</u> .	It's a musical, and it's set in France in the 1800s. Hugh Jackman plays a man who escapes from prison. Russell Crowe is the police officer who chases him. I really enjoyed the movie. It has wonderful music, and the costumes are amazing.
2. <u>The war with Grandpa</u> is playing right now.	It's a comedy story, is about a boy that has to live with is grandfather and has to give him his bedroom. The boy will try to have his bedroom back
3. The best movie I've ever seen is <u>the pursuit of happiness</u> .	It's a drama movie, is a story about a salesman that has financial problems. He has a son and he will do the impossible to recover
4. I didn't like <u>cat woman</u> .	It's a science fiction about a woman who dies and revive by egyptian cats that gave her superpowers.

4 I still haven't see it.

Grammar and vocabulary | Complete the conversation with *already*, *still*, or *yet*.

Ann There are so many movies that I ___<u>still</u>___ haven't seen. Do you want to go see one tonight?

Gus Yeah, OK. Let's see. How about Brad Pitt's new movie? I haven't seen that ___<u>yet</u>___.

Ann Oh, I've <u>already</u> seen that one. It was good. How about the new horror movie that's out? Have you seen that <u>yet</u>?

Gus No, I don't like scary movies. I'm 25, and I <u>still</u> haven't seen a horror movie.

Ann Well, there's a new animated movie out. I haven't seen that one <u>yet</u>, either.

Gus Oh, great. Let's go. I've been dying to see it!

1 Favors

Complete the conversations with the expressions in the box.

I wanted to	I was wondering,
✓ I was wondering if I could	Would it be all right if I
I was wondering if you could	Would it be OK

1. **Victor** Hi, Raoul. What can I do for you?

   Raoul *I was wondering if I could* talk to you for a moment. Is now OK?

   Victor No problem. Come on in.

   Raoul Thanks. _____ worked from home tomorrow?

   Victor Tomorrow?

   Raoul Yes. Someone is coming to fix my stove, and I need to be home to let him in. _____ with you?

   Victor Yeah, sure. I don't see why not.

   Raoul Thanks, Victor. I really appreciate it.

2. **Dad** Hi, Josie. What's up?

   Josie Hey, Dad. _____ ask you a favor.

   Dad Sure, what is it?

   Josie Well, _____ lend me some money – if that's OK.

   Dad Hmm. It depends. How much? And for what?

   Josie Well, I was thinking, your birthday is next week, right?

   Dad Yes, it is.

   Josie So, _____ could I borrow $50 to buy you your present?

2 Can I borrow the car?

Conversation strategies

Stephanie's friend Ally is coming for a visit. Stephanie needs to ask her roommate Jenny for some favors. Look at her list, and complete each of her requests.

Things I need to do:
1. Ask Jenny if Ally can stay here.
2. Pick up Ally at airport — borrow Jenny's car.
3. See if Jenny wants to go sightseeing with us Saturday.
4. Organize a party Saturday night — check with Jenny.
5. Check Ally's return flight online — use Jenny's computer.

1. I wanted to _ask you if Ally could stay here_ .
2. I was wondering if I could _____ .
3. I was wondering, _____ ?
4. Would it be all right _____ ?
5. Would it be OK with you if I _____ ?

3 All right. What time?

Conversation strategies

Choose the best sentence to continue each conversation. Then write *A* if the speaker is agreeing, *M* if the speaker is moving the conversation along, or *U* to show the speaker understands.

1. A I'm going grocery shopping later, and I was wondering if you could come and help me.
   B ☑ All right. What time?
   ☐ That's OK.   [A]

2. A Do you have time to talk now?
   B Sure. Let me just put these papers away.
   ☐ Um, OK, I guess so.
   ☐ All right. What did you want to talk about?   ☐

3. A This pasta is delicious! Could you give me the recipe?
   B ☐ Sure. It's very easy.
   ☐ That would be OK.   ☐

4. A Can you help me with something?
   B ☐ OK. What do you need?
   ☐ That's all right.   ☐

5. A I'm leaving early today.
   B ☐ Right. I remember you have an appointment.
   ☐ OK. I think so, too.   ☐

1 Weekend favorites

Reading **A** Read the reviews. What things are reviewed? Check (✓) the boxes.

☐ a book ☐ a movie ☑ a phone app ☑ a video game ☑ a Web app

Weekend Blog

THINGS TO KEEP YOU BUSY ON WEEKENDS

1. MOVIE EFFECTIVE

With Movie Effective, you can add special effects to your videos. Simply record a video with your smartphone camera. Then add exciting effects — just like they do in the movies. <u>The app comes with two effects</u> — lightning and slow motion — but you can also buy others, like sound effects. Even though I don't usually shoot or share videos personally, I found this to be a lot of fun. So, be careful — it's addictive, and you may get totally hooked!

2. ACCUSED

I really enjoyed playing this game. It combines a science-fiction setting with great action. You are a character who is wrongly accused of a crime. You have to find out who the real criminal is and get justice. Your choices determine the storyline. <u>The action is fast-moving and there are some sad moments, so if you're very sensitive, this may not be the video game for you.</u> However, the amazing setting and the ability to create your own story make this a great game for most players.

3. RECORDYOURRUN

If you are serious about running, hiking, biking, or even skiing, and have been wondering how to keep track of your progress, this phone app is the answer. It records your pace, distance, and time, and you can save your results and compare different exercise sessions. You can set goals for each time you go out and share your progress with friends. There's also a feature that lets your friends and family follow your progress in a race on a map. This app is the perfect way to mix technology and exercise.

4. FRETENDS

FretEnds has a fabulous Web app that will teach you how to play the guitar. <u>You can</u> choose to play a real guitar or a virtual one. There are eight levels of play. If you start at the beginner level, you will learn to play "Brown Eyed Girl." You need to let the app access the microphone on your computer, so it can "hear" you play. Each song is broken down into small parts. After you've learned one part, you can move on. This app is great for everyone, <u>whether you've never played or even if you've been playing for years.</u>

B Read the article again. Write *T* (true) or *F* (false) for each sentence. Then correct the false sentences.

1. Movie Effective helps you record videos on your smartphone. ___F___
2. The special effects on Movie Effective are all free. ___F___
3. *Accused* is a romantic comedy. ___F___
4. *Accused* is suitable for everyone. ___F___
5. RecordYourRun is for people who take exercise seriously. ___T___
6. With RecordYourRun, people can see if their friends are winning a race. ___T___
7. You need to buy a guitar before you can use the FretEnds app. ___F___
8. The FretEnds app is not for experienced players. ___F___

2 Music review

A Read the music review. Complete the sentences with *although*, *even though*, or *even if* to contrast ideas. Sometimes more than one answer is possible.

_____ *Come Away With Me* was amazingly successful and really introduced Norah Jones to the world, *Little Broken Hearts* is a much better album. Most of her earlier work uses a lot of piano, but this album focuses more on the guitar, so the sound is different. _____ most of these songs are about heartbreak, the music is beautiful and sweet. _____ you don't like sad romantic songs, you will find something to enjoy in this new collection.

– *Music Scene* magazine

B Write a review of a movie, an album, or a TV show. Use *although*, *even though*, and *even if* to contrast ideas.

Unit 10 Progress chart

What can you do? Mark the boxes. ✔ = I can . . . ? = I need to review how to . . .	To review, go back to these pages in the Student's Book.
Grammar	
☐ use the present perfect and present perfect continuous.	98 and 99
☐ use *since*, *for*, and *in* with the present perfect to show duration.	99
☐ use *already*, *still*, and *yet* with the present perfect.	101
Vocabulary	
☐ name at least 6 different kinds of movies.	100 and 101
☐ talk about movies using at least 15 new words and expressions.	100 and 101
Conversation strategies	
☐ ask for a favor politely.	102
☐ use *All right*, *OK*, and *Sure* to agree to requests; *All right*, *OK*, and *So* to move a conversation to a new phase or topic; and *Right* to show I agree or understand.	103
Writing	
☐ use *although*, *even though*, and *even if* to contrast ideas.	105

It could be . . .

Grammar | Complete the sentences with the expressions in the box. Then write a second
sentence using the cues and an appropriate modal.

can't be the winners	~~may be taking a driving test~~	✓ must be learning to drive
could be taking a hard test	~~might be the best student~~	must be the winners

1. He _must be learning to drive_ .
   It could / might / may be his first lesson.
   (It / be / his first lesson)

2. He _may be taking a driving test_ .
   It could be his first lesson
   Can / must not
   (It / be / his first lesson)

3. She _might be the best student_.
   She must feel proud
   (She / feel proud)

4. She _could be taking a hard test_.
   She must be nervous
   might be
   (She / be nervous)

5. They _must be the winners_ .
   They must practice a lot
   (They / practice a lot)

6. They _can't be the winners_ .
   They must be dissappointed
   (They / be disappointed)

2 He must be crazy!

Grammar | **Circle the correct words to complete the sentences.**

1. **Mandy** What's he doing? He (must be) / can't be crazy!

   Molly He (might be) / can't be an acrobat with the circus.

   Mandy You're right. He must practice / (must be practicing) for tonight's show.

   Molly That's amazing! I mean, it (can't be) / might be easy to bend like that.

   Mandy Yeah, it (could be) / must not be painful, too.

   Molly Well, I certainly won't try that!

2. **Jason** How old is that kid? She must be / (can't be) more than five years old.

   Peter Yeah, you're right. She must not be / (might be) about four or five.

   Jason She's really good. She (must play) / must be playing *routine* every day for hours and hours.

   Peter She makes it look so easy, too. I wonder what her parents think. They could be / (must be) so proud.

   Jason Yeah, she (could be) / can't be the youngest professional piano player in the world.

3 About you

Grammar | **Think of someone you know who is not in the room with you now. Answer the questions about him or her using *must*, *may*, *might*, *could*, or *can't*.**

1. Where do you think he or she is right now? *She might be lying in bed*
   She can't be cooking.
   It's Saturday afternoon, so he might be on the golf course. He can't be at work.

2. What do you think he or she is doing?
   She might be watching T.V

3. How do you think he or she is feeling?
   She may be feeling tired.

4. What do you think he or she is wearing?
   I think, She might be wearing pajamas

5. Who do you think he or she is with?
   She must be with her husband

6. What do you think he or she is thinking about right now?
   She could be thinking about me,

1 Scrambled up

Grammar and vocabulary

A Write the adjective for each definition. You can check your answers in a dictionary. Then use the letters in the boxes to answer the question below.

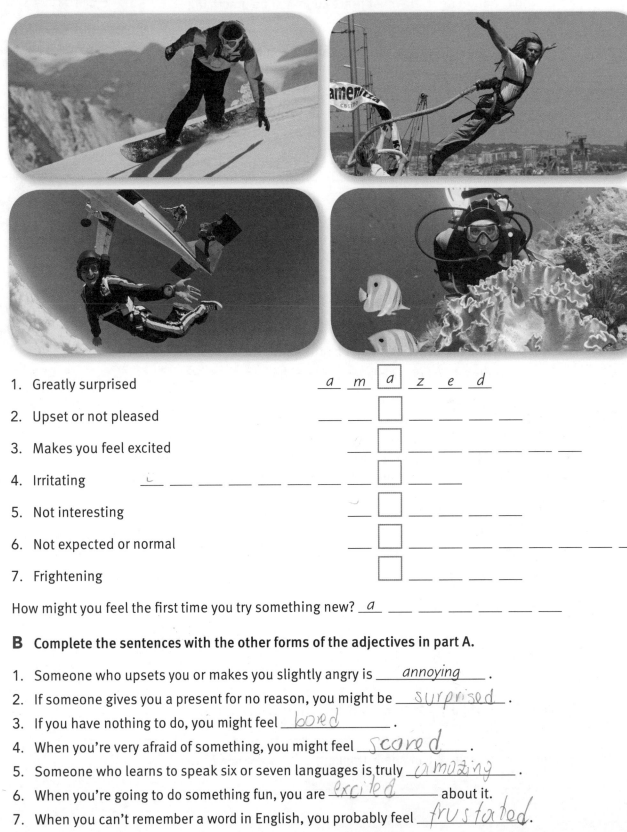

1. Greatly surprised   _a_ _m_ [_a_] _z_ _e_ _d_

2. Upset or not pleased   __ __ [ ] __ __ __

3. Makes you feel excited   __ [ ] __ __ __

4. Irritating   __ __ __ __ __ __ [ ] __ __

5. Not interesting   __ [ ] __ __ __

6. Not expected or normal   __ __ [ ] __ __ __ __ __ __

7. Frightening   [ ] __ __ __ __

How might you feel the first time you try something new? _a_ __ __ __ __ __ __

B Complete the sentences with the other forms of the adjectives in part A.

1. Someone who upsets you or makes you slightly angry is ___annoying___ .
2. If someone gives you a present for no reason, you might be ___surprised___ .
3. If you have nothing to do, you might feel ___bored___ .
4. When you're very afraid of something, you might feel ___scared___ .
5. Someone who learns to speak six or seven languages is truly ___amazing___ .
6. When you're going to do something fun, you are ___excited___ about it.
7. When you can't remember a word in English, you probably feel ___frustrated___ .

2 Good news, bad news

Grammar and vocabulary | **Complete the emails. Use the correct forms of the adjectives.**

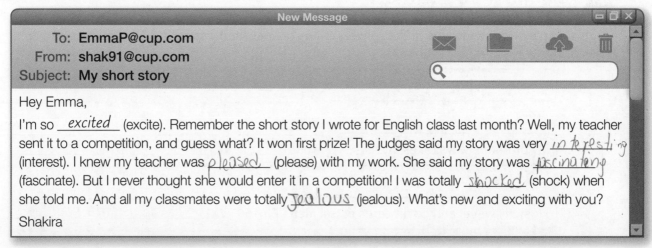

New Message

To: EmmaP@cup.com
From: shak91@cup.com
Subject: My short story

Hey Emma,

I'm so __excited__ (excite). Remember the short story I wrote for English class last month? Well, my teacher sent it to a competition, and guess what? It won first prize! The judges said my story was very _interesting_ (interest). I knew my teacher was _pleased_ (please) with my work. She said my story was _fascinating_ (fascinate). But I never thought she would enter it in a competition! I was totally _shocked_ (shock) when she told me. And all my classmates were totally _jealous_ (jealous). What's new and exciting with you?

Shakira

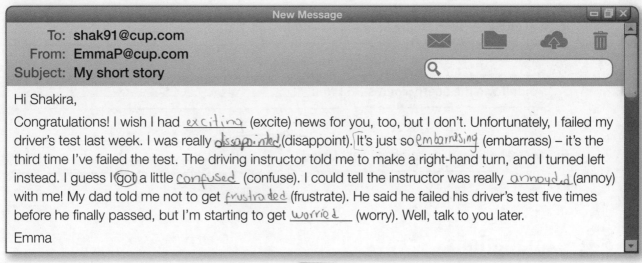

New Message

To: shak91@cup.com
From: EmmaP@cup.com
Subject: My short story

Hi Shakira,

Congratulations! I wish I had _exciting_ (excite) news for you, too, but I don't. Unfortunately, I failed my driver's test last week. I was really _disappointed_ (disappoint). It's just so _embarrassing_ (embarrass) – it's the third time I've failed the test. The driving instructor told me to make a right-hand turn, and I turned left instead. I guess I got a little _confused_ (confuse). I could tell the instructor was really _annoyed_ (annoy) with me! My dad told me not to get _frustrated_ (frustrate). He said he failed his driver's test five times before he finally passed, but I'm starting to get _worried_ (worry). Well, talk to you later.

Emma

3 About you

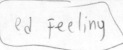
ed Feeling

Grammar and vocabulary | **How would you feel in these situations? Complete the sentences with true information.**

1. You fail a test that you have studied very hard for.
   I would feel _disappointed if I failed a test that I thought I was prepared for_ .
   It might be _embarrassing if my friends found out_ .

2. Your friend doesn't show up for a date.
   I would get _frustated because is not the first time that happened_
   I might feel _dissapointed. I had to cancel a doctor's appointment for this date_

3. You are home alone during a storm.
   I might feel _anxious. I might not prepare for this kind of situation_
   It could be _demanding because I have to move quickly to be safe_ .

4. Someone is telling you a story you've already heard ten times.
   I might feel _annoyed. This story is not funny anymore_ .
   I would probably think _that the situation is embarrased because I'm not laughing_

1 You must be excited.

Conversation strategies | Complete the responses in the conversations to show understanding. Use *must be* and an adjective.

1. I'm learning how to design a website. | *That must be hard* .

2. My brother always takes my stuff. | That <u>must be annoying</u> .

3. I lost my wallet and credit cards at the mall. | You <u>must be shocked</u> .

4. I'm going to climb Mount Rainier next month. | You <u>must be excited</u> .

5. I didn't win the poetry contest. | You <u>must be sad</u> .

6. My ex-boyfriend is dating my best friend. | That <u>must be dissapointing</u> .

2 Explanations

Conversation strategies | Complete the conversation with *you see* or *I see*, or leave a blank where neither one is appropriate.

Walt Hi, Reg. I'm sorry I'm late. I didn't hear my alarm.
<u>You see</u> , I was working on my report until about 3:30 this morning.

Reg Uh-huh, <u>I see</u> . So, will it be ready for the meeting with the boss?

Walt _____ Yes. I just have to make some copies. What time is the meeting?

Reg Well, it was at 11:00, but the boss called me about half an hour ago, and it's now at 2:30. She's meeting someone for lunch, <u>you see</u> , and she has to leave at 11:30.

Walt Oh, <u>I see</u> . So, I guess I didn't have to rush.

Reg Well, at least it's all done now, and you can relax.

3 An author in Paris

Complete the conversation with the expressions in the box. Use each expression twice.

I see	that must be	you must be	you see

Akina Hey, Omar. I hear you're going away for a while. Where to?

Omar Yeah, I'm leaving for Paris next week.

Akina You're kidding! Wow, _you must be_ excited!

Omar I am. I've never been there before. _you see_, I'm going to do some research for my next book. That's always the best part – the research.

Akina I bet. _that must be_ fun. So, what's your book about?

Omar It's a love story, of course.

Akina _I see_. Uh . . . can you share any details yet?

Omar I guess. Hmm . . . let's see. It's about a young girl who goes to visit a friend in Paris. And well, you know, she meets a mysterious young man, they fall in love, and lots of things happen.

Akina Really? What kind of things?

Omar Well, I don't want to say yet. _you see_, I want to keep the details a surprise.

Akina I understand. But, gosh, _that must be_ hard. I can never keep secrets.

Omar I know what you mean. It's difficult sometimes.

Akina So, tell me what else you're doing in Paris.

Omar Oh. I'm going to read from my last novel at an English-language bookstore.

Akina Great! _you must be_ pleased about that. Will you be nervous?

Omar No, not at all. I've done it several times. It's part of the job of being a writer.

Akina _I see_. Well, have a wonderful trip. Good luck with your research.

Omar Thanks. I'll tell you all about it when I get back.

1 Child prodigies

Reading | **A** Read the article. What does "child prodigy" mean?

☐ someone under the age of 15   ☐ a child with a special talent   ☐ a child who is famous

CHILD PRODIGIES:
Nature OR Nurture?

Mozart wrote his first minuet at age six. Cellist Yo-Yo Ma first performed in public at the age of five. William James Sidis read Homer in Greek at age four and was the youngest person ever to attend Harvard University at 11. Ukrainian chess player Sergey Karjakin became the youngest international grand master at 12. Pablo Picasso first publicly exhibited his paintings at age 13.

Many parents may hope for a genius child, but there can be a price to pay. Some child prodigies never experience a normal childhood, often because it's difficult for them to make friends, and they suffer socially. Some genius children even have mental breakdowns at an early age, and gifted child athletes or musicians can be permanently injured from practicing too hard.

We often hear stories of parents who push their children too hard. However, some experts say that for the most part, "pushy parent" is an unfair label: Parents don't push prodigies, prodigies push parents. Many gifted children quickly become bored with school and homework that is too easy. For these kids, school is frustrating, and they risk losing interest in it altogether. It's better to allow these children to skip grades, experts say, than to let them become disappointed in school.

Are prodigies born, or are they created? The short answer is: we don't know. Certainly, many parents of gifted children provide a stimulating environment: They read to their children at an early age, take them to museums and concerts, and give them a lot of independence. But experts advise parents not to be disappointed if their child isn't an early genius. Mozart was a child prodigy; Einstein was not. But the world is still amazed by them both.

B Find a word or expression in the article for each meaning below.

1. go to, or be present at (a place or an event) (paragraph 1) _attend_

2. psychological problems (paragraph 2) _____

3. talented; exceptional (paragraph 3) _____

4. interesting; encouraging you to learn (paragraph 4) _____

C Read the article again. Then answer the questions.

1. Who's the youngest prodigy mentioned in the article?

   _____

2. What are three disadvantages of being a child prodigy?

   _____

3. What problems do some gifted children have with school?

   _____

4. How do some parents help their gifted children develop?

   _____

2 My child is a prodigy!

Writing | **A** Read the letter from a parent to a school principal. Circle the expressions that give impressions or opinions. Underline the statements that are stated as fact.

_MT_

Dear Dr. Evans,

<u>My child is enrolled in your school.</u> ⟨I believe that⟩ he is a very gifted student, and I feel that he is bored in his classes. It seems to me that he is becoming increasingly frustrated and anxious because he has lost interest in school. Last year he was the top student in his class, but this year his grades are slipping. My impression is that he needs to take more difficult classes. In my opinion, he is not finding his current classes challenging enough. Can you help?

Sincerely,

Marsha Taylor

B Write a letter to the editor of a local newspaper about one of the topics below or your own idea. Use the expressions from part A.

- There aren't enough leisure facilities for local teens.
- We need healthier food options in schools.
- There's too much litter on city streets.

Unit 11 Progress chart

What can you do? Mark the boxes. ✓ = I can . . . ? = I need to review how to . . .	To review, go back to these pages in the Student's Book.
Grammar ☐ use the modals *must*, *may*, *might*, *can't*, and *could* to speculate.	108 and 109
☐ use adjectives ending in *-ed* to describe how someone feels.	110 and 111
☐ use adjectives ending in *-ing* to describe someone or something.	110 and 111
Vocabulary ☐ name at least 12 adjectives to describe feelings and reactions.	110 and 111
Conversation strategies ☐ use *That must be* or *You must be* + adjective to show I understand.	112
☐ use *You see* to explain something and *I see* to show I understand.	113
Writing ☐ use expressions like *I feel* to give impressions or opinions.	115

In the news

Lesson A / Local news

1 And now, the news . . .

Grammar | Complete the news reports. Use the simple past passive.

1. Newtown Park train station ___was closed___
   (close) this morning after a bag _____
   (find) on a train. Several trains _____
   (delay), and some _____ (cancel). The
   bag _____ (remove) from the station
   and _____ (search). Police said later
   that the bag was full of clothes. The train station
   _____ (reopen) after two hours.

2. A woman _____ (rescue) earlier today
   after she climbed onto her roof to repair her
   chimney. Firefighters _____ (call) to the
   scene after neighbors heard the woman shout
   for help. Fortunately, the woman _____
   (not hurt), but she _____ (take) to the
   local hospital and _____ (release) later
   this afternoon.

3. The National Museum _____ (break into)
   last night, and three valuable paintings
   _____ (steal). The area around the
   museum _____ (close off) following the
   incident, and bystanders _____
   (interview). Police are now looking for two young
   men who _____ (see) nearby.

2 More news

Grammar | **Rewrite the sentences using the simple past passive.**

1. They delayed the game for two hours.   *The game was delayed for two hours.*

2. Someone stole a ring from an exhibit.   _____

3. They canceled the rock concert.   _____

4. A woman found a wallet on a bus.   _____

5. They took two people to the hospital.   _____

6. Someone rescued a man from a fire.   _____

3 What happened?

Grammar | **Look at the picture. What do you think happened? Write a news report. Use the verbs in the box or your own ideas. Use the simple past passive. Be creative with your facts!**

break into
close
find
hurt
open
rob
steal
take

News Report: Stolen Goods!

A downtown jewelry store was robbed yesterday.

1 All kinds of weather

Vocabulary | **Look at the pictures. Complete the sentences with the words in the box.**

aftershocks	floods	hurricane	✓rains	tornado
earthquake	hailstorm	lightning	thunderstorm	winds

1. The region was hit by heavy _____*rains*_____ earlier today. Several roads were closed because of flash _____ .

2. Farmers say their crops were badly damaged by the ice from a freak _____ that passed through the area today.

3. Parts of the country were damaged by a _____ yesterday.

4. Airports were closed today due to _____ Albert. Flights were canceled because of strong _____ and rain.

5. The area was hit yesterday by a major _____ , measuring 5.6 on the Richter scale. _____ were felt throughout the area.

6. Electricity throughout the city was disrupted by thunder and _____ from a severe _____ .

2 What was the cause?

Grammar and vocabulary | Look at each pair of pictures. What caused the damage? Write a sentence using the given word and *by*.

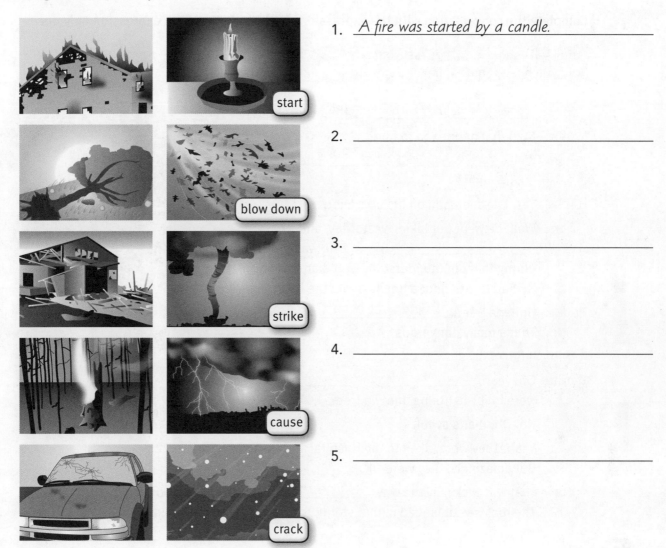

start

blow down

strike

cause

crack

1. _A fire was started by a candle._

2. _____

3. _____

4. _____

5. _____

3 In the news

Grammar | Rewrite the sentences using the simple past passive and the adverb given.

1. The fire damaged the building. (partially)
   The building was partially damaged by the fire.

2. The storm disrupted train services. (temporarily)
   _____

3. Flash floods damaged several houses in the area. (badly)
   _____

4. A wildfire injured three firefighters. (seriously)
   _____

5. A tornado destroyed a small farm. (completely)
   _____

1 News travels fast!

Conversation strategies Complete the conversation with the expressions in the box. Use each expression only once.

did I tell you	guess what	you know
did you hear about	✓have you heard	you know what

Don _Have you heard_ the news about Henry?

Nadia No. What happened to him?

Don Well, _____ he goes mountain biking, right?

Nadia Yes. I've seen him on his bike a lot.

Don Well, he went out biking yesterday, and _____ ? He was in the mountains during that big thunderstorm in the afternoon. He had to sit under a tree to avoid the lightning. . . .

Nadia Under a tree? _____ ? That's really dangerous.

Don It is?

Nadia Oh, yeah. _____ those golfers who were hit by lightning under a tree?

Don No. Oh, that's awful.

Nadia Yeah. They were taken to the hospital and everything. But amazingly, they were OK.

Don That was lucky. By the way, _____ about my car? The roof was damaged in that storm, too. It was hit by the hailstones.

2 About you

Conversation strategies Write sentences introducing some news. Use true information.

1. _You know my friend Callie? She got a new laptop for her birthday._
    (good news about a friend)

2. _____
    (fun news about yourself)

3. _____
    (bad news about a local sports team)

4. _____
    (news about the local weather)

5. _____
    (interesting news about your favorite actor or singer)

6. _____
    (news about a family member)

7. _____
    (news about another city)

3 The funny thing was . . .

Conversation
strategies Circle the best way to complete each sentence.

1. I lost my bag last week, and then I found it outside my dorm room. The funny thing was, **everything was stolen** / (**nothing was stolen**).

2. Thieves broke into my car last week, and the worst thing was, **they took my favorite bag** / **the inside of the car was completely cleaned**.

3. Some neighbors of ours got married last month, and the weird thing is, **they didn't tell anyone about it** / **we all had a great time**.

4. We had a great weekend at the beach. The best thing was, **the water was so warm** / **it rained**.

5. That movie was incredible. The only thing was, **the ending was the best** / **the ending was disappointing**.

6. We went out for dinner last night, and the food was terrible. The other thing was, **the waiters were helpful** / **it was really expensive**.

4 The whole story

Conversation
strategies Complete the conversations with the expressions in the box.

Did I tell you?	The best thing is,
✓ Did you hear	The funny thing is,

1. A *Did you hear* _____ about the new vacation schedule?

   B No, I didn't. What about it?

   A We get an extra week of vacation.

   B Great!

   A _____ the extra week is in February. That means we can plan a nice, long ski vacation!

2. A _____ There was a small fire at school yesterday.

   B Really? Where?

   A It was in the science lab. Some students were doing an experiment, and it exploded.

   B I hope no one was hurt.

   A Everyone is fine. _____ the students all got A's!

1 Only the news that interests you

Reading | **A** Read the article. Which news sources do young people use?

CHANGING SOURCES OF NEWS

Far fewer people, especially the young, get their news from traditional news sources (either print or television), according to the most recent surveys. Instead, they are getting news from online sources and social networking sites, using their cell phones, tablets, and other mobile devices. In just two years, the number of people who get news from social networks doubled, and now about a third of young readers get their news this way. Although half of all Americans still watch TV to keep up with events, only 28% of people between the ages of 18 and 29 do so.

This use of social networks for news can be seen in Europe also. One in five people in the United Kingdom, and 43% of young people, get their news from the most popular social networking and microblogging sites. According to a recent study in Spain, three-quarters of the people between the ages of 16 and 30 got their news from a social networking site, as compared to only 28% from newspapers.

The addition of these news channels may contribute to "news fatigue," or a feeling of being overloaded with news. A study that was conducted by the University of Texas found that the way we get the news affects whether we feel information overload. People who got their news from computers and tablets were much more likely to feel overloaded, while people who got their news from TV or read it on their cell phone were less likely to experience this. The study showed that reading the same news on a computer was felt to be more tiring than reading it on a phone, perhaps because options seem more limited on a phone, and so more manageable. People on computers and tablets usually see many more links than people who use phone apps.

News organizations have adapted their news presentation style to try to prevent or reduce news fatigue. Some provide news in three forms: breaking headlines, short present-tense stories, and links to longer stories. By cutting down the number of headline updates, they also hope to reduce news fatigue.

B Read the article again. Circle the best alternatives to complete the sentences.

1. The author suggests in the article that young people and older people _____ .
   a. get news the same way   (b.) often get their news from different sources

2. One news source that is growing in popularity is _____ .
   a. microblogging sites   b. television news

3. Three out of four young people get their news from social networks in _____ .
   a. Spain   b. the United States

4. People who get their news on computers are more likely to be overloaded than if they get their news on _____ .
   a. tablets   b. smartphones

5. One way that people get news fatigue is by reading too many _____ .
   a. headline updates   b. longer stories

2 News survey

Writing **A Read the survey. Then complete the article below with the expressions in the box.**

Barnesville News Survey:

1. Do you read the *Barnesville News* every day?   👍**Yes** 49%   👎**No** 51%
2. What's your favorite section?

Weather	0%
Local	9%
Sports	10%
Arts	20%
International	59%
Travel	2%

almost
✓ half
majority
none
out of
20%

About ___*half*___ of the people we surveyed read the *Barnesville News* every day. The _____ of *Barnesville News* readers prefer the international section. Only one _____ ten readers chose the sports section as their favorite. _____ 10% of readers enjoy the local section, while _____ of them are interested in the arts section. _____ of them chose the weather as their favorite.

B How many of your friends read a local or national news website?
   Write a paragraph like the one in part A to show the statistics.

Unit 12 Progress chart

What can you do? Mark the boxes. ✓ = I can . . . ? = I need to review how to . . .	To review, go back to these pages in the Student's Book.
Grammar ☐ use the simple past passive to discuss the news.	118, 119, and 120
☐ use the passive + *by* to introduce the "doer" or cause of an action.	120 and 121
Vocabulary ☐ name at least 10 types of extreme weather or natural disasters.	120 and 121
☐ name at least 4 adverbs with the simple past passive.	120 and 121
Conversation strategies ☐ introduce news with expressions like *Guess what?*	122
☐ use expressions like *The thing is* . . . to introduce issues.	123
Writing ☐ write about statistics.	125

97

Illustration credits

Harry Briggs: 22, 42, 80   **Cambridge University Press:** 21, 50   **Steve Cancel:** 93   **Chuck Gonzales:** 13, 37, 58, 82, 83
Frank Montagna: 2, 26, 27, 44, 67, 86, 87   **Marilena Perilli:** 6, 7, 20, 28, 46, 62, 63, 74   **Greg White:** 14, 35, 78, 91
Terry Wong: 5, 38, 39, 54, 68, 69, 94, 95

Photo credits

3 ©Andresr/Shutterstock   **4** ©Erin Patrice O'Brien/Getty   **8** *(top to bottom)* ©Michael Tran/FilmMagic/Getty Images; ©Eros International/courtesy Everett Collection   **9** ©Monirul Alam/ZUMAPRESS.com/Alamy   **10** *(left to right)* ©Alexandra Lande/Shutterstock; ©GoodSportHD.com/Alamy   **11** ©Eyecandy Images/Alamy   **12** *(top to bottom)* ©Yadid Levy/age fotostock/SuperStock; ©Andrew Bain/Getty Images; ©Manfred Grebler/Getty Images; ©Universal Images Group/SuperStock   **15** *(left to right)* ©Philip Lee Harvey/Getty Images; ©Punchstock   **16** *(top to bottom)* ©Oktay Ortakcioglu/Getty Images; ©leungchopan/Shutterstock   **18** *(top row, left to right)* ©Francesco Dazzi/Shutterstock; ©Medioimages/Photodisc/Thinkstock; ©Maurilio Cheli/Associated Press; ©Max Nash/Associated Press *(bottom row, left to right)* ©Jerritt Clark/WireImage/Getty Images; ©Randy Faris/Corbis; ©Alik Keplicz/Associated Press; ©Mike Segar/Reuters/Newscom   **19** ©Andrzej Gorzkowski Photography/Alamy   **20** *(clockwise from top left)* ©Punchstock; ©Thinkstock; ©Digital Vision/Thinkstock; ©Thinkstock; ©AAMIR QURESHI/AFP/Getty Images; ©Galen Rowell/Corbis   **23** ©Thinkstock   **24** ©Photo Courtesy of NOAA *(background)* ©Serg Zastavkin/Shutterstock *(icicles)* ©April Cat/Shutterstock   **25** ©Thinkstock   **29** ©imagebroker.net/SuperStock   **32** ©Frank Herholdt/Getty Images   **34** ©George Kerrigan   **35** ©George Kerrigan   **36** *(top to bottom)* ©ifong/Shutterstock; ©Stockvision/Shutterstock   **40** ©Thinkstock   **41** *(top to bottom)* ©Robyn Mackenzie/Shutterstock; ©Lucky Business/Shutterstock   **50** *(top to bottom)* ©Thinkstock; ©Punchstock; ©Dennis MacDonald/Age Fotostock; ©Sherrianne Talon/istockphoto; ©Jurgen Reisch/Getty Images   **53** ©Rich Legg/Getty Images   **55** *(all photos)* ©Thinkstock   **59** ©x7vector/Shutterstock   **61** ©Andrew D. Bernstein/NBAE via Getty Images   **62** ©John Giustina/Getty Images   **66** ©MediaBakery   **70** ©PBS/Courtesy: Everett Collection   **75** ©Clark Brennan/Alamy   **77** ©Jupiterimages/Thinkstock   **80** *(top)* ©DircinhaSW/Getty Images *(bottom, left to right)* ©JGI/Getty Images/RF; ©Cultura Limited/SuperStock   **81** ©David Wolff-Patrick/WireImage/Getty Images   **84** *(clockwise from top left)* ©Punchstock; ©Nick Chaldakov/Alamy; ©Thinkstock; ©Digital Vision/Thinkstock   **90** *(top to bottom)* ©Mike Finn-Kelcey/Newscom; ©RubberBall/SuperStock; ©Thinkstock   **92** *(clockwise from top left)* ©Sandra Mu/Getty Images; ©David Cole/Alamy; ©Thinkstock; ©Thinkstock; ©Thinkstock; ©Eric Nguyen/Jim Reed Photography/Corbis

Text credits

While every effort has been made, it has not always been possible to identify the sources of all the materials used, or to trace all copyright holders. If any omissions are brought to our notice, we will be happy to include the appropriate acknowledgements on reprinting.

The top 500 spoken words

This is a list of the top 500 words in spoken North American English. It is based on a sample of four and a half million words of conversation from the Cambridge International Corpus. The most frequent word, *I*, is at the top of the list.

1.	I	40.	really	79.	see
2.	and	41.	with	80.	how
3.	the	42.	he	81.	they're
4.	you	43.	one	82.	kind
5.	uh	44.	are	83.	here
6.	to	45.	this	84.	from
7.	a	46.	there	85.	did
8.	that	47.	I'm	86.	something
9.	it	48.	all	87.	too
10.	of	49.	if	88.	more
11.	yeah	50.	no	89.	very
12.	know	51.	get	90.	want
13.	in	52.	about	91.	little
14.	like	53.	at	92.	been
15.	they	54.	out	93.	things
16.	have	55.	had	94.	an
17.	so	56.	then	95.	you're
18.	was	57.	because	96.	said
19.	but	58.	go	97.	there's
20.	is	59.	up	98.	I've
21.	it's	60.	she	99.	much
22.	we	61.	when	100.	where
23.	huh	62.	them	101.	two
24.	just	63.	can	102.	thing
25.	oh	64.	would	103.	her
26.	do	65.	as	104.	didn't
27.	don't	66.	me	105.	other
28.	that's	67.	mean	106.	say
29.	well	68.	some	107.	back
30.	for	69.	good	108.	could
31.	what	70.	got	109.	their
32.	on	71.	OK	110.	our
33.	think	72.	people	111.	guess
34.	right	73.	now	112.	yes
35.	not	74.	going	113.	way
36.	um	75.	were	114.	has
37.	or	76.	lot	115.	down
38.	my	77.	your	116.	we're
39.	be	78.	time	117.	any

The top 500 spoken words

118. he's	161. five	204. sort
119. work	162. always	205. great
120. take	163. school	206. bad
121. even	164. look	207. we've
122. those	165. still	208. another
123. over	166. around	209. car
124. probably	167. anything	210. true
125. him	168. kids	211. whole
126. who	169. first	212. whatever
127. put	170. does	213. twenty
128. years	171. need	214. after
129. sure	172. us	215. ever
130. can't	173. should	216. find
131. pretty	174. talking	217. care
132. gonna	175. last	218. better
133. stuff	176. thought	219. hard
134. come	177. doesn't	220. haven't
135. these	178. different	221. trying
136. by	179. money	222. give
137. into	180. long	223. I'd
138. went	181. used	224. problem
139. make	182. getting	225. else
140. than	183. same	226. remember
141. year	184. four	227. might
142. three	185. every	228. again
143. which	186. new	229. pay
144. home	187. everything	230. try
145. will	188. many	231. place
146. nice	189. before	232. part
147. never	190. though	233. let
148. only	191. most	234. keep
149. his	192. tell	235. children
150. doing	193. being	236. anyway
151. cause	194. bit	237. came
152. off	195. house	238. six
153. I'll	196. also	239. family
154. maybe	197. use	240. wasn't
155. real	198. through	241. talk
156. why	199. feel	242. made
157. big	200. course	243. hundred
158. actually	201. what's	244. night
159. she's	202. old	245. call
160. day	203. done	246. saying

The top 500 spoken words

247. dollars	290. started	333. believe
248. live	291. job	334. thinking
249. away	292. says	335. funny
250. either	293. play	336. state
251. read	294. usually	337. until
252. having	295. wow	338. husband
253. far	296. exactly	339. idea
254. watch	297. took	340. name
255. week	298. few	341. seven
256. mhm	299. child	342. together
257. quite	300. thirty	343. each
258. enough	301. buy	344. hear
259. next	302. person	345. help
260. couple	303. working	346. nothing
261. own	304. half	347. parents
262. wouldn't	305. looking	348. room
263. ten	306. someone	349. today
264. interesting	307. coming	350. makes
265. am	308. eight	351. stay
266. sometimes	309. love	352. mom
267. bye	310. everybody	353. sounds
268. seems	311. able	354. change
269. heard	312. we'll	355. understand
270. goes	313. life	356. such
271. called	314. may	357. gone
272. point	315. both	358. system
273. ago	316. type	359. comes
274. while	317. end	360. thank
275. fact	318. least	361. show
276. once	319. told	362. thousand
277. seen	320. saw	363. left
278. wanted	321. college	364. friends
279. isn't	322. ones	365. class
280. start	323. almost	366. already
281. high	324. since	367. eat
282. somebody	325. days	368. small
283. let's	326. couldn't	369. boy
284. times	327. gets	370. paper
285. guy	328. guys	371. world
286. area	329. god	372. best
287. fun	330. country	373. water
288. they've	331. wait	374. myself
289. you've	332. yet	375. run

The top 500 spoken words

376. they'll	418. company	460. sorry
377. won't	419. friend	461. living
378. movie	420. set	462. drive
379. cool	421. minutes	463. outside
380. news	422. morning	464. bring
381. number	423. between	465. easy
382. man	424. music	466. stop
383. basically	425. close	467. percent
384. nine	426. leave	468. hand
385. enjoy	427. wife	469. gosh
386. bought	428. knew	470. top
387. whether	429. pick	471. cut
388. especially	430. important	472. computer
389. taking	431. ask	473. tried
390. sit	432. hour	474. gotten
391. book	433. deal	475. mind
392. fifty	434. mine	476. business
393. months	435. reason	477. anybody
394. women	436. credit	478. takes
395. month	437. dog	479. aren't
396. found	438. group	480. question
397. side	439. turn	481. rather
398. food	440. making	482. twelve
399. looks	441. American	483. phone
400. summer	442. weeks	484. program
401. hmm	443. certain	485. without
402. fine	444. less	486. moved
403. hey	445. must	487. gave
404. student	446. dad	488. yep
405. agree	447. during	489. case
406. mother	448. lived	490. looked
407. problems	449. forty	491. certainly
408. city	450. air	492. talked
409. second	451. government	493. beautiful
410. definitely	452. eighty	494. card
411. spend	453. wonderful	495. walk
412. happened	454. seem	496. married
413. hours	455. wrong	497. anymore
414. war	456. young	498. you'll
415. matter	457. places	499. middle
416. supposed	458. girl	500. tax
417. worked	459. happen	

TOUCHSTONE

MARCIA FISK ONG

SERIES AUTHORS
MICHAEL McCARTHY
JEANNE McCARTEN
HELEN SANDIFORD

VIDEO ACTIVITY PAGES

CAMBRIDGE
UNIVERSITY PRESS

Contents

Introduction: To the Student

Character descriptions

Touchstone Video is a fun-filled, compelling situational comedy featuring a group of young people who are friends. David Parker is a reporter. His roommate is Alex Santos, a personal trainer. David's friend Gio Ferrari is a student visiting from Italy. Liz Martin is a singer and Web designer. She lives with Yoko Suzuki, a chef. Kim Davis is David's co-worker. She works in an office.

Through the daily encounters and activities of these characters, you have the opportunity to see and hear the language of the Student's Book vividly come to life in circumstances both familiar and entertaining.

This is David Parker.
He's a reporter.

This is Yoko Suzuki.
She's a chef.

This is Alex Santos.
He's a personal trainer.

This is Gio Ferrari.
He's a student.
He's from Italy.

This is Liz Martin.
She's a Web designer
and singer.

This is Kim Davis.
She's David's co-worker.

The Video

Welcome to the *Touchstone* Video. In this video you will get to know six people who are friends: David, Liz, Yoko, Alex, Kim, and Gio. You can read about them on page iv.

You will also hear them use the English that you are studying in the *Touchstone* Student's Books. Each of the four levels of the Video breaks down as follows:

Episode 1	Act 1	Student's Book units 1–3
	Act 2	
	Act 3	

Episode 2	Act 1	Student's Book units 4–6
	Act 2	
	Act 3	

Episode 3	Act 1	Student's Book units 7–9
	Act 2	
	Act 3	

Episode 4	Act 1	Student's Book units 10–12
	Act 2	
	Act 3	

Explanation of the DVD Menu

To play one Episode of the Video:
- On the Main Menu, select *Episode Menu.*
- On the Episode Menu, select the appropriate *Play Episode.*

To play one Act of the Video:
- On the Main Menu, select *Episode Menu.*
- On the Episode Menu, select *Act Menu.*
- On the Act Menu, select the appropriate *Play Act.*

To play the Video with subtitles:
- On the Main Menu, Episode Menu, or Act Menu, select *Subtitles.*
- On the Subtitles Menu, select *Subtitles on.* The DVD will then automatically take you back to the menu you were on before.

To cancel the subtitles:
- On the Main Menu, Episode Menu, or Act Menu, select *Subtitles.*
- On the Subtitles Menu, select *Subtitles off.* The DVD will then automatically take you back to the menu you were on before.

The Worksheets

For each Act there are *Before you watch*, *While you watch*, and *After you watch* worksheets.

For *While you watch* worksheets:
- Find **DVD** 0 on your worksheet.
- Input this number on the Video menu using your remote control. The DVD will then play only the segment of the Video you need to watch to complete the task.

We hope you enjoy the *Touchstone* Video!

Episode 1 A Day in the Park

Act 1

Before you watch

A Complete the crossword puzzle with the words in the box.

Word box:
- challenging
- ✓ creative
- down-to-earth
- generous
- genius
- impatient
- practical
- talented

Crossword: 3 across spells CREATIVE

Across

3. Danny is an incredible artist. He always comes up with new ideas. He's _____ .
4. Anna never likes to wait for anything. She's _____ .
6. Tim always gives good advice because he's honest and _____ .
7. Carrie likes to give her friends things. She's very _____ .

Down

1. Albert Einstein was extremely intelligent. People call him a _____ .
2. Lisa dances, sings, and plays the guitar very well. She's _____ .
3. I have to work really hard and learn a lot of new things at school. It's _____ .
5. Sean is sensible and good at dealing with problems. He's really _____ .

B Read the horoscopes. Find and circle the personality and behavior words from Exercise A.

http://www.gemini/leo.com - Horoscope - Gemini & Leo

File   Edit   View   Favorites   Tools   Help

Weekly Horoscope

Gemini

Your life is very challenging right now. Don't be impatient with friends, and don't take things too seriously. Try to relax and everything will be OK soon! If a friend asks to borrow something, be generous and give it to him or her.

Leo

You're so talented – you're always doing many different things. You'll feel very creative today, so it's a good day to start a new project. Friends come to you for help because you're so practical and down-to-earth. They think you're a genius when you help.

While you watch

DVD 1
VHS 00:05
−04:21

A Whose horoscope talks about these things? Check (✓) the correct answers.
(You will check one of the items more than once.)

| | Yoko | David | Liz | Alex | Gio |

Whose horoscope talks about . . . ?	being generous	enjoying life more	a future decision	good news	hard work	success
1. Yoko's					✓	
2. David & Liz's						
3. Alex's						
4. Gio's						

DVD 2
VHS 00:05
−04:21

B Circle the correct answers.

1. Alex has been to the park _____ .
   a. once   b. many times

2. The park is _____ to get to.
   a. hard   b. easy

3. Yoko reads horoscopes for _____ .
   a. advice   b. fun

4. Yoko reads _____ horoscope.
   a. a fake   b. the wrong

5. David says that Yoko is always _____ .
   a. doing many different things   b. helping other people

6. Liz _____ read her horoscope.
   a. has already   b. hasn't

7. Alex is always borrowing David's _____ .
   a. laptop   b. MP3 player

8. Liz thinks her horoscope sounds _____ .
   a. wrong   b. right

9. Alex's horoscope says he's always _____ .
   a. having a lot of fun   b. working hard

10. Gio is _____ to hear his horoscope.
    a. afraid   b. excited

11. Gio's horoscope says he's _____ part of his personality.
    a. developing   b. ignoring

While you watch

DVD 3
VHS 00:13
−01:46

C Listen for these sentences. What do the people say exactly? Circle the correct answers.

1. *Alex* It's **an incredibly / a really** nice park.
2. *David* And it's **totally / pretty** easy to get here.
3. *Alex* Yeah, that was **pretty / very** lucky. I get **so / pretty** impatient when I have to drive in heavy traffic.
4. *Yoko* Well, this one's for me. It's **surprisingly / amazingly** true.
    "You're **extremely / really** talented, practical, down-to-earth, a wonderful chef . . ."
5. *David* And you do them all **very / really** well.
6.   *Liz* I already read it. It's not **good at all / very good**.

DVD 4
VHS 02:38
−04:04

D Listen for what the horoscopes say about these things. Complete the sentences with the correct adverbs and adjectives.

1. Work is _____ .	a. big
2. Your boss is _____ to keep up with.	b. challenging
3. Success is _____ to you.	c. creative
4. Everything is _____ in your life.	d. very important
5. But you have a(n) _____ decision to make soon.	e. impossible
6. You're a(n) _____ genius.	f. absolutely wonderful

DVD 5
VHS 00:05
−00:37

E Put the conversation in the correct order. Then watch the video and check your answers.

_____ *Alex* Have you been to this park before?

_____ *Alex* Yeah, many times. It's a really nice park. It has the most incredible view.

_____ *Gio* It sure is. It feels good to be outdoors.

_____ *Alex* Yeah, that was pretty lucky. I get pretty impatient when I have to drive in heavy traffic.

_____ *Gio* No, I haven't. Have you been here before?

_1_ *Alex* Ah! It's a perfect day for a picnic!

_____ *David* And it's pretty easy to get here. I mean, we got here fast. There wasn't much traffic.

After you watch

A What can you remember? Write one thing the horoscopes said about each person.

1. Yoko   _She always works hard._
2. David   _____
3. Alex   _____
4. Gio   _____

B Match the questions to the answers. Then practice with a partner.

> a. He's great, but he's always borrowing my things.
> b. Yes, she is. She's an artist and a musician. She's extremely talented.
> c. She's nice, but she's very demanding. She's always working late.
> d. It's a little challenging. I'm working pretty hard.

1. How's your new roommate? _____
2. Is your sister an artist? _____
3. How's work? _____
4. How's your new boss? _____

C Write two or three sentences to describe the habits and qualities of two people you know well. Then compare sentences in small groups.

Name _____	Name _____

"My brother James is a musician. He's really talented. He's always performing at local events and parties."

Episode 1 A Day in the Park

Act 2

Before you watch

A Complete the sentences with the words in the box.

| balanced | demanding | ✓ high-powered | lucky | rewarding | workaholic |

1. Bill is an executive with a large company. He has a lot of power and makes important decisions. He has a _high-powered_ job.
2. Cindy loves her job at the animal hospital. She doesn't make a lot of money, but she helps people and their pets. Her job is _____ .
3. Teachers work long hours and have a lot of extra work to do outside of school hours. Their work is very _____ .
4. James works all the time and finds it hard to stop working. He never takes vacations. He's a _____ .
5. Marion has a lot of money, so she only works when she wants to! She's _____ .
6. Sometimes I'm stressed because I have too much work, and sometimes there isn't any work at all. My life isn't very _____ .

B Complete the sentences with the present perfect. Use contractions.

1. I _'ve been_ (be) to Thailand, but I _____ (not be) to Bali. I _____ (hear) it's beautiful.
2. We're going to New Zealand for three weeks. I _____ (want) to go there for a long time.
3. I'd like to go somewhere unusual, like Laos. I _____ (take) some trips, but I _____ (not go) anywhere like that.
4. My cousin _____ (do) a lot of amazing things. He _____ (travel) all over South America, and he _____ (try) hang gliding.

While you watch

DVD [6]
VHS 04:26
−08:33

A What topics do David and Gio talk about? Check (✓) the correct topics.

1. ☐ hobbies
   ☐ work
2. ☐ David's boss
   ☐ David's co-worker
3. ☐ travel
   ☐ entertainment
4. ☐ South Africa
   ☐ South America
5. ☐ a family member
   ☐ a close friend
6. ☐ a blog
   ☐ a magazine article
7. ☐ goals
   ☐ regrets

DVD [7]
VHS 04:26
−08:33

B Check (✓) true or false.

1. David's boss is easy to work for.	☐ True	☐ False
2. David doesn't like his job.	☐ True	☐ False
3. David has traveled to a few places.	☐ True	☐ False
4. David has visited Machu Picchu.	☐ True	☐ False
5. David recently became interested in ancient cities.	☐ True	☐ False
6. Gio's sister Monica is a world traveler.	☐ True	☐ False
7. Monica works for a computer company.	☐ True	☐ False
8. Gio is finishing school in about a year.	☐ True	☐ False
9. Gio wants to earn a lot of money when he graduates.	☐ True	☐ False
10. David feels worse after talking to Gio.	☐ True	☐ False

DVD [8]
VHS 05:33
−06:53

C Listen for these sentences. Complete the sentences with the correct form of the verbs in the box. (You will use one verb more than once.)

be	go	hear	take	travel	want

1. *Gio* Really? But you've <u>been</u> to a lot of places.

   David Uh, I've _____ a few trips with friends, I guess. But I've never _____ anywhere, you know, exciting.

2. *David* Well, I've always _____ to go backpacking in South America.

3. *Gio* Wow. I've _____ it's the most amazing place.

4. *David* Well, I've always _____ interested in ancient cities.

5. *Gio* You know, my sister Monica's _____ there.

6. *Gio* Actually, she's _____ all over the world. She's _____ scuba diving in Costa Rica, hiking in the Himalayas . . .

While you watch

D Who says these things? Check (✓) the correct name.

	David	Gio
1. I also want time to enjoy life.		
2. I've learned a lot about myself.		
3. What do you want to do?		
4. I think it's important to do something useful with your life.		
5. You have to keep your life balanced.		
6. I also want to help people.		
7. You're the best.		
8. That's what friends are for.		

E Listen for these parts of Gio and David's conversation. Match the sentences with the responses.

1. Well, I've tried that, but he doesn't really listen. It's so unfair. _____
2. Well, I don't know. I've always wanted to travel more. _____
3. I really want to see Machu Picchu. _____
4. Cool. You know, my sister Monica's been there. _____
5. She's been scuba diving in Costa Rica, hiking in the Himalayas . . . _____
6. She works for herself. She's a computer specialist. _____
7. I know what you mean. _____

a. Do you?
b. It sure is.
c. Really?
d. You're kidding.
e. She has?
f. You do?
g. I think that's great.

After you watch

A What can you remember? Answer the questions.

1. What would David like to do?

   David wants to travel more.

2. What would Gio like to do?

   _____

3. What advice would you give David and Gio about their plans?

   _____

   _____

B Complete the conversations with a response from the box. Then add a follow-up question. Practice with a partner. Try to keep the conversation going.

Do you?	He has?	✓She does?	They have?	You have?

1. *A* Alison wants to go to Hawaii.

   B She does? Why does she want to go there? _____

2. *A* I really want to have my own business.

   B _____

3. *A* I've always wanted to try hang gliding.

   B _____

4. *A* My brother has been to Peru five times.

   B _____

5. *A* My parents have lived in a lot of different countries.

   B _____

A Alison wants to go to Hawaii.

B She does? Why does she want to go there?

A She's always wanted to learn how to surf.

C Complete the sentences. Then compare your answers with a partner.

1. I've always wanted to _____ .
2. I've never gone _____ .
3. I've never been to _____ .
4. My dream is to _____ .

"I've always wanted to learn to play the piano."

Episode 1 A Day in the Park

Act 3

Before you watch

A Write the adverb form of these adjectives.

1. careful _____
2. correct _____
3. easy _____
4. fast _____
5. good _____
6. quick _quickly_____
7. serious _____

B Complete the sentences with adverbs from Exercise A.

1. When the bell rang, Meg finished her work _quickly_____ and ran to the door.
2. Frances got upset when I made that joke. She takes everything so _____ !
3. If you answer all the questions _____ , you'll win $2,000!
4. You play the piano _____ . Where did you learn how to play?
5. Please don't drive so _____ ! You're making me nervous.
6. I always listen to people very _____ .
7. Your password should be a word that you can remember _____ .

C Match each trivia question with the correct category. Can you answer any of the questions?

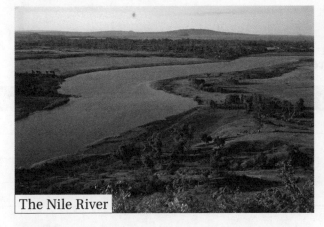

The Nile River

International departures

The busiest international airport

Question

1. What movie has won the most Academy Awards? _____
2. When did World War I begin? _____
3. How long is the Nile River? _____
4. How many players are on a volleyball team? _____
5. What is the busiest international airport in the world? _____

Category

a. transportation
b. sports
c. entertainment
d. history
e. geography

While you watch

DVD 11
VHS 08:38
–13:47

A Circle the correct answers. (You can guess.) Then watch the video and check your answers.

1. Where is the fastest passenger train in the world?
   a. France   b. Japan   c. the U.S.
2. How fast can the train go?
   a. 50 miles an hour   b. 500 miles an hour   c. 500 kilometers an hour
3. What is Tiger Woods's real name?
   a. Eldon   b. Eldrick   c. Derrick
4. Who won the Academy Award for best actress in 2004?
   a. Halle Berry   b. Nicole Kidman   c. Hilary Swank
5. What's the highest mountain in the world?
   a. K2   b. Mount Everest   c. Mount Kilimanjaro
6. What is *Into Thin Air*?
   a. a book   b. a TV show   c. a movie
7. How long is a tennis court?
   a. 22 meters   b. 24 meters   c. 26 meters

DVD 12
VHS 08:38
–13:47

B Watch the video. Check (✓) the correct people.

Who . . . ?	Alex	David	Gio	Liz	Yoko
1. really likes "Brain Power"		✓			
2. likes to eat slowly					
3. has ridden the TGV train					
4. plays a lot of sports really well					
5. is pretty competitive					
6. can remember names pretty easily					
7. is a fast reader					
8. takes the game pretty seriously					
9. can do math in his or her head pretty quickly					
10. has the lowest score					

While you watch

DVD 13
VHS 08:38
−13:16

C Why does each person say the following? Watch the video and match the sentences to the reasons.

1. "Oh, excellent!"
   Gio says this because ___d___

2. "I, uh, like to eat slowly."
   Liz says this because _____

3. "Darn it!"
   David says this because _____

4. "That was fun!"
   Yoko says this because _____

5. "Be careful."
   Alex says this because _____

6. "Ah, ha! Try this one."
   David says this because _____

7. "You're pretty good at this game after all."
   Gio says this because _____

8. "Wow, that was quick."
   Alex says this because _____

9. "I'm sorry."
   Yoko says this because _____

10. "Wow! I'm impressed!"
    Yoko says this because _____

a. he doesn't answer a question fast enough.

b. she's impressed by Alex's math skills.

c. he thinks Yoko is competitive.

d. he likes to play games.

e. Yoko answered a question fast.

f. she doesn't want to play the game.

g. she enjoyed playing the game.

h. he's surprised at Liz's ability.

i. David gave the wrong answer.

j. he thinks the question is hard.

DVD 14
VHS 09:39
−12:19

D Watch the video and listen for these sentences. Match the underlined expressions with the things they refer to. (One answer is not used. Another answer is used twice.)

1. *David* Hold on. I think I know <u>this one</u>. ___a___

2. *Liz* I've never heard of <u>it</u>. _____

3. *Yoko* <u>That</u> was fun. _____

4. *Liz* I actually know <u>this</u>! _____

5. *Liz* But I've heard <u>it's</u> pretty good. _____

6. *Yoko* I just read a book about <u>it</u> last weekend. _____

a. the answer

b. the badminton game

c. Mount Everest

d. "Brain Power"

e. the movie

f. the TGV train

After you watch

A What can you remember? Write one thing that you learned about each person. Do you have any similar qualities or interests?

1. Gio   *He loves to play games.*
2. David _____
3. Alex _____
4. Liz   _____
5. Yoko _____

B Answer the questions and add a comment. Then compare with a partner. How are you the same? How are you different?

1. Do you walk quickly or slowly?
   _____

2. Do you read quickly or slowly?
   _____

3. Do you play any sport well?
   _____

4. Do you remember names easily, or do you have difficulty remembering them?
   _____

5. Do you take things seriously, or do you like to make a lot of jokes?
   _____

6. Do you think carefully before you make a decision?
   _____

A *Do you walk quickly or slowly?*
B *Actually, I walk extremely quickly – especially after work. I like to get home fast.*
A *I walk pretty fast, too. . . .*

Episode 2 Food and Family

Act 1

Before you watch

A Complete the sentences with the correct expressions.

a choice	a living	a lot of thinking	✓ a mess	some research	up my mind

1. Please don't make _a mess_ . I just cleaned the house.
2. You have a lot of good possibilities. You just need to make _____ !
3. I did _____ to find out about good vacation spots.
4. I can't make _____ if I want to see a movie or stay home tonight.
5. I'd like to take a class or something, but I'm too busy trying to make _____ .
6. I've done _____ , and I've decided to move back to Tokyo.

B Match the statements with the responses. Then practice with a partner.

1. It seems like people are too busy to cook. _____
2. I don't eat enough healthy foods. I'm going to have to make changes in what I eat. _____
3. You shouldn't eat so much fast food. _____
4. I think most people want to eat better. _____
5. You'd better eat a good breakfast, or you'll be tired all day. _____

a. You're right. I don't want to be tired today.
b. Absolutely! Look at how many people want to learn about healthy food.
c. I know, but it's so convenient!
d. That's for sure. I know I don't have time to cook.
e. That's true. But you do eat some healthy stuff.

C Number the lines of the conversation in the correct order.

_____ Um, I don't know. Whatever you're having, I guess.

_____ I'm having a ham sandwich.

_1_ I'm going to get something to eat. Do you want anything?

_____ The deli across the street. What would you like?

_____ No. You can pay me when I get back.

_____ Yeah, sure. I'm a little hungry. Where are you going?

_____ That sounds fine. Thanks. Should I pay you now?

While you watch

DVD [15]
VHS 13:52
−18:18

A Circle the correct answers. Circle *c. don't know* if the answer isn't mentioned.

1. David is having a _____ and coffee for breakfast.
   a. donut   b. roll   c. don't know
2. David gets stir-fried noodles with _____ .
   a. chicken   b. shrimp   c. don't know
3. David is writing a story about _____ life.
   a. city   b. modern   c. don't know
4. David has to decide on his story today because _____ .
   a. he's going on vacation   b. it's due at 5:00   c. don't know
5. The first idea is about _____ .
   a. eating habits   b. making a living   c. don't know
6. The second idea is about _____ .
   a. marriage   b. families   c. don't know
7. Kim likes the _____ idea.
   a. first   b. second   c. don't know
8. David decides to interview _____ .
   a. a junk food addict   b. a chef   c. don't know

DVD [16]
VHS 13:52
−15:10

B Listen for these parts of David and Kim's conversation. Complete the sentences.

1. *Kim* Hey, David. I'm going out to get lunch. Do you want anything?
   David Um, I'm <u>OK</u> for <u>now</u> . But thanks.
   Kim Are you sure? It's no problem.
   David I'm _____ . _____ . Besides, I'm still finishing my breakfast.

2. *Kim* What would you like?
   David Um, I don't know. I'll _____ whatever you're _____ , I guess.
   Kim Stir-fried noodles? They're pretty good.
   David Yeah, that _____ good.
   Kim With chicken or shrimp?
   David _____ _____ is fine. Um, should I pay you now?
   Kim Oh, you can pay now or when I get back. Whichever is _____ for _____ .

While you watch

C Listen for these sentences. Circle the ones you hear.

DVD 17
VHS 15:19
−16:59

1. a. You made a mess in here.
   b. You're making a mess in here.
2. a. I did a lot of thinking.
   b. I've done a lot of thinking.
3. a. I can't make up my mind what to write about.
   b. I couldn't make up my mind what to write about.
4. a. Everyone is too busy just making a living.
   b. Everyone is too busy just trying to make a living.
5. a. So people make bad food choices.
   b. So people are making bad food choices.
6. a. I could do some research.
   b. I did some research.

D Listen for the sentences and complete them with one of the expressions in the box. Then match the sentence with the responses.

DVD 18
VHS 15:19
−16:36

'd rather	going to have to	might want to	've got to

1. I _____ get it done before Thursday. _____
2. And I'm _____ decide today. _____
3. I mean, you _____ talk to someone about your ideas – to brainstorm. _____
4. I _____ not cook unless I have to. I just don't have the time. _____

a. Well, can you get some help?
b. That's a great idea!
c. Exactly.
d. What are you working on?

E Listen for these sentences. Match the two parts to complete the opinions.

DVD 19
VHS 16:41
−18:18

1. It seems like __c__
2. If you ask me, _____
3. It seems to me that _____
4. I could _____
5. But I don't think _____
6. I can _____
7. Maybe you'd better _____

a. interview a nutrition expert, or . . .
b. interview Yoko.
c. people are getting married much later these days.
d. talk to her about your food choices, too.
e. that will help people improve their diets.
f. everyone wants to know how to eat better.
g. the first idea is better.

After you watch

A What can you remember? What were David's two story ideas? Which idea does Kim like? Why?

Story ideas

1. _____

2. _____

Kim likes the **first / second** idea because _____

B Read the problems. Write advice using the expressions in the box. Then compare your answers with a partner.

You might want to . . .	You should / shouldn't . . .
You're going to have to . . .	Maybe you'd better . . .

1. *A* My boss wants me to work late most days.

   B _____

   _____

2. *A* My roommate always borrows my CDs, but she never returns them.

   B _____

   _____

3. *A* My parents want me to be a lawyer so I can earn a lot of money.

   B _____

   _____

4. *A* My roommate never washes the dishes after he cooks dinner.

   B _____

   _____

C Think of two things you want advice about. Work in pairs, share your problems, and offer your advice and opinions. Use expressions from Exercise B and the boxes below.

Giving opinions	Agreeing	Disagreeing
If you ask me . . .	Absolutely.	I know, but . . .
It seems like . . .	Definitely.	That's true, but . . .
It seems to me that . . .	That's for sure.	That's interesting, but . . .
I think / don't think . . .	You're right.	

A My roommate never helps around the house. I have to do all the cleaning.
B If you ask me, you should talk to him.
A I know, but I don't want to start a fight . . .

Episode 2 Food and Family

Act 2

Before you watch

A Complete the two paragraphs with the correct expressions.

| ✓ deadline | decision | disappointed | expert | proud | sense | stressed |

1. I had a big ___deadline___ for work today. The project didn't make any _____ , so last night I had to work until 10:00 to figure it out. I was pretty _____ ! When I handed it in today, the boss congratulated me. I was pretty _____ of my work.

2. Last month I spoke to an _____ to get some professional advice. After that, I quit my job and got a new one. I hope I made the right _____ . I mean, I don't want to be _____ with my new job!

B Match the two parts of the sentences.

1. We asked the teacher __c__
2. The receptionist told us ____
3. My boss made us ____
4. Have the students ____
5. I can't get my parents ____
6. My friend lets me ____
7. My dad wants me ____
8. Could you please help me ____

a. carry these boxes to my car?
b. work late last week.
c. to explain the assignment.
d. to wait in the waiting room.
e. borrow her car all the time.
f. wait in the classroom until the bell rings.
g. to understand how I feel.
h. to study medicine, but I don't want to.

C Write three more sentences like the ones in Exercise B. Use the patterns in the chart.

let / make / help / have + object + verb	get / want / ask / tell + object + to + verb
1. My friend lets me use her computer.	1. We asked him to give us a day off!
2.	2.
3.	3.
4.	4.

While you watch

DVD 20
VHS 18:23
−23:21

A Circle all the correct answers. (One, two, or three answers are possible.)

1. Gio tells Yoko about _____ .
   a. a problem   b. a phone call   c. an interview
2. Gio talks about his parents' _____ .
   a. business   b. house   c. dream
3. Gio says his parents don't _____ him.
   a. talk to   b. visit   c. understand
4. Yoko thinks _____ is important.
   a. honesty   b. pressure   c. money
5. David plans to _____ .
   a. write an article   b. interview Yoko   c. learn some recipes
6. David and Yoko agree to meet _____ .
   a. tomorrow   b. in the morning   c. on Thursday

DVD 21
VHS 18:23
−22:29

B Check (✓) true or false. Then try to correct the false sentences.

1. Yoko's boss asks her to stay late. ☐ True ☐ False
   _____
2. Gio is a little upset. ☐ True ☐ False
   _____
3. Gio's parents own a toy company. ☐ True ☐ False
   _____
4. Gio wants to work in the U.S. for a few months. ☐ True ☐ False
   _____
5. Yoko's parents hoped she would become a doctor. ☐ True ☐ False
   _____
6. Gio's parents are going to be proud. ☐ True ☐ False
   _____
7. David's article is about how to cook simply and eat better. ☐ True ☐ False
   _____
8. David has a meeting at noon. ☐ True ☐ False
   _____

While you watch

DVD 22
VHS 18:45
−20:59

C Listen for these sentences. Complete each one with the correct form of a verb in the box and the object that follows it. (Some verbs will not be used. Others will be used more than once.)

ask	get	have	let	make	tell	want

1. *Gio* They __want__ __me__ to move back to Italy after I graduate.
2. *Gio* My parents _____ _____ to work in the family business.
3. *Gio* They've always _____ _____ to be a part of it.
4. *Gio* I can't _____ _____ to understand.
5. *Yoko* They did not _____ _____ to be a chef.
6. *Yoko* After that, they _____ _____ make my own decision.
7. *Yoko* _____ _____ to give you some time to think.
   And _____ _____ , really nicely, not to pressure you.

DVD 23
VHS 21:40
−22:55

D Listen for these sentences. Circle the ones you hear.

1. a. It'll be fun!
   b. It's going to be really fun!
2. a. I'm going to talk to my boss . . .
   b. I'll have to talk to my boss . . .
3. a. Well, uh, what are you doing tonight?
   b. Well, uh, what do you want to do tonight?
4. a. I'm working, but I'll have some free time tomorrow morning.
   b. I'm working, but I have some free time tomorrow morning.
5. a. Uh, I have a meeting at 8:00, but it should only take an hour.
   b. Uh, I have a meeting at 8:00, but it will only take an hour.
6. a. So I'll just meet you at the restaurant around 9:30 tomorrow, OK?
   b. So let's just meet at the restaurant around 9:30 tomorrow, OK?
7. a. Actually, I think this will be fun!
   b. Actually, I think this is going to be fun!
8. a. I'll talk to you later.
   b. I'll see you later.

After you watch

A What can you remember? Answer the questions.

1. What was Gio's problem, and what was Yoko's advice?

   _____

   _____

2. Do you agree with her advice? What do you think Gio will do?

   _____

   _____

B Make plans to do something with your partner. Decide on a date and a time. Write your conversation using the ideas below. Try to add at least three more lines.

A What are you doing on _____ ? Would you like to go to _____ ?

B I'd love to. But I can't go on _____ . I'm _____ . How about _____ ?

A That sounds great. What time should we meet? Is _____ OK?

B Actually, I _____ , so I can't meet that early. Can we make it _____ ?

A Sure . . .

> What are you doing on Tuesday night? Would you like to go to dinner?

> I'd love to. But I can't go on Tuesday. I'm taking a photography class. How about Thursday?

C Talk about things your parents made you do. Complete the sentences for yourself. Then compare your answers with a partner.

1. When I was younger, my parents didn't let me _____ .
2. They made me _____ .
3. They wanted me to _____ .
4. My _____ is always telling me to _____ .
5. _____ didn't want me to _____ .

Before you watch

A Match each food on the grocery list to a picture. Which two things on the list are not in the picture?

Shopping List

1. frozen dinner ___h___
2. fresh fruit _____
3. fresh vegetables _____
4. fish _____
5. a carton of eggs _____
6. a carton of milk _____
7. a few onions _____
8. rice _____
9. a loaf of bread _____
10. a bottle of soy sauce _____

B Match the questions and answers. Then practice with a partner.

1. How did you learn to cook? _____
2. Do we have any eggs? _____
3. Did you have big holiday dinners when you were a child? _____
4. I need some soy sauce for this recipe. Do we have any? _____
5. Do you cook the vegetables with a lot of olive oil? _____

a. Yes, there's a bottle in the fridge.
b. Yes, my relatives used to come over for Thanksgiving every year.
c. No, I just use a little.
d. Yes, I think there are a few in the fridge.
e. I used to work in my family's restaurant when I was a child.

While you watch

DVD 24
VHS 23:26
−28:03

A Listen for these topics. Cross out the word or expression that <u>isn't</u> mentioned.

1. **interview topics**

   Yoko's experiences, how to diet safely, how to cook simply

2. **Yoko's childhood**

   helped in the kitchen, stirred things, didn't like cooking

3. **the Japanese diet**

   tofu, fish, rice

4. **Yoko's advice**

   prepare meals on the weekend, buy frozen dinners, make simple dishes

5. **vegetables**

   delicious, roasted, raw

6. **in David's refrigerator**

   milk, eggs, soy sauce

7. **today's menu**

   baked chicken, grilled vegetables, wild rice

DVD 25
VHS 23:26
−25:44

B Circle the correct answers.

1. Yoko is **excited / nervous**.
2. David is doing a **feature / human-interest** story.
3. Yoko, her mother, and her aunts used to cook for **a few / a lot of** relatives.
4. Yoko's mother learned to cook from her **aunt / mother**.
5. Yoko says people don't **eat out / cook at home** a lot.
6. David **eats out / cooks** a lot.
7. Yoko says busy people can **order takeout / plan ahead**.

DVD 26
VHS 24:49
−27:33

C What do David and Yoko say about these things? Match the objects to the sentences that describe them. (One item matches to two sentences.)

1. Japanese food _____
2. frozen meals made on the weekend _____
3. frozen dinners from the store _____
4. vegetables _____
5. *tamago donburi* _____

a. David's never tried them.
b. David doesn't like them.
c. Yoko says it has fewer calories.
d. David loves them.
e. Yoko thinks it's quick and easy.
f. Yoko thinks they're expensive.

While you watch

DVD 27
VHS 24:49
−27:17

D Circle the correct answers.

1. Japanese food is healthy because it _____ .
   a. uses very little salt   b. has very little fat
2. Yoko thinks people _____ too much nowadays.
   a. eat   b. eat out
3. David doesn't have enough _____ to cook.
   a. time   b. energy
4. Yoko likes to make _____ simple dishes and freeze them.
   a. a few   b. a lot of
5. Yoko thinks people eat too much _____ food.
   a. fast   b. junk
6. Yoko likes roasted vegetables with a little _____ oil.
   a. olive   b. vegetable
7. David has a carton of eggs and _____ onions.
   a. some   b. a few
8. He also has _____ rice.
   a. some   b. a lot of

DVD 28
VHS 23:59
−24:36

E Watch the video. Circle the correct words to complete Yoko's memories.

When I was a little kid, I used to (1) **cook with** / **help** my mother in the kitchen. She would (2) **let** / **have** me open packages and measure and stir things. I always had a lot of fun.

When I got older, we used to (3) **eat** / **have** big family meals. All my aunts and uncles used to (4) **come over** / **visit**. My cousins would all (5) **tease me** / **be playing**, but I wouldn't (6) **leave** / **help in** the kitchen. I would (7) **work** / **stay** with my aunts and my mother. We would (8) **serve** / **cook for** everyone.

After you watch

A What can you remember? Write three or four sentences about how Yoko learned to cook.

Yoko used to help her mother in the kitchen.

_____

_____

B Write questions to ask a partner about their food and cooking experiences when they were younger. Then work with a partner. Take turns asking and answering your questions.

1. Who used to cook in your house when you were growing up?
2. _____
3. _____
4. _____

A *Who used to cook in your house when you were growing up?*

B *My mother used to do most of the cooking, but once in a while my dad would cook.*

C Think of a favorite memory of something that you did regularly as a child and write a paragraph about it. Use *used to* and *would* where possible. Then share your stories in groups.

_____

_____

_____

_____

"My parents used to take me to my grandfather's house every Saturday.
My grandfather would always make cookies for me. . . ."

Episode 3 I'm Having a Problem!

Act 1

Before you watch

A Label the picture with the words in the box.

cable	✓ hard drive	keyboard	manual
monitor	mouse	screen	software

1. hard drive
2. _____
3. _____
4. _____
5. _____
6. _____
7. _____
8. _____

B Cross out the expression that does <u>not</u> go with each phrasal verb.

1. **hook up**   a computer   ~~some music~~   a phone
2. **look up**   a book   an answer   a word
3. **open up**   a book   a box   a light
4. **plug in**   a button   a keyboard   a monitor
5. **throw away**   a box   an answer   a book
6. **turn on**   a box   some music   a light

C Match the problems on the left with the advice on the right. Then practice with a partner.

1. There's no picture on the TV. _____
2. I keep getting this error message on my computer. _____
3. My computer is too slow. _____
4. I need to check my e-mail when I'm out of town. _____
5. Do you think I should get a desktop or a laptop computer? _____

a. Why don't you call tech support? They'll tell you what it means.
b. You know what you should do? Just find an Internet café. That's what I'd do.
c. If I were you, I'd get a laptop. It's a lot more convenient.
d. I would check that it's plugged in.
e. You might want to think about getting a faster one.

While you watch

DVD 29
VHS 28:08
−32:07

A Circle the correct answers.

1. Alex buys a new _____ .
   a. computer   b. printer
2. The machine _____ .
   a. keeps freezing   b. doesn't work properly
3. David tells Alex to turn it off and _____ .
   a. turn it back on again   b. wait a few minutes
4. David says the problem might be the _____ .
   a. cable   b. hard drive
5. Alex calls _____ first.
   a. tech support   b. Liz
6. Alex has to _____ .
   a. hold for someone   b. call back later
7. The phone call _____ Alex.
   a. helps   b. doesn't help
8. Liz has helped _____ before.
   a. David   b. Alex
9. Alex reads an _____ aloud.
   a. error message   b. instruction manual
10. Liz thinks it's a _____ problem.
    a. keyboard   b. software

DVD 30
VHS 28:08
−28:36

B Watch the video. Then check (✓) the things you saw Alex do.

Alex . . .
- [ ] put the boxes down
- [ ] threw the boxes away
- [ ] put the keyboard on the desk
- [ ] put the monitor on the desk
- [ ] looked something up in the manual
- [ ] plugged in the computer
- [ ] hooked the cables up
- [ ] turned the computer off

While you watch

DVD [31]
VHS 28:36
–31:54

C Listen for these sentences. Match the two parts to complete the suggestions and advice.

1. Have you _____
2. Just turn it off and then _____
3. If I were you, I'd _____
4. You know, you might want to _____
5. Well, why don't you _____
6. Oh, I'd _____
7. Based on what you're saying, I _____

a. call tech support.
b. checked the instruction manual?
c. give her a call anyway.
d. take the computer back to the store.
e. turn it back on again.
f. think it's probably a software problem.
g. call Liz?

DVD [32]
VHS 28:36
–29:43

D Listen for these parts of the conversation. What do David and Alex say exactly? Complete the sentences.

1. *Alex*   It turns on, but the screen is blank except for this. See? Do you have any idea __what__ it _____ ?

   David   No, I have no idea. Have you checked the instruction manual? It might say _____ the problem _____ .

   Alex   Yeah, I checked the manual – but nothing.

   David   You know _____ you should _____ ? . . .

2. *Alex*   Here goes. Cross your fingers!

   David   I wonder _____ _____ something wrong with the hard drive.

   Alex   Oh, no! Don't say that. That _____ be terrible.

   David   Well, I'm sorry. I really don't know. If I were you, I'd call tech support. Do you know _____ their phone number _____ ?

DVD [33]
VHS 29:48
–30:13

E Listen to the recorded message. Complete it with the correct form of the verbs in the box. (You will use one verb more than once.)

be	help	hold	reach

> You have (1) _____ the tech support line. Currently, all operators (2) _____ other customers. Your call (3) _____ very important to us. Please (4) _____ and someone (5) _____ with you in a minute.

After you watch

A What can you remember? What different kinds of advice does David give Alex? What else could Alex do?

David tells Alex to check the manual. _____
_____
_____

B Read about the problems. Complete suggestions and advice with your own ideas.

1. My computer is very slow.
   You might want to _get a new one._____ .
2. I can't get a good connection on my cell phone.
   I would _____ .
3. My car is making a strange noise.
   If I were you, I'd _____ .
4. My DVD player isn't working.
   You might want to _____ .
5. I need a new camera.
   Why don't you _____ ?

C Write down two problems like the ones in Exercise B. Then take turns sharing your problems with a partner. Give advice and suggestions for your partner's problems.

1. _____
2. _____

D Work in small groups. Discuss these questions. Find out how tech savvy your classmates are.

1. How many electronic gadgets do you own? How often do you use them?
2. How often do you go online? What do you go online for?
3. Do you know how to buy something online?
4. What do you do when you have a tech problem?
5. Can you remember when you first learned to use a computer?

Act 2

Before you watch

A Read the course description. Then complete the chart.

NEW THIS SEMESTER

Design Basics (online)

This beginning-level course is for designers who would like to use software and computer graphics and to help them become more creative.

Design Basics is an online course: participants download the lectures and material to work when it is convenient. Students can also communicate with the instructor and other participants in a chat room specially-designed for the course. If your schedule is unpredictable, this is the class for you!

Course Catalog

Find a word that means	
1. designs or drawings	graphics
2. able to make art or to think about things in a new way	
3. to move data from the Internet to a computer	
4. something fits easily with your needs and schedule	
5. a place on the Internet where people can talk with other people	
6. something irregular or changing	

B Match the two parts of the sentences.

1. If I had time and money, __h__
2. I wish I could speak Spanish, ____
3. I don't have a computer at home, ____
4. You'd probably make more money ____
5. I'd come to the party ____
6. We'd get there faster ____
7. It's Monday today, ____
8. If you could have three wishes, ____

a. but I've never studied a foreign language.
b. but I wish I did.
c. but I wish it was Friday.
d. if I didn't have to work this weekend.
e. if we took the car.
f. if you got a better job.
g. what would you ask for?
h. I'd travel around the world.

While you watch

DVD 34
VHS 32:12
−36:14

A What topics are mentioned? Use the words in the box to complete the topics.

art	city	class	✓ computer	Europe
home	Internet	job	Web page	Web site

1. Alex's __computer__ problem
2. an online _____ course
3. downloading _____ lectures
4. going to _____ to study
5. _____ design

6. working at _____
7. a(n) _____ connection
8. Liz's terrific _____
9. David's _____
10. a(n) _____ news Web site

DVD 35
VHS 32:12
−36:14

B Circle the correct answers.

1. Alex got a new computer because his old one ____ .
   a. was broken
   b. wasn't fast enough
2. Alex can ____ in his online art course.
   a. go into a chat room
   b. paint on the computer
3. Alex chose an online course because it's ____ .
   a. more convenient
   b. cheaper
4. Alex picked up a brochure to learn about programs in ____ .
   a. Rome
   b. Florence
5. Liz can't spend time on her music because ____ .
   a. she's changing jobs
   b. her job is too demanding
6. Alex wants a Web site to ____ .
   a. show his art
   b. find new clients
7. David is ____ his current job.
   a. worried about
   b. bored with
8. David likes Liz's job because ____ .
   a. she's always learning something new
   b. she can decide her own hours

While you watch

DVD 36
VHS 33:30
−36:14

C Listen for these sentences. Match the two parts to complete the sentences. Who says each sentence? Write *A* (Alex), *L* (Liz), or *D* (David) next to each sentence.

_A_ 1. Sometimes I wish I could just quit my job and _C_
____ 2. If I had enough time and money, I'd ____
____ 3. You'd probably ____
____ 4. If I worked for myself, I'd ____
____ 5. I wish I had a Web site – you know, to ____
____ 6. It seems like I'm ____
____ 7. If I were you, I'd definitely ____

a. show my art.
b. go to grad school.
c. paint all the time.
d. check this out.
e. learn a lot that way.
f. not doing anything new.
g. worry about that.

DVD 37
VHS 34:03
−35:19

D Listen for these parts of the conversation. What do they say exactly? Circle the correct answers.

1. *Liz*   I wish I **wasn't / weren't** so busy with *my* work. Web page design is interesting, but **I want / I'd love** to spend more time on my music.

2. *Liz*   . . . it's easy to work too much **if / when** you're not careful. You know what **I mean / I'm saying**?

   Alex   Uh-huh. But **on the other hand / then again**, you can choose when and where to work.

3. *Liz*   Well, **I could / I'd be happy to** help you design one. Just let me know when you're ready.

   Alex   That **sounds / would be** great!

   David   You know, you're both so artistic. I wish I **was / were** more creative.

DVD 38
VHS 34:48
−36:14

E Listen for these sentences. Match the sentences and the responses.

1. My Web site! ____
2. What's more creative than that? ____
3. Well, maybe you could talk to your boss. ____
4. If you could have any job, what would you do? ____
5. You're always learning something new. ____
6. I've seen sites like this. ____
7. If I were you, I'd definitely check this out. ____

a. I'm not sure.
b. Cool!
c. Well, maybe.
d. Hmm. Maybe I will!
e. Or start looking around . . .
f. Huh. . . .
g. That looks terrific. Wow!

After you watch

A What can you remember? How do they want their lives to be different? Which person do you think is the most likely to achieve his or her dream? Why?

1. Alex wishes he could _____
   _____

2. Liz wishes she could _____
   _____

3. David wishes he could _____
   _____

B Complete the sentences about yourself.

"I wish I could sing!"

1. I wish I could _____
   _____

2. If I had a lot of money, I'd _____
   _____

3. If I could have any job, I'd _____
   _____

4. If I had more free time, I'd _____
   _____

5. If I had the chance to move to another country, I'd
   _____

6. If I could meet a famous person, I'd want to meet
   _____

C Work with a partner and compare your answers in Exercise B. Give your opinions about your partner's wishes. Use the expression in the box.

> That would be great / cool / interesting / exciting / fun!
> I know what you mean, but . . .
> Maybe. On the other hand, . . .
> I don't know. Don't you think . . . ?

A If I had a lot of money, I'd never work again. You know what I mean?
B Well, I don't know. I like to work. I think I'd get bored.

Before you watch

A Complete the sentences with the words in the box.

Adjectives		Verbs	
demanding	uncomfortable	apologize	ignore
✓ hot and cold	weird	get along with	interrupt
rude			

Adjectives

1. Sometimes Tim is friendly, and sometimes he isn't. He's _hot and cold_ .
2. My new job is really _____ . I have to work a lot of hours.
3. The boss was really angry, so everyone in the office was _____ .
4. If you forget to say "Please" and "Thank you," it's a little _____ .
5. This TV show is _____ . I don't understand it.

Verbs

6. Please say "Hello." Don't _____ me.
7. I'm really sorry for getting angry. I want to _____ .
8. It's a good idea to be nice and to _____ your co-workers.
9. Please don't _____ the speaker when he's talking.

B Match the sentences with the responses. Then practice with a partner.

1. My new boss is sort of rude sometimes. ____
2. How's your new job? ____
3. Do you think it's important to like the people you work with? ____
4. I'm sorry if I was rude. I want to apologize. ____
5. It's kind of uncomfortable if you don't get along with another student in class. ____

a. Yeah, I do. It's important to get along with your co-workers.
b. That's OK. Don't worry about it.
c. Yeah, it is. I know what you mean.
d. It's great, but it's a little demanding.
e. Maybe he's just stressed out.

While you watch

DVD 39
VHS 36:19
−41:07

A Circle the correct answers.

1. What does the man do after he bumps into Yoko?
   a. He says nothing to Yoko.
   b. He apologizes for his behavior.

2. What does Kim do with the cell phone she finds?
   a. She leaves it on the table.
   b. She gives it to a waiter.

3. What does Kim think of her new job?
   a. It's too easy.
   b. It's really interesting.

4. What does Kim say about her co-worker, Nina?
   a. She's sort of hot and cold.
   b. She's busy and stressed out.

5. How does Kim feel about the situation with Nina?
   a. She's not worried about it.
   b. She's uncomfortable.

6. What does Liz do when the waiter gives her too much change?
   a. She returns the money.
   b. She doesn't notice at first.

7. How does Kim feel when she sees Nina?
   a. She's happy.
   b. She's embarrassed.

8. Why has Nina had a bad week?
   a. She broke up with her boyfriend.
   b. Everything has gone wrong lately.

9. What does Kim do when Nina apologizes?
   a. She accepts the apology.
   b. She apologizes too.

DVD 40
VHS 36:19
−41:07

B Who says these things? Check (✓) Liz, Yoko, Kim, or Nina.

	Liz	Yoko	Kim	Nina
1. I guess it was just an accident.				
2. Is this cell phone either of yours?				
3. Are things not going well?				
4. I'm working in the research department now.				
5. Oh, now that's challenging.				
6. Oh! You gave me too much change.				
7. Could you find something you have in common with her?				
8. It's sort of funny that you're here.				
9. I think I made a horrible impression on you.				
10. Um, would you like to join us?				

While you watch

DVD 41
VHS 37:22
−39:50

C Listen for these sentences. Circle the ones you hear.

1. a. Do you remember the promotion my boss talked to me about?
   b. Do you remember the promotion that I talked to my boss about?
2. a. And she's someone who has to work with me every day.
   b. And she's someone I have to work with every day.
3. a. Do you really think it's important to like the people you work with?
   b. Do you really think it's important for people at work to like you?
4. a. . . . you need to get along with people who do good work.
   b. . . . you need to get along with people to do good work.
5. a. I get along well with people who have the same interests as me.
   b. I get along well with people when we have the same interests.
6. a. That's Nina, the woman that I was just talking to.
   b. That's Nina, the woman that I was just talking about.

DVD 42
VHS 37:52
−38:53

D Listen for these parts of the conversation. What do they say exactly? Circle the correct answers.

1. *Kim* One of my new co-workers, Nina, she's **kind of** / **sort of** hot and cold.
2. *Yoko* Huh. **Maybe** / **I guess** she's just busy or stressed out.
   Kim Mm, yeah, maybe. Don't you think it's kind of **strange** / **weird**, though?
3. *Liz* I mean, **maybe you** / **you probably** shouldn't worry about it too much.
   Kim Yeah, maybe. In a way, I **guess** / **think** it's not that important. On the other hand, it's **just** / **a little bit** uncomfortable when someone won't speak to you.
   Yoko I know what you mean. And I **guess** / **think** it is important because you need to get along with people to do good work.

DVD 43
VHS 36:46
−39:09

E Match the underlined words and the things they refer to. (You will use some things more than once.)

1. Oh, I guess someone lost <u>it</u>. _____
2. I'll put <u>it</u> in the lost and found. _____
3. <u>That</u> sounds good. Me too. _____
4. Well, I got <u>it</u>! _____
5. <u>It's</u> pretty demanding. _____
6. Don't you think <u>it's</u> kind of weird, though? _____
7. Let me buy <u>these</u>. _____

a. the new job
b. Nina's behavior
c. the drink(s)
d. the cell phone
e. the promotion

After you watch

A What can you remember? Answer the questions about the story.

1. What happened to Yoko at the beginning? _____

   _____

2. What recently happened to Kim at work? _____

   _____

3. What problem is Kim having at work? _____

   _____

4. What has happened to Nina this week? _____

   _____

B Answer the questions with your own ideas. Then compare with a partner.

1. What would you do if someone bumped into you and didn't apologize?

   _____

2. What would you do if you found a lost cell phone?

   _____

3. What would you do if a friend offered to pay for something?

   _____

4. What would you do if a waiter gave you too much change?

   _____

5. What would you do if someone was ignoring you?

   _____

A What would you do if you found a lost cell phone?
B I'd probably call the last number dialed on it.

C Work in small groups. Discuss these questions.

1. Do you think it's important to like the people you work with or the students you study with? Why or why not?
2. What are three suggestions for someone who doesn't get along with a co-worker or classmate?

Episode 4 What's Happening?

Act 1

Before you watch

A Read the movie blurbs. Then complete the chart.

Stop the Clock

Bruce Mills gives an excellent performance as a spy who uncovers a plan to change the future of the world. This is an old-fashioned action movie with a lot of suspense and incredible special effects. The stunts are amazing.

The Happy German

This lighthearted musical is set in Germany in the 1800s. It's about two people who work in a circus together and fall in love. It won an Academy Award for its costumes, and the music is excellent. It is subtitled.

Find a word or expression that means . . .	
1. a person who tries to find out secret information	SPY
2. traditional or customary	
3. a feeling of worry or excitement that something is going to happen	
4. tricks or technology used to create an illusion or artificial image	
5. a play or movie that uses singing and dancing to tell the story	
6. takes place	
7. the clothes that actors wear in plays or movies	
8. to have words on the movie screen that translate the dialog	

B Complete the conversation with the expressions in the box. Then practice with a partner.

ask you a favor	✓ do you have a moment	get your work done
if I could leave	need you to	

A Excuse me. (1) Do you have a moment ?

I wanted to (2) _____ .

B Sure. What did you want to talk about?

A Well, I was wondering (3) _____ the office early today.

You see, it's my father's birthday and . . .

B Well, I (4) _____ finish that report before you go.

Will you be able to do that?

A Oh, yes. I'm almost done with it already.

B OK, then. As long as you (5) _____ before you go.

A Great. Thanks.

While you watch

DVD 44
VHS 41:10
−46:36

A Check (✓) all the correct answers.

1. What do Kim and David talk about at the beginning of the story?

☐ movies ☐ a horror movie ☐ going to lunch
☐ DVDs ☐ an action movie ☐ going back to work

☐ a musical ☐ plans for the weekend ☐ their boss
☐ a foreign film ☐ a new job ☐ a co-worker

2. What do David and Gary talk about?

☐ an e-mail ☐ extra work ☐ a day off ☐ working on the weekend
☐ voice mail ☐ a co-worker ☐ a promotion ☐ working late

DVD 45
VHS 41:10
−43:15

B Watch the video and complete the chart about the two movies. Then answer the questions.

	92 Minutes	Three Months in Paris
1. Who has seen it already?	David / Kim	David / Kim
2. What language is it in?	English	_____ with subtitles
3. What's it about?	It's about some people who are trying to take over the government. This guy plays a _____ . He only has ninety-two minutes to save the _____ .	It's about a girl who wants to be famous. She goes to _____ to _____ in a nightclub.
4. When does it take place?	in the future	in the _____
5. What does he or she say about it?	It's pretty exciting.	The costumes, the dancing, and the _____ are amazing. It has a really _____ ending.

6. Does Kim like action movies?

Sometimes – _____

7. Does David want to see the movie that Kim saw? Why or why not?

Maybe, but _____

While you watch

DVD 46
VHS 43:15
−46:36

C Circle the correct answers.

1. InterNews is an _____ .
   a. online news Web site   b. international news magazine
2. Kim thinks David should take _____ .
   a. the day off   b. the job
3. Gary asks David to write an article about natural _____ .
   a. foods   b. disasters
4. Martin can't write the article because he's _____ .
   a. sick   b. busy
5. The article is due on _____ .
   a. Monday   b. Tuesday
6. Working on the weekend is _____ idea.
   a. David's   b. Gary's
7. David _____ that he won't be able to see *Three Months in Paris*.
   a. is upset   b. doesn't care

DVD 47
VHS 44:21
−46:36

D Listen for these sentences. Match the two parts to complete them. Then say which sentences are used to ask for a favor politely.

1. I was wondering if I could __f__ .
2. Actually, I'm glad you _____ .
3. I wanted to _____ .
4. . . . unfortunately, he's very sick and he won't _____ .
5. Would it be OK with you if I _____ ?
6. As long as you _____ .
7. Now I won't be able to _____ .

a. ask you a favor
b. be able to finish it
c. finish it by Tuesday morning, it's OK with me
d. go and see *Three Months in Paris* with you
e. stopped by
f. talk to you for a second
g. took Monday off

After you watch

A What do you think? Why does David want to change jobs? Do you think he will get the new job? Why?

_____

_____

_____

B Write the words in the box under the movie types. (Some words can describe more than one movie type.) Then try to add one or two words to each category.

aliens	costumes	dancing	fight scenes	monster
songs	special effects	stunts	suspense	

Thriller	_Musical_	_Science-fiction movie_

C Work with a partner. Use some of the words in the box in Exercise B to write a description of a movie that you saw recently.

_____

_____

_____

_____

> The Drummer is a new thriller. It's set in England in the
> 1950s. It's about a young man who discovers a drum full
> of money. The police think he stole the money, so they
> chase him all over the country. . . .

Episode 4 What's Happening?

Act 2

Before you watch

A Write the adjectives in the correct category.

✓ amazing	✓ anxious	awful	beautiful	bored	disappointed
excited	fantastic	frustrated	interested	motivated	scary

Positive	Negative
amazing	anxious

B Compare the two sentences about Kate. Which sentence describes her job? Which describes her feelings about the job?

    a. *Kate is really <u>excited</u> about her new job.*
    b. *Kate's new job is really <u>exciting</u>.*

Choose the correct form in each sentence.

1. We were **amazed / amazing** by Luke's stories about his trip to Africa.
2. The little boy was **scary / scared** by the big dog.
3. The movie was so **bored / boring** that I fell asleep.
4. Pam was so **interested / interesting** in her book that she lost track of the time.

C Number the lines of the conversation in the correct order. Then underline the two questions used to ask about news.

____ Really? Do you have midterms or something?
____ Thanks! Anyway, what about you? What have you been up to?
_2_ Well, I've been studying a lot.
____ Really? That's fantastic! You must be so excited!
____ Not much. But guess what? I'm going to Australia this summer!
____ Oh, you'll do well. You're so motivated!
_1_ What have you been doing lately?
____ Yeah, I do. Actually, I'm a little worried about them.

While you watch

DVD 48
VHS 46:40
−51:32

A Listen to each person's activities. Write *D* if the person has done or is doing the activity. Write *P* if he plans to do it.

Gio

1. _____ finish school
2. _____ study for his finals
3. _____ get work experience
4. _____ talk to his parents

Alex

1. _____ work at the gym
2. _____ take an online course
3. _____ take a trip
4. _____ get a scholarship

David

1. _____ interview at InterNews
2. _____ get a job
3. _____ start his first report
4. _____ shoot a video

DVD 49
VHS 46:40
−51:32

B Who says each sentence and why does he say it? Circle the correct name and then match the sentence to its topic. (You will use some topics twice.)

1. "I have so much reading to do."
   Gio / Alex / David says this about _____ .

2. "To be honest, I'm a little anxious about it."
   Gio / Alex / David says this about _____ .

3. "The scary thing was, I didn't know how to tell my parents that."
   Gio / Alex / David says this about _____ .

4. "Um, to be honest, it's a little disappointing."
   Gio / Alex / David says this about _____ .

5. "Well, maybe it will get better."
   Gio / Alex / David says this about _____ .

6. "The thing is, I thought I missed the deadline."
   Gio / Alex / David says this about _____ .

7. "I know they'd love to meet you."
   Gio / Alex / David says this about _____ .

8. "I've been learning something new every day."
   Gio / Alex / David says this about _____ .

9. "Yeah, it's really beautiful."
   Gio / Alex / David says this about _____ .

10. "Well, I can't wait to see it."
    Gio / Alex / David says this about _____ .

a. the online course

b. David's video story

c. his job

d. the garden

e. studying for finals

f. his parents

g. staying in the United States

h. the scholarship

While you watch

DVD [50]
VHS 46:40
–50:02

C Listen for these questions. Match them to their answers.

1. What have you been up to? _____
2. You're studying for finals already? _____
3. So you're not going to go back to Italy right after you graduate? _____
4. What have you been doing lately? _____
5. How long have you been taking the class? _____
6. What trip? _____
7. What?! What are you talking about? _____
8. What about your job? _____
9. Have you heard David's big news? _____

a. No, what?
b. Oh, did I tell you . . . ? I'm going to Italy for a month.
c. Well, you won't believe it – I've been studying a lot!
d. Yeah. Since the beginning of the semester.
e. Well, I've been working at the gym, of course.
f. For about two weeks.
g. Oh, they're being really encouraging.
h. No, I'm going to stay here and . . .
i. I wanted to surprise you.

DVD [51]
VHS 49:08
–51:06

D Listen for these sentences. Circle the ones you hear.

1. a. So when they called me, I was really surprised.
   b. So when they called me, it was really surprising.
2. a. You must be so excited!
   b. That must be so exciting!
3. a. Well, you know what? I got the job!
   b. Well, guess what? I got the job!
4. a. So far, it's been really interesting.
   b. So far, it's really interesting.
5. a. I was so bored with my old job.
   b. It was so boring at my old job.
6. a. Did you hear about the garden in our neighborhood?
   b. You know the garden in our neighborhood?
7. a. But the thing is, now someone wants to buy the lot.
   b. But the thing was, someone wanted to buy the lot.

DVD [52]
VHS 49:49
–51:15

E Watch the video. Then correct four more errors in the description of David's new job.

    David got a new job at InterNews. He started working there ~~two weeks~~ *about a week* ago. So far, he likes the job and thinks it's interesting. His first story is going to be a newspaper report about a garden in the neighborhood that used to be a parking lot. The people who created the garden love it. Unfortunately, someone wants to put an apartment building there and destroy the garden. David hopes his story will make him famous.

After you watch

A What can you remember? Write the news in each person's life. Then write what you think will happen.

	He's . . .	He's going to . . .	We think he'll . . .
1. Gio	He's been studying for final exams.	He's going to stay in the U.S. after he graduates.	
2. Alex			
3. David			

B Work with a partner. Use the prompts and your own ideas to make a conversation. Ask about one another's news.

> *A* Ask your partner about his / her news.
> *What have you been . . . ?*

> *B* Say what you've been doing lately.
> *I've been . . .*

> *A* Respond. Use an adjective. Then ask a question
> *That sounds . . .*

> *B* Answer the question.
> Then ask your partner about his / her news.
> *Anyway, what about you? What . . . ?*

> *A* Say what you've been doing.
> *I've been . . .*

> *B* Respond. Use an adjective. Then ask a question.
> *That sounds . . .*

> *A* Answer the question.

A What have you been up to?
B Not much. Just working a lot. I've been working
   ten hours a day, and even on weekends!
A Oh yeah? That sounds . . .

Act 3

Before you watch

A Work with a partner. Complete the crossword puzzle.

	¹·G						²·D						
			³·G							⁴·C			
												⁵·T	
	⁶·D							⁷·C					
						⁸·L							
	⁹·N												
	¹⁰·F												
		¹¹·B											
	¹²·C												

Across

3.

6. Not clean
7. The place where crimes are judged
9. An area in a town where you live, work, and shop
11.

12. Activities that break the law, such as robbery or damaging property

Down

1. A place where people grow plants and flowers
2. Not safe
4. Too many people in one space
5.

8. A place to park your car is called a parking _____ .
10.

While you watch

DVD [53]
VHS 51:36
−56:10

A Watch the entire story. Then check (✓) the sentences that best summarize the story.

1. ☐ David is doing a story about a new garden that is being developed.
   ☐ David is doing a story about a garden that is in danger.

2. ☐ The garden was created because the parks in the area were all dirty and dangerous.
   ☐ The garden was created because there were no other parks or gardens in the area.

3. ☐ The people love the garden and the neighborhood is safer.
   ☐ The people love the garden, but the neighborhood is more expensive.

4. ☐ The city owns the land and plans to build on it.
   ☐ A construction company wants to buy the land and build on it.

5. ☐ If the two sides cannot reach an agreement, the land will be sold.
   ☐ If the two sides cannot reach an agreement, they may go to court.

6. ☐ David and his friends think that the garden should be saved.
   ☐ David and his friends can't agree on what should happen.

DVD [54]
VHS 52:25
−56:10

B Match the questions and the responses.

1. What was the neighborhood like when you moved here? _____
2. Were there any parks or gardens in the area? _____
3. What did this space look like before? _____
4. So, what did you do to fix it up? _____
5. How do the people in the neighborhood like the garden? _____
6. Your company wants to destroy the Berry Street Garden and build a parking lot on it. Isn't that true? _____
7. Why can't you just build the parking lot somewhere else? _____
8. Why don't we all walk over there now? _____

a. Everyone loves it.
b. Oh, it was a big mess.
c. No, but there were a couple of empty lots.
d. That's a great idea!
e. This is the perfect location.
f. Well, first we had to clean up all the garbage and stuff.
g. Well, it was really different.
h. Yes, it's a crowded neighborhood.

DVD 55
VHS 52:25
−54:01

C In what order does Susan say these things happened? Number the sentences in order.

_____ Susan and her friends built a fence.

_____ Susan moved to the neighborhood.

_____ Susan and her friends cleaned up garbage.

_____ The garden brought people together.

_____ Susan and her friends chose a lot.

_____ Susan and her friends planted trees.

_____ There were no injuries.

DVD 56
VHS 52:03
−54:15

D Listen for these sentences. Circle the ones you hear.

1. a. The garden is in danger and might be destroyed.
   b. The garden is in danger and could be destroyed.

2. a. There was a lot of crime.
   b. There was too much crime.

3. a. It was completely filled with garbage.
   b. They filled it completely with garbage.

4. a. . . . and then we planted all the trees and flowers.
   b. . . . and then all the trees and flowers were planted.

5. a. You must feel pretty good about that.
   b. You should feel pretty good about that.

6. a. It's very upsetting that the garden might be destroyed.
   b. It's very upsetting that the garden may be destroyed.

DVD 57
VHS 54:42
−56:10

E Match the statements with the reasons.

1. Granix is buying the land now because _____
2. Granix wants to build a parking lot because _____
3. Granix likes this location because _____
4. Susan doesn't want to start over because _____
5. David wants to visit the garden because _____

a. it takes years to develop a garden.
b. it's near several main streets.
c. the neighborhood is crowded and needs it.
d. it's a beautiful day.
e. they want to build a parking lot on it.

After you watch

A What can you remember? What arguments does Susan use in favor of keeping the park? What arguments does Mr. Smith use in favor of building a parking lot on the site?

Susan Douglas

It looks beautiful.

_____

_____

_____

Mr. Smith

Susan's group doesn't own the land.

_____

_____

_____

B Complete the news article with the past passive form of the verbs in the box.

ask	clean	✓ close	damage	involve
make	plant	reopen	replace	

Lake Park Reopens

Lake Park has finally reopened after an extensive renovation. The park (1) ___was closed___ for several months, and a lot of improvements (2) _____ .

"The Park Building (3) _____ and painted, and we installed a new fence all around it because the old one (4) _____," said Mike Chen of the City Parks Authority. "We brought new sand into the play area, and the old play structures (5) _____ with safer ones. The park is a lot greener now because more trees and flowers (6) _____ around the edges of the park."

The neighbors are very happy with the new park. "We (7) _____ for our opinions and the city listened to what we said," said Gloria Garcia of the Lake Park Community Association.

"We (8) _____ at every stage of the project."

The park (9) _____ last weekend.

C Write a short paragraph about a place that you know that was improved in some way. Use some of the verbs in Exercise B above.

_____

_____

_____

_____

_____

Illustration credits

Irregular verbs

Base form	Simple past	Past participle
be	was/were	been
beat	beat	beaten
become	became	become
begin	began	begun
bite	bit	bitten
bleed	bled	bled
blow	blew	blown
break	broke	broken
bring	brought	brought
build	built	built
burn	burned/burnt	burned/burnt
buy	bought	bought
catch	caught	caught
choose	chose	chosen
come	came	come
cost	cost	cost
cut	cut	cut
dig	dug	dug
do	did	done
draw	drew	drawn
dream	dreamed/dreamt	dreamed/dreamt
drink	drank	drunk
drive	drove	driven
eat	ate	eaten
fall	fell	fallen
feed	fed	fed
feel	felt	felt
find	found	found
fight	fought	fought
fly	flew	flown
forget	forgot	forgotten
forgive	forgave	forgiven
freeze	froze	frozen
get	got	gotten
give	gave	given
go	went	gone
grow	grew	grown
hang	hung	hung
have	had	had
hear	heard	heard
hide	hid	hidden
hit	hit	hit
hold	held	held
hurt	hurt	hurt
keep	kept	kept
know	knew	known
lead	led	led
leave	left	left
lend	lent	lent
let	let	let
lie	lay	lain

Base form	Simple past	Past participle
light	lit	lit
lose	lost	lost
make	made	made
mean	meant	meant
meet	met	met
pay	paid	paid
prove	proved	proven/proved
put	put	put
quit	quit	quit
read	read	read
ride	rode	ridden
ring	rang	rung
rise	rose	risen
run	ran	run
say	said	said
see	saw	seen
sell	sold	sold
send	sent	sent
set	set	set
sew	sewed	sewn/sewed
shake	shook	shaken
shine	shone	shone
shoot	shot	shot
show	showed	shown/showed
shut	shut	shut
sing	sang	sung
sink	sank	sunk
sit	sat	sat
sleep	slept	slept
speak	spoke	spoken
speed	sped	sped
spend	spent	spent
spill	spilled/spilt	spilled/spilt
spring	sprang	sprung
stand	stood	stood
steal	stole	stolen
stick	stuck	stuck
strike	struck	struck
swim	swam	swum
take	took	taken
teach	taught	taught
tear	tore	torn
tell	told	told
think	thought	thought
throw	threw	thrown
understand	understood	understood
wake	woke	woken
wear	wore	worn
win	won	won
wind	wound	wound
write	wrote	written